Quarantine Access

QUARANTINE
ACCESS

A Novel of Faction

ISBN–13 Softcover: 978-1546771944
Published by Amazon.com,
Amazon.UK, Amazon.FR
Order Today!
Available Online at:
Amazon.com
e-books at Amazon.com
and KDP Bookshelf.
or visit your local bookstore.

EDWARD A. DRUM MD

This is a work of historic fiction. Many referenced events are true, but some characters, places and incidents are the product of the author's imagination and are used fictitiously to carry the story. Some characters are real as the story line would be lost if fictional characters did not carry events that are perceived connected. Medical jargon is limited to inform of historically events in the mismanagement of the AIDS epidemic. This is a novel of faction as ideologies collide with what is known factual information.

Author's Note

I began writing <u>Quarantine Access</u> three decades ago as a young practicing physician. I was stunned that the AIDS epidemic not being treated as an epidemic. Political correctness quickly dominated the dialogue controlling the message of this epidemic.

Strangely enough, the epidemic has now morphed into "Living with HIV".

I ask you to consider how distortions refocus societies' attention and misinform? More importantly, why and how was AIDS repackaged for your consumption?

Were it not for my wife, Penny-Re, discovering this manuscript in a dusty cardboard box forgotten under a stairwell, it might never have found the light of day. After you've read this Novel of Historical Faction, you may wish it remained under the stairwell!

Historically, open discussion of controlling the AIDS epidemic quickly eroded into a crafted message that ignored time tested effective solutions. It became socially unacceptable to consider quarantine of sexual behavior as a viable option, arguing it violated sexual expression. This mantra controlled the conversation in an era of revolutionary sexual extremes, where "the stranger the better" was endorsed and applauded as the new norm!

Responsible sexual behavior was rejected by social and political

Planners. This epidemic in many cases was encouraged. The question is Why?

"Quarantine Access", traces this historic epidemic during a cold war atmosphere. The United States was in an epic conflict with the former Soviet Union on the high seas, in the air, and in bio-warfare. Real events are portrayed with some fictional characters to move this story.

Many medical professionals bought into distortions as did much of society. The epidemic was superficially discouraged by then San Francisco Mayor, Diane Feinstein but allowed the bath houses with anonymous sex. National Blood Banks targeted donations from well-intended homosexuals in the Castro District of San Francisco. Donated blood from high risk homosexuals were comingled into the national blood bank pool. Thousands received these transfusions and died of AIDS. This was not limited to the USA but was on an international scale.

Thomas Sowell once said, "Some books you write for pleasure, and others you write out of a sense of duty, because there are things that need to be said." This is one of those occasions!

Very Respectfully,
Edward A. Drum MD Captain (MC) USNR-ret

Copyright:

ISBN: 13: 978-1546771944…
       10: 1546771948

Dedication

To:

My mother, Kitty Drum who defined love.

DLS, who rekindled it. My

Lord and my Country.

Reference Proverbs 1:4-7

"To give insight to gullible people.

To give knowledge and foresight to the young.

A wise person will listen and continue to learn,

And an understanding person will gain direction-

The fear of the Lord is the beginning of knowledge.

Stubborn fools despise wisdom and instruction."

Acknowledgements with special gratitude
and love to: Penny-Re, my wife for
inspiration, believing and her daughter
Katy for graphics.

CONTENTS

PROLOGUE

A sliver of moonlight pierced the corner of the bedroom window. Nancy Brewer lay in bed listening to her daughter Kristen's slumber party. There are things a young girl will tell a friend, but not her mother. Nancy wanted to know her daughter's thoughts. She listened intently through a floor vent as she repositioned herself in bed. The girls were in the basement recreation room.

The concert had been wonderful. Kristen and her friends belonged to La Bella Core, an interdenominational girls' choir from the south end of Bainbridge Island. The girls were between eleven and thirteen. They were interested in boys, music, gossip, talking and singing.

Refreshments had followed the concert at the Trinity Presbyterian Church in Winslow. This was heartland America on the edge of the Pacific Rim. This steepled white church overlooked Eagle Harbor at the ferry terminal west of Seattle bound traffic.

"Don't spill the popcorn. You'll get grease all over the place "said Kristen. "You sound like my mother, "Lana shot back. Abby asked, "He's so cute, don't you think?" "Who's cuter, Michael or Aaron?" Someone from a corner asked.

"Well, Aaron of course and I like his ear rings. He smiled and talked to me yesterday. " What did he say?" "Hi, Sweetie?" No stupid, he asked if I was a virgin."

They giggled.

Jessica tried to change the subject. "We were pretty good tonight, weren't we?"

"Jessie, we're talking boys, not choir," said Kristen. Golda put her hand over her mouth and giggled.

Elizabeth reached for popcorn. "Aaron's cool. I think he's kind of an artist. Probably smokes dope, too. I smelled him when he brushed me going to third period."

"Whoa, brushed against you? How close?"

"No way! Aaron isn't like that. I think he's radical, carries a condom too. He showed me his wallet!" You're so dense, listening to the school nurse again. Condoms don't do anything except keep you from getting pregnant," Jessica declared.

Nancy Brewer fluffed her pillow and strained for more information.

"Oh, No, he's not doing it."

"So, why's he carrying them around, just showing off?" "They keep you from getting AIDS," someone said.

"No, silly, AIDS is from a green monkey.", Elizabeth insisted. "Well, it's really from the African black man, I mean the Africans. The green monkeys bite the Africans, and they have sex and transmit AIDS. Most of Africa has it now," Jessica added with her usual authoritative tone.

"I think Aaron's really cute—do you think he

likes me?" Elizabeth asked.

"We're talking about AIDS, not Aaron."

"Come on, let's all sing. We're the choir, aren't we?" Lana asked wishfully.

"I don't want to sing—we practiced enough. I want to know about sex and AIDS," Golda said. "Aaron is so, well... mature. He's older than the other boys. Bet you he goes to law school," Elizabeth interjected.

"The guy is gay, Liz! Watch the way he walks. He's probably the only guy in our class with the virus."

"You're all wrong. It came from an African monkey. It's got nothing to do with being gay or anything like that," someone in the dark corner offered.

"My daddy says it's from the gays," Lisa declared. "My schoolteacher says it's from, it's from Africa."

"You're all wrong. My mom, you know, thinks it was caused by the Health Department vaccinating the blacks in Africa. Yeah, to avoid all the starving children that might be born." "Kristen, don't you worry about AIDS?" Jessica offered from the far corner.

"Come on, you guys, this is supposed to be a slumber party, not a health class. Give me another Coke."

"Let's play twister again."

"No, that's a stupid game. You girls are really

bad, talking like that," Laura said.

"I'm tired; I want to go to bed. Turn the radio down."

"I think Laura's a suck-up. Did you see her brown-nose the teacher yesterday?"

"You don't know how good it feels", Jessica announced. "What are you talking about?" asked Abby.
"Well sex of course"

"Come on, you guys, let's go to sleep."

"Yeah, knock it off. Mom's probably listening anyway," said Kristen.

Nancy Brewer adjusted her position. She felt guilty. "Pass me the pizza, no, the pepperoni one."

"Well I think this stuff about monkeys is pure bull"! Jessica said, "Look its late, it's from Africa and a monkey. That's what my school nurse says, and she's got to be right."

"I still like Kevin. I'm going to corner him by the lockers."

"Whoever falls asleep first, gets frozen underwear."

Nancy Brewer listened closely. The night seemed to last forever. *We live in confusing times, she thought. I want my daughter to believe in something. But what? Parents have an obligation to teach the truth. I just don't know what the truth is?*

She rolled over onto her back, pulled the blanket support to her chin and thought of Charles. Like most Navy wives, she was again alone raising their child. Charles had been away on deployment now over four months in Guantanamo Bay. Cuba. She wiped

15

a tear away with the leading edge of her sheet. There were seven more years of payback for his Navy medical residency training in surgery. They both felt owned, but he was a good surgeon and well trained.

The digital clock read 2:37 am.

Nancy Brewer felt uncertain and insecure as Charles had lost weight and his last few letters were distant. Something had changed. A wife can sense these things.

CHAPTER 1

"Man Down!...Man Down!"

The corpsman shielded his eyes while adjusting the brilliant overhead surgical lamp. Lieutenant Commander Pete Tierney, U.S. Navy physician, was probing and exploring a bullet wound that was wet, ugly, and necrotic.

The corpsman admired Tierney. The doctor's hands were gentle and experienced. His words were measured and controlled.

"Hmmm...shit! Hand me a culture tube for aerobes and anaerobic bacteria.

Tierney adjusted his horn-rimmed glasses with his arm to avoid touching his sterile gloved hands. He examined the wound. The young Marine's right arm was swollen from wrist to shoulder. Yellow pus oozed from the entrance and exit sites just above the elbow. The Marine could not flex his elbow. Tierney placed his palm against the young man's forearm, applied traction, and then relaxed the pressure. The arm was rigid as stone, but the tissue was soft and puffy with the odor of decay. The Marine had a fever and the lymph nodes in his right armpit were tender and enlarged. His arm was rapidly becoming a useless appendage. For an eighteen-year-old private first class this was the end of a military career. It was the end of the use of his dominant arm.

"What happened here?" asked Tierney.

"I tried to get him to surgery at the Navy hospital," said Lieutenant Scott Weaver, "but they wouldn't admit him. They didn't consider it a gunshot wound." Weaver was fresh from his medical internship on this, his first operational tour with the Navy. He was as green and impressionable as a new ensign crossing the North Sea.

"What are you talking about Scott? It's obviously a gunshot wound". "Well, his roommate put an unspent shell on the stove in the guard shack and it blew up, "explained Weaver. I still don't get it."

"So, I sent the guy to the Navy Hospital." Weaver paused and looked at his notes. "It was another screw up. The surgical team said it wasn't a gunshot wound because it didn't come out of a rifle. They did a quick cleanup of the wound and just put him on a broad-spectrum antibiotic. They said something about it lacking velocity and projectile mass while encountering flesh."

"Look, I don't want to sound dense, but why didn't they treat this like a gunshot wound?" asked Tierney.

"Because, it didn't come out of a gun barrel"! "It's cost effective health; they avoid surgically opening the wound and the cost of a hospital stay." Pete replied, "Its managed care and our front-line warriors aren't cared for!" "It's cheaper not to hospitalize them." Weaver sighed. "They just said it was based on management protocols. But the hospital collects his BAQ"? (Basic Allowance for Quarters) offsetting the cost of a hospital stay." said Peter. "They collect his housing costs."

"What they really mean, Scott, is save a buck and waste a Marine. They're forcing us to sell shoddy medicine as cost-effective health care. It's bottom-line political medicine. Yeah, real high-quality stuff and do you have any idea how little a private first class is paid for housing? Not much if he is living in the Barracks."

Tierney leaned over the counter and dialed the Naval Hospital in Bremerton. He had a long reach for a man who stood five feet nine inches. He was thirty-seven, with quick smiling green eyes. His sandy brown hair would be curly except for his Navy cut. His angular face was sun-freckled, as a second-generation Irishman.

Lieutenant Commander Pete Tierney had lost the trust factor!

"Surgical department, please!"

"That would-be Captain Johnson, one moment please," said the receptionist.

Tierney did not want to speak with Johnson. They had disagreed in the past on how to treat a sailor with hemorrhoids. His hemorrhoids were so bad the man had to crawl into his medical office. Johnson wouldn't see him . "Put him in a knee-chest position" was his advice. Crawling didn't seem therapeutic.

"Captain Johnson, Pete Tierney here....,   With due respect Captain, I have a week old, dirty, infected gunshot wound that your department didn't attempt to debride. Everybody knows that wide debridement and drainage are fundamental for gunshot wounds. What we've got now is a man who's going to lose the use of his arm."

"Now wait a minute, Tierney. We treated the Marine and sent him back to you guys for follow-up. What the hell did you do to him? You screwed it up again, didn't you?"

Tierney's conflicts with Johnson had been memorable and historic. He didn't relish the prospect of another one, but if he avoided the issues, the Marine would be lost. He was lost in the cracks of a system that focused on the bottom line.

"You can't pass the buck, Captain. You missed the only opportunity any of us would ever have with this man. Why wasn't he treated properly? Was it the DRGs (Diagnostic Related Groups) or something else? Was it hospital policy, bottom-line cost-containment stuff?"

Everybody had learned that lesson in Vietnam. Debridement is the only way to save viable tissue after a gunshot wound.

"Tell you what, Captain, I'm sending this Marine back to you guys in surgery to get this wound treated properly, before he loses what's left of a useless arm."

"Dam you Tierney, you're playing holier than thou, aren't you? Rubbing me and my department's nose in it. Hell, you know as well as I do, we don't control what happens at this hospital. The administrators don't listen to us! Why should they listen to you? They love hiding behind policy--they can't create it fast enough."

"Well, Captain, someone has got to listen. I'll have the duty driver bring this man back over to the surgical department ASAP."

"Word's out Tierney. The hospital owns your clinic and won't support it."

Tierney hung up, shaking with anger. He adjusted his glasses and scolded himself for his loss of control.

Maybe the surgeon was right. Maybe it's useless, he told himself. Johnson's in charge of credentialing, after all, he'll make my life miserable. He will QA me to death. Tierney sighed. Nobody listens to the docs, not the administrators, and certainly not the politicians. Nobody in the whole damn Navy listens. Not a soul. They think they know what medicine is about, but not one of them has a clue. But they sure want to control it!

Tierney walked away from the emergency room. The Marine gazed vacantly at the ugly wound and his motionless arm.

"Doc, I'll be okay, won't I?"

Tierney was taken by the fear in the young Marine's eyes. They were needy, pleading for reassurance. Tierney nodded a hesitant yes and hoped the reassurance appeared genuine. He sensed the Marine was young enough to hold on to the image of indestructibility. Although Navy medicine fed the myth that its technology could fix almost anything, no one would be able to fix this man's arm. That opportunity was lost ten days ago to the politics of cost containment. Another casualty, another statistic recorded in an impersonal ledgered column. Soon it will be the VA's problem following a medical discharge from further service.

Lieutenant Scott Weaver was grateful his patient would have a second chance with surgery, the minimum of care necessary. The Marine would keep his arm, but it would become a useless remnant of a bad experience, and a bad policy, a bad political system. Maybe when the elbow healed, it would at least remain fixed in a functional position. The VA hospital would have a new customer before the month was over.

It wasn't a true gunshot wound; as a result it seemed a moot point. For the moment, it was enough that the captain and his surgical department would reconsider in the face of managed care protocols.

Tierney imagined a time in the future, a time when the Marine as an old man would rock in a wicker chair on his back porch telling sea stories to his grandkids. He would have to explain his arm. Tierney could imagine the story. "I lost my arm in the Marine Corps to a system error." Not a good story.

To Tierney and Weaver, obtaining proper attention for the Marine seemed a hollow victory. The Marine had no idea he'd lost the use of his arm to an empty concept euphemistically called *managed care.*

It might have been more tolerable if this were only a bad outcome, but it was not. Every other day, became a battle to have sailors attended properly at the naval hospital. Yesterday it had been the sailor from the nuclear Polaris submarine SSBN *Alabama* who had kidney stones. Urology would not see him unless he was vomiting, febrile, and without urinary output for twenty-four hours or more. One symptom was not enough; he had to show all three. The poor shipmate had spent three months under the seas defending his country, welcome home, sailor!

Wednesday brought the boson's mate with a penetrating splinter from the creosoted dock at Delta Pier. The splinter, six inches long, had impaled his left palm and exited the back of the wrist. It felt as big as the Trident submarine he was helping secure at the dock, the sailor told Tierney. He ended up losing the median nerve controlling the use of his thumb. Tierney's efforts to get him admitted to the hospital degenerated into a shouting match with the orthopedic department.

Trying to gain acceptance of a patient became a ritualized ordeal. Ultimately the boson's mate was medically retired from the Navy. He remained grateful for Tierney's efforts. Still, the VA would gain another customer.

Word at the Naval Hospital was out. If a case came from Bangor, it would be ignored. "Operational needs" became the buzzword to ignore. Johnson was right; the hospital would not support the clinic. Tierney felt agitated and anxious as he walked back to his office.

There seemed a lot of voids in his personal life. Navy medicine was becoming one of them. He knew he was out of balance. Nobody liked to see his own dark side and Tierney was no exception. He didn't want to look in the mirror. He was tired of fighting a system that didn't care. Like many of his colleagues, he loved the Navy, but Navy medicine was a different matter.

12 April 1992

Lieutenant Commander Pete Tierney, U.S. Navy Medical Corps, found himself pacing the tiled floor in the hallway outside his cluttered, confined office. Tierney was the senior medical officer of the largest, strategic nuclear submarine base in the world. The base was peacefully nestled in the evergreen forests on the eastern shore of Hood Canal in Washington State. Tierney was uneasy and preoccupied. He scuffed the floor. The in basket stacked with charts required attention. Two corpsmen had patients to present. The waiting room was full.

At the Sub Base Medical Clinic, it was a routine day by all measures, but banal it was *not* thought Tierney. Already Lieutenant Tatum, his administrative boss though his military junior had found a way to cross paths with him. Tatum had issued his usual volley of sarcastic remarks, which seemed to cast a lingering shadow in Tierney's mind. This time the criticism had something to do with devotion to *total quality management.* Tierney had neglected to fill out the correct box on a government form.

Tierney felt his professional integrity draining away. He was being managed by an administrative bean counter, a man who couldn't hope to share Tierney's sense of professionalism. Tatum had a mindless passion to comply. He was a parrot, symbolic of what was wrong with Navy medicine. The real Navy was not like this suffering medical system, he tried to assure himself. Rank meant more than pay. It meant responsibility and dedication. It stood for more than simply control. It reflected applied wisdom. Tatum was more than a balding annoyance; he reflected all that was wrong with the Medical Service Corps, which administered Navy medicine.

The Bangor Submarine Base was home to the Trident submarine, the stealthy black-hulled nuclear sneak manned by devoted Rickover-trained professionals. Everything at Bangor was a secret. Even its hollow sidewalks resonated with cavernous mystery. None asked what was underground. The atmosphere was cloaked in security. Even the jokes were secret, private, laced with hidden meanings.

The Tridents carried the nuclear firepower to destroy a world. Their crews were trained to launch the missiles never knowing if it was a real attack or just a drill. Power contrasted with the powerless.

Tierney felt himself becoming part of the unheard, the desperate, and the powerless. He felt managed professionally. He felt controlled.

He did not need to be managed, and hated being controlled. He complied even worse. He was too much like his colleagues, an individualist applying a science. A creative thinker didn't fit well with procedural types who quoted chapter and verse as if it were the Bible. His mood reflected this conflict. Tierney grew sullen, felt rejected, his spirit drooped. Surely, he thought leadership and management as concepts, are in conflict. Managed care suppressed initiative. You cannot manage creative, professional minds. Stimulating creativity fosters leadership. Managing creativity suppresses its energy.

Maybe his mood was a reaction to the pressures and distractions of the moment. Maybe it was a reaction to Shawn Carole, the woman who had mesmerized him, and then left without word. His usual tennis partners were not available; he needed the escape, the social contact, the freedom to blast balls at an opponent. Tennis was a great release. Tierney was quick, agile and loved the competition.

Yes, he was working himself into a frenzied stew. At this rate, it surely would become another troublesome, frustrating day. He had best find a tennis game.

His good friend and tennis partner Phillip Legé was recovering from arthroscopic surgery to his knee. Legé, a retired naval aviator and member of the Judge Advocate Corps, was celebrated for his astute legal mind. He now devoted his enthusiasm and energies to searching for bargains at estate sales and trying to get back on the tennis court. Tierney had helped him with his knee problem. Legé in turn had been a good ear when it came to Tierney's problems with Shawn. The two men trusted each other.

Charles Brewer, another favorite tennis partner, had been unexpectedly deployed to Guantanamo Bay (GITMO), Cuba, for six months. Some clandestine surgical exercise, Tierney had been told. Brewer was always full of surprises, even in tennis. He played a deceptive game, commensurate with his personality.

Lately, Brewer had seemed to lack his usual vigor. Maybe it had something to do with his involvement at Guantanamo Bay. Then again, maybe it was his weight loss. He looked sick and gaunt. Though he tried to deny it, the weight loss was unmistakable.

Tierney was a studious observer of people in general and of what a man's tennis game said about his personality. As a flight surgeon, he prided himself for having diagnosed a young hotshot pilot's excessive impatience. This fellow's every shot had to be a perfect winner. Tennis brought out the very best and the very worst of a hidden personality. Perfectionism set up people for mishaps. *Mishap* was aviation jargon for crashing and burning. *Accident* was too neutral a word, Tierney had decided; *mishap* suggested a trail of accountability. Having the right stuff in the cockpit required flexibility. Perfection was not a requirement of a Navy pilot.

Tierney was aware; he too had a dark side. There were demons within that he tried carefully to veil. The loss of Shawn had exposed this raw, vulnerable area.

Tierney phoned Roy Ariva, another good tennis partner.

"Roy, want to hit some balls around? Say, ten o'clock Saturday morning?"

"Saturday morning? Sure. Alice wants me out of the house anyway. Sounds like some friends are coming over."

"See you at the club, then?"

"Okay, just let me know if you can't get an inside court. Weather's miserable, no way we'll find an outside court," replied Roy.

A typically sloppy Puget Sound day, thought Tierney. Good, chasing balls around the court is a lot more fun than jogging and certainly more social. Better yet, it gets my mind off the damn clinic. Shawn had not been in touch for months. She had never been like this before.

Tierney was at a loss but did not wish to press her. He should have pressed, but his confidence had been shaken. Her sudden disappearance had left him with raw emotions he could not digest.

Tierney had gone through a divorce. His wife never adapted to the constant transfers. Tierney would have given up his Navy career for her, but the problems went deeper. He never learned to his own satisfaction what they really were.

Tierney had been stationed at the Bangor sub base for sixteen months. The Naval clinic there had its own personality, mostly austere and hazardous, but with wonderfully adaptive characters.

Tierney stopped pacing when he saw Senior Chief Elliott approaching. Senior Chief was just such a valued gem in a rough shore of jagged stones. He could move people with a whisper yet retained much of his paternal growl.

The senior chief had a hesitation in his gait, He looked worried.

"Okay, Senior, what is it?" asked Tierney.

"Jamie again...another ear infection I think...you know, cranky all night, tugging at his ear."

"Well, bring him in and I'll have a look, unless you want to take him to the naval hospital."

"No way! That's almost as bad as a trip to Group Wealth!" exclaimed the Senior Chief

Nobody, professionally that is, admired the large local HMO.

"Say, Doc, you don't look so happy yourself. More trouble with your girlfriend?"

"There's a lot going on, decision time again. Do I stay in the Navy and get more training? Or do I get the hell out of this canoe club? I've got a decent chance of getting a residency in infectious disease by next summer if I punch the right tickets; that tropical disease course and the leadership management training course at Bethesda would help my chances."

"I'm worried about Jamie, Doc, not your career!" "You're always so direct, Chief."

"There he is now. I called the wife and told her to skip the naval hospital and bring him to see you."

"Always one step ahead of me, Chief." Tierney knew he could trust the senior chief.

A car had pulled up in front of the clinic. Out of it spilled a cute little towheaded lad.

"Speaking of moves, Doc, how *is* that lady friend of yours? Shawn, is it?"

"All right, Chief! Don't press the issue. Bring that kid of yours in, or I'll send you to N-A-V-B-R-E-M-H-O-S-P!" he threatened. "What is it with you today, trying to play the role of Rumor Central?!"

"Doc, that's your dark side talking."

Elliott, a hand on Jamie's shoulder, guided his son inside.

Tierney lifted Jamie on the exam table.

The boy looked fine, except for his usual ear infection. He held his father's hand and was visibly attached. This bonding could be especially close in families torn by long separations dictated by the "needs of the Navy".

Tierney gave Jamie a pat on the tummy and then a big lift to the sky and down to the floor. The boy climbed to his father's lap and awaited his pink antibiotic and a cue from his father that it was time to go home.

Jamie was always a joy to see. He knew, even at age five, that his father was a very important man. After all, Elliott was a chief hospital corpsman, and a senior chief at that. He is One of the men who risked everything to answer the call for "Medic!" on the battlefield or the decks of a pitching ship.

Nice to have a slow moment for a change, thought Tierney. He took up the *Bremerton Sun* and focused on the headline: "AIDS Toll 100 a Day and Climbing." In two short years, the Center for Disease Control projected, 300 a day would die. The total dead now was over 200,000 already exceeding the sum of all those killed in action in Vietnam and Korea combined.

None of it made any sense, thought Tierney as he reviewed a medical journal. It didn't seem to make sense to his colleagues either, ignoring an obviously lethal epidemic. The medical literature of 1982 was ancient by now. What were the so-called experts saying about AIDS?

AIDS had started as an oddity, an object of almost academic interest, seemingly innocuous, scarcely noticed, except by some astute physicians who tried desperately to call attention to this new, developing disease.

Tierney shook his head in dismay. Acquired Immunodeficiency Syndrome was first described in the late 1970s and was first placed under active surveillance by the CDC in June 1981. In that first year, a mere 593 cases had been recorded. Almost all of them involved homosexual males or IV drug addicts.

Two years later, an estimated one million cases were known. Almost twelve years later, contrary to political rhetoric, the statistics hadn't changed. The CDC reported 93 percent of all AIDS cases in the U.S. belonged to the same groups: homosexual males, IV drug users, or those who received blood from such people.

Women had proved they were at severe risk from bisexual males, this was the heterosexual connection. Nothing else had changed in over a decade of public awareness of AIDS. Yet it was still such a hot political subject, you couldn't openly talk about it. Everybody talked, to be sure, but openness and honesty were restrained by political correctness.

Blunders of colossal proportions had occurred in the management of this epidemic, as cited in the chronology of _And The Band Played On_ written by Randy Shilts. The prevalent approach was one of absolute disregard. Neglect by design, the author said in so many words.

Lord knows how many in the United States are HIV- positive, thought Tierney. And with the secrecy surrounding any genuine scientific investigation, we may never really know.

The clinical descriptions of the disease were all too familiar. The details were unimportant, or so it seemed. Society had a mess on its hands, one that awaited a label, like _crisis!_ Tierney had long ago learned that Congress loved to use this word when it wanted to legislate a solution. He felt it would take more time and a good measure of political pressure, something more than statistics. Certainly, more was required; a lot more than blind neglect, condoms, safe sex, empty clichés, and clean needles.

It had been a rough two years for Pete Tierney. He measured the turmoil in years; no other unit of time seemed to fit. He had no idea of what was to come. He was not a fatalistic, but Irish. There was an intensity about him that captured attention. He was almost always a bit optimistic even when the situation didn't exactly warrant it. A wry humor helped him through rough spots. His words were measured and direct. Still, he was considered outspoken, at times even dangerous, but the twinkle in his eye smoothed over any abrasiveness.

He usually carried a light smile and a laugh that suggested insight, despite accusations of naiveté.

The restraint in his language was a learned experience. The medical profession had a way of using descriptive terminology to add impact where directness would not suffice. It was a bit subtle, but obvious to the informed. To a larger audience, such language lacked clear impact and was often ignored, or so Tierney thought.

He often thought he should have studied public speaking. Then he would be able to reach a wider audience. The whole profession was in trouble anyway. No one seemed to listen or to care.

Being flexible and malleable only made you more vulnerable to criticism and legislative control.

"MAN DOWN! .... MAN DOWN!" shattered the silence.

"Better get your gear, Doc. The ambulance is ready to roll and you're on tap."

Tierney grabbed his stethoscope and his khaki cover, moved quickly down the hall and climbed into the right front seat of the waiting ambulance. Just as the corpsman was about to step on the accelerator, there was a pounding on the rear double doors.

"Now what the hell!" demanded the corpsman.

"It's the OIC," said Petty Officer Tice, looking out the rear door window.

And there he was, Lieutenant Isaac Tatum, the administrative service corps officer-in-charge (OIC), banging his fist on the rear white doors with determined frenzy. The standard joke was that Tatum was born worried, or his life's goal was to become a speed bump. No one cared much for him. He was tolerated, preferably from a distance. Being in the same ambulance was too close.

"Find out what he wants," someone said, just as Petty Officer Tice opened the door with an inquisitive look. Before he could ask, the OIC had climbed inside, found a vacant bench seat, secured a clipboard against his cheek, and attached the seat belt.

"Okay, let's go!" he commanded.

Now this is strange, thought Tierney. This guy Tatum had become a pain to everyone. Even his verbal commands rang hollow and seemed measured, as if he were practicing leading a staged charge up a hill that would be captured in all its glory on video. Tatum must have watched too many war movies.

"What's going on, Lieutenant? " asked Tierney.

"Well, I thought it was about time I saw firsthand what you people really do. You know, kind of observe."

Tierney paused, reflected, and searched the expressions of his trusted corpsmen for a sign of mutual understanding. They all had a puzzled and distant vacancy to their eyes.

Maybe I've been a little too harsh on the guy, thought Tierney. Maybe he really is interested. Give him a break.

"All right, you heard the man, let's go," Tierney said.

Before the words were out of his mouth the acceleration buried him in the cushioned seat. The siren wailed its urgent message, familiar to riders of these top-heavy vehicles that teeter round corners. Someone had added a new cadence to the siren, the variable pitch of a British police car in a London fog. The corpsmen loved the high visibility and the rush of driving with lights on and sirens howling.

The corpsmen remained strangely subdued and avoided each other's gaze. Worse than strangers on an elevator, Tierney thought. He chalked it up to the presence of the OIC.

Tatum had a way of casting a dark shadow of disapproval, even in the darkened confines of an ambulance. He always seemed to be measuring something. Ready to report his bean count to a medical service corps officer higher up the chain of command. It seemed nothing ever slipped his hawkish, critical, measuring eye, it invited contempt.

Tierney wondered. Why Tatum? Why this run? He must be collecting data to appraise, no, assess, performance. *Assess* had become one of those overused, politically correct, noncommittal words suggesting continual study without conclusion. Just a process word. *Knock it off,* Tierney silently scolded himself. *Give the guy a break. So then, why did he bring the clipboard?* The man was probably preparing some administrative report critiquing the expediency of response by the ambulance team. Observer indeed, he thought. *Snoop* is a better description.

Tierney's experience coincided with others who felt medical administrators were always on the hunt and not to be trusted. They were not much different from the feared political officer in the Soviet military whose job it was to ensure each soldier towed the official communist line. It was a KGB mentality. What really was Tatum's reason for being there? Tierney could feel tension build in the silent confines of the ambulance.

The radio sputtered and chattered. Amid the noise were clear directions to the Bachelor Officer Quarters (BOQ).

Responding to a *"Man Down"* always seemed charged with anxious moments. Tierney and the corpsmen prepared themselves mentally. They recalled and recreated scenes from the past, then downplayed them with their chatter, seeking a sense of control perhaps over "whatever unexpected situation might occur."

Scenes from the recent past flashed through Tierney's mind. The Marine in the guard tower at Trident Training Facility who blew his brains out while on guard duty. That damnable, short-tempered submariner who shot two fellow sailors in the Bachelor Enlisted Quarters.   30

That marine calmly drove into Bremerton, purchased a gun, and shot the store attendants, killing one, all for no apparent reason. The Naval Investigative Service went crazy with this Flail-EX (flailed-exercise). There were more agents and messages flying that month than the *Bremerton Sun* could handle. The Personal Reliability Program had come under close public scrutiny. There was much concern over nuclear submarines and trigger-happy sailors. The public and the *Sun* had a hot story and neither would let it go away. Not surprisingly, fear sold newspapers.

At the BOQ the ambulance crew, Tatum, and Tierney were escorted by a burly security guard to a second-deck room styled like all the rest. The rooms on the right were mirror images of those on the left. It was applied efficiency, symmetry gone amok. Adjacent to the living area was a room with a single bed. Of course, Tierney thought, only real submariners would sleep in a narrow rack, even ashore. A black man lay on the floor between the bed and a double-closeted door. Tierney saw an intravenous line and a piggybacked 50 ml vial of Anectine, (a paralytic drug) now empty. The line was connected to a 250-ml plastic bag of normal saline. Two other spent syringes lay next to the body. The first one, Ketamine and the second, amyl barbiturate. Everything was clearly labeled. A very professional job, thought Tierney, A clean suicide.

The man's head was turned toward the closet door. Rigor mortis had set in like cold concrete, like a cast on a broken leg. No matter how hard you tried, you would not find warmth or softness. The body was stiff and cold to the core.

Tierney struggled to position himself to examine the head without disturbing the body or the suicide scene.

Shit...its Charlie! Charles Brewer, a general surgeon, best friend, tennis partner and neighbor. Charlie, what the hell did you do to yourself? We had played tennis together, mowed our lawns together, and told each other racial jokes, forgetting which color we were supposed to be, as it never seemed important. We were more than friends, we were brothers.

What was Brewer doing here? When had he returned from GITMO? Tierney felt tears; he didn't know what to do with them.

I can't believe he'd just quit like this! Look how thin he is. He was never a quitter. I knew him better than this! Charlie wouldn't back out like this! No damn way!

Suddenly the room was full of official types directed by the large, pendulous investigative officer in charge of security. None allowed Tierney to search the area for clues. The room became a controlled, sterile environment.

"Hey Doc, look here!"

Hospital Corpsman Petty Officer HM-2 Vasques indicated a sheet of yellow legal paper on the cherry desk in the living room.

It was part of a letter to Brewer's wife, Nancy, and their child. Brewer sounded morose and guilt-ridden. He had sexual encounters in Pattaya Beach, Thailand, in Bangkok, Naples, and Olongopo. He was HIV-positive. He admitted to being bisexual, predicted he would have AIDS and feared he would no longer be allowed to practice surgery. He had lost hope and now life itself.

"Must have hit the Samurai on Mic Si Si Street in Olongopo." Petty Officer Vasques arched his eyebrows, as if to declare that he kept a girl in every port. "Doc, I bet he made the Sabailand massage parlor in Pattaya Beach."

"Shut up! This man was my friend. Show some respect!"

Tierney was shaken. How strange to have known someone so closely for so long and not really have known him at all.

And not just Brewer--there was Shawn as well.

"I don't believe it," he murmured.

Tatum nodded to the security guard at the door. "This'll be an easy one, "Suicide, open and shut case, suicide note and all."

Tierney whirled toward Tatum but managed to stop himself. What's the son of a bitch doing now? Assessing and documenting? Probably, with a stopwatch and full report to follow. Tierney reflected. He'd never known this surgeon to write so legibly. Was that how Brewer had written his farewell to the world? Sloppy penmanship was Brewer's trademark. He and Tierney had joked about whose writing was worse. Tatum must have been going for some sort of efficiency award.

The security officer placed the letter in a plastic bag for evidence. The Naval Investigative Service would soon arrive. Nothing is to be disturbed until then.

From the living room, Tierney glanced back his last time. The body was supine, clothed in pajamas, a white T-shirt underneath, head fixed in full right lateral rotation, eyes wide open as if in full startle. Tierney returned, knelt beside the stiff corpse and pulled the eyelids down. Funny, how the eyelids remained soft despite rigors.

Then he noticed a patch of denuded skin from the back of the left ear lobe.

"Doctor, don't you think you've seen quite enough? Shall we call it quits?" It was Tatum's typically stilted squawk.

Pete recognized the language and the message.

"What do you suppose this lesion is on his ear?" Tierney asked himself aloud. "Why? Are you in such a hurry, Lieutenant?"

Tierney reflected in a long pause; this was no ordinary abrasion as there was no evidence of bleeding about the denuded area, it also had sharp surgical like margins. This had to be a post mortem change and it had to be deliberate!

"What is it that you see, Doctor?" asked Tatum, fearing to display any sudden sense of respect for Tierney's powers of observation. Tatum appeared anxious.

"Nothing!" Tierney paused. "Oh, Nothing at all."

The OIC left after reminding the guard that no one was to disturb any evidence. The guard himself was to stay with the body until the coroner released it. Since the body was on government property, this was not really a burning issue, but simply a formality. Tatum seemed renewed with a born-again devotion to duty.

Tierney could not stop thinking about Brewer.

This guy was one of my closest friends. I didn't have the slightest sense that he was gay. You'd think I would know that after four years together. *What was he doing in Cuba?*

Tierney could not bring himself to return directly to his office. Medicine at the clinic had grown repetitious, tedious. The managers had left it barely tolerable. On a personal level medicine, still had meaning if he looked hard enough. The people sometimes made it worthwhile. Today, however, was a tragic turning point.

There must be a reason behind all these losses. Tierney left his pager with Senior Chief Elliott and walked past the security guards

and the yellow barrier tape about the rear of the brick BOQ.
He needed time to think.

The brisk, moist wind cooled his cheeks and ears. He liked the chilling vigor of a fresh breeze. It reminded him of sailing the waters of Puget Sound. The wind was a pleasant distraction. You could always tell its direction by how it played on your ears. If the wind was on your nose, it played equally on both ears. If it was off center, then one ear was protected from the air flow. Kind of like a personal wind vane. The saltwater smell and the freshening breeze reminded him this was home.

It had been a very rough year: The sudden loss of Shawn, the struggle with his mother's death and the closing of her estate.

But now, Charlie!

Tatum had never gone on any of the other runs, not for the Marine who committed suicide, not for the gun slinging submariner. What was so special that required his presence with Brewer? This was becoming a bitch of a year!

Tierney strode off, determined to separate himself from the suicide scene. Soon he found himself at the edge of Trident Lake. The walkway led up a hill and became a path through a forest of hemlocks, Douglas firs, and cedars, a tranquil nature trail.

Questions about Shawn flew through his head. They used to take afternoon walks along this path. Questions about Charles, how would he ever find the words to tell Nancy? How would he explain Charlie's letter of remorse, his fear of AIDS? Nancy would need to be tested herself. The practicality of it all flooded over him and the veil seemed unreal. How to ask such technical questions of people so close? Tierney knew the obligation was his alone.

Why do we only deal with the victims of this disease? He tried to remember what he had learned at that last Infectious Disease Conference in Seattle. The lecturer, a specialist in infectious diseases at San Francisco General Hospital, spoke candidly of the terror he felt every day when he checked himself for the Kaposi's sarcoma eruption of the skin that characterized active AIDS. Tierney had long since forgotten the man's name, but he would always remember his presentation. The intensity of his fear was palpable. He worked on the front lines of this infectious disease as a consultant at San

Francisco General. Every day was a new and almost certain risk. Each morning, this doctor would study his naked body in the full-length mirror of his bathroom, looking for the telltale violaceous spots of a Kaposi's sarcoma. Then it was called Gay-Related Immune Disease, Wasting Disease, or Slim Disease. They were the same, just described differently from various perspectives. Whatever the name, it meant certain death.

Tierney respected this lecturer. He was not pompous; he didn't flaunt his appearance by draping a stethoscope around a starched, button-down collar, and avoided white jackets. Like Tierney, he worked in the trenches of health care, struggling to make sense of it all.

What struck Tierney strangely was how useless it was for Brewer to have committed suicide. I could have at least talked to him. I might have given him some hope, enough to get him around the corner of another day. He did not need to kill himself.

What was it this lecturer had said? Oh yes. "We consider quarantine inappropriate." Damn, I hate the misuse of the word inappropriate. It's overused and wrung out, Tierney thought. It kills good ideas in the civilian world just as quickly as in the Navy.

Well, Tierney reminded himself, back to the clinic to make a report for the investigative types who will soon surround it.

Tierney entered the double glass doors on the west side of the clinic. Seeing no OIC, he asked Senior Chief Elliott his whereabouts.

"He's still at the scene."

"How will I ever be able to tell Nancy?" Tierney muttered to himself. "Better call the chaplain."

"Not to worry, Doc. Lieutenant Tatum already put in a call to the Naval Hospital Command and the chaplain's office. Seems Tatum has a personal interest. He must have thought of everything."

"So it seems, Chief, so it seems!" Tierney turned away and tried to convince himself it was all real.

CHAPTER 2

Non-Hostile, Class Alpha Casualty

A Navy chaplain accompanied Tierney to the home of Nancy Brewer.

It's an oft repeated scene, a black official sedan with a driver stopping outside the home of a Navy family. The neighborhood grows silent as the sedan circles, looking for the home of the lost sailor. Shades close and drapes are pulled. Nancy, unaware, smiled at the sight of Tierney approaching the front door. It took only a moment for her to realize the visit was ominous and official.

She opened the screen door, and then let it slam behind her. She wiped her hands on her apron and placed her arm around her daughter Kristen's shoulder. She searched Tierney's eyes. The twin boys next door stopped their game and looked on from a distance, sensing something was wrong. They kept their distance instinctively fearful of bad news. Peter never appeared at the Brewer's home in a dress blue uniform.

As Tierney removed his dark glasses, Nancy could see the tears in his eyes, the sorrow in his face.

She shook her head, turned away, and buried her face in the apron.

"Nancy, I'm so sorry." Pete extended his right hand.

She turned to face Peter, the chaplain stood behind.

"Charlie's dead?" she asked, knowing the answer.

Tierney nodded and extended the other hand. Nancy fell into his arms, sobbing. He gathered her in, with Kristen holding onto her mother's waist; Pete reached around Kristen's shoulder.

It was a soul-wrenching experience, telling Nancy what had happened to her husband. Her life abruptly and instantly shattered. Pete felt her loss, Charlie was his closest friend.

Tierney planned to return over the next few days. Both were crushed and incensed to learn the funeral would be delayed.

Nancy could not believe that Charles was dead: A suicide, much less because of homosexual guilt trips and HIV sero- conversion.

She pointedly snapped, "A wife ought to know if her husband is gay, and Charles could not possibly have hidden this from me. Even if he was bisexual, I would have of all people, known!"

Pete mused in indecision. Initially he believed her without really knowing why. *Maybe she's right, and I should trust her instincts.* Then he reevaluated options, possibly Charlie had deceived me, he just as easily could have deceived his wife. Maybe she's stuck in denial?

"Something is wrong, terribly wrong." Nancy continued, "I don't care what the Navy or the JAG (Judge Advocate General₁) says, Charlie was not gay, bisexual, or any other alternative, politically correct persuasion," she snarled. "I'm sick to death of lies, euphemisms. My husband is dead! He was not bisexual, gay, nor a drug user! After thirteen years I ought to know! How the hell did he get AIDS?"

She paused, rubbed her forehead. Her anger seemed to fade. "Peter," she asked, calmly and politely, "will you please check the hospital morgue? Make sure he's really there? Help me, Peter. Charles was not homosexual! If anything, he knew something he shouldn't have known and was too honest to keep it quiet."

"Okay, Nancy, I'll look into it, the weekend is coming. I won't have anyone to talk to over the weekend not until Monday. I'm sure the pathologist won't be around. Nancy, I know how hard this is on you. I too feel the loss. You know how close we were."

"Pete, you're not listening to me! No! Something is very, very wrong! I'm his wife. I would know, don't you think! I would know if he was even mildly gay? This is crazy, and I will not wait till Monday!"

"Okay, Nancy, Okay, I'll do my best. I noticed two details that prove suspicious. I noticed a patch of denuded skin on the back of his left ear lobe and a legible suicide note. Nancy, it really looked like a suicide, it was done very professionally, like Charles was a professional anesthesiologist, not a surgeon." Tierney noticed his reflection in the patio window. Neither his gestures nor his logic were convincing.

Tierney paused and listened to what he had just said, "Like a professional anesthesiologist." Charlie doesn't know shit about the drugs used by the gas man. He's a cutter, not a gas man.

"Let me know what you learn Peter. I do not trust the Naval Investigation Service and I don't trust this Medical Command. Right now, I don't trust anyone. Something is very wrong, badly wrong. Charles needed me, I was not aware of what was happening to him. Peter, I don't have anyone else to turn to, only you."

Nancy turned toward the window overlooking the narrow passage between Keyport and Poulsbo She held her arms closely around her chest, as if Charles were holding her.

Peter felt he had done enough damage for one day and made his apologies to Nancy kissing her on the cheek and Kristen on the forehead. He promised to visit the morgue on the weekend and report his findings to Nancy.

She had several days, before the weekend, to find some solace. She took Peter's phone number in case she thought of something.

"Peter, give me a little time to think about what to do and what arrangements to make."

Peter nodded in agreement. "I'll see you this weekend". He left via the kitchen door, forgetting his cover and walked to the waiting black official vehicle. The Navy Chaplin was next in line to assist Nancy and her daughter. When he had done the miracle work that only a man of God can do, both departed for the Submarine Base Bangor. Peter guessed that Navy Legal would be her next visitor.

Pete thought, *there did seem to be a lot of secrecy about Brewer's death.* He returned to her cottage, he felt rattled and had forgotten his cover.

Nancy turned to Peter and glared at him. "I had no idea he was back. No phone call from him, no notification to pick him up at the airlift from McCord, AFB. I thought he was still in GITMO. For all I know he died there and they shipped him back." Her tone was shot with anger and sarcasm.

Pete nodded recognition, turned away and searched for his hat. Nancy led him to the back door. He opened the screen door, the cool air of the sea breeze awakened his realization, and he knew what she was talking about.

Tierney chastised himself. *I know I shouldn't get involved in this matter. I feel it in my bones; this is going to get dirty. I just don't need this right now!* "Why me?" he asked aloud. "Why me?"

Back at Subbase Bangor, Tierney slipped into the form-fitting seat of his Fiat Spider and gently accelerated onto the winding road. The radio blared the nasal whine of Michael Bolton. He switched stations. An unknown station reported that Haitian refugees were being taken to Guantanamo Bay (GITMO), Cuba.

It was quiet back at the clinic. Tierney reviewed the message traffic to the Bureau of Naval Personnel. The preliminary reports had been written in typical Navy format; an abbreviated description of the non-hostile death of Commander Charles Brewer, an apparent suicide. Next of kin in Norfolk, Virginia, and immediate family notified.

From: NavBremHosp
To: Bureau Naval Personnel
Bureau of Medicine Surgery
Subj: Death of Active Duty Member/ Casualty Report
    Reg:
Charles L. Brewer CDR (MC) USN SS#555-12-1220
Via:
CO NAVBREMHOSP
CO BANGORSUBMARB
CO SUBMARGRP NINE

THE NAMED MEMBER WAS FOUND DEAD 2 APRIL 92 AT BANGOR BOQ. THIS IS CLASS ALPHA SERVICE CONNECTED NON-COMBAT CASUALTY. NIS INVESTIGATION IN PROCESS. NEXT OF KIN NOTIFIED AND BELONGINGS RESTORED. BODY LOCATED AT NAVHOSPBREM MORGUE. AUTOPSY AUTHORIZED DUE TO EVIDENT SELF- INFLICTED WOUNDS.

by direction
R. Sharon

Pete reflected and knew this is the typical stale language of Navy official jargon. It was much too routine, impersonal, and unimaginative for such a close friend, but such messages were always impersonal. Still, he was offended as he placed the message back on the reader board walls mounting hooks.

The following day, Lt. Isaac Tatum interrupted Tierney as he finished a rereading of the same message board.

"Doc Tierney, this is Lieutenant Kim Kelly, the investigative officer assigned by the naval hospital. She has been waiting since 1330, to ask you questions about CDR Brewer's suicide."

Lt. Kelly and Tierney shook hands.

"Can you tell me what you found at the scene Tierney?" Did you notice anything unusual can you offer some comments on the suicide letter?"

"Well the letter was clearly written and spoke of Charlie's fear of getting AIDS."

The interview was rapidly concluded within seven minutes and appeared it was a mere formality for a sudden and unexplained death.

Kelly did not sit nor take notes
Strange Peter thought *for an investigator.*

"Lt. Kelley are you from the local command?"

"No, I'm from D.C. and it was a long flight!"

"But, don't we have a local JAG corps in the northwest region?" Peter asked

Kelly's abrupt manner, appeared more of an urgency to complete the forms, than to investigate the death.

Tierney attempted a few more questions and was quickly put in his place:

"That is not pertinent to this official inquiry, Commander! The questions I am asking *are* necessary, and quite routine."

Tierney noticed Tatum had not left the room. Pete turned to him and asked, "Is it necessary that you be present for this interview Lieutenant Tatum?"

"Please excuse me"! He rubbed his balding head and exited with a twitch to his upper lip. Tierney found this annoying and revealed some pressure on the man.

When alone, Tierney turned his attention to Kelly, and launched a final try. "Why did CDR Brewer return from GITMO so notably early in his assignment? I mean two months early?"

"Orders from the Commanding Officer!" Kelly responded.

"Now, come on, Lieutenant. His wife didn't even know he had returned home. Why, the big secret?"

There was a long, uncomfortable pause.

"Commander Tierney, I am the one conducting this investigation and it is at command request. It is for me to ask the questions, not you. I want you to tell me exactly what you saw at the suicide scene. I want it in detail, and I want it in writing. Do we understand each other?"

This will get me nowhere fast, thought Tierney. *Better chill out.*

"Yes, Lieutenant, I understand."

Peter decided to give Kelly what she wanted, and then visit the pathologist at the Navy Hospital, as Nancy had asked. *I' ll just pop in there and see what I can learn. Might as well try to give Nancy some peace of mind, but this may be a witch hunt.*

Late Friday:

Morgues were always submerged in the dark recesses of hospitals, usually in basements, sometimes under lock and key, rarely visited by the living, and mostly unoccupied. This evening was no exception. The logbook at the front desk was attended by a second-class corpsman who registered visitors, but not hospital staff. Tierney was therefore hardly noticed. The pathologist had apparently gone home, and the only available record of Charles was a simple register with a vault number.

The first thing Tierney noticed was that the autopsy hadn't been performed locally. This was odd, because there was almost always a local pathologist on duty. An autopsy was required for all unexplained cases of traumatic death.

Maybe, too much risk with an HIV-positive corpse? Tierney considered.

He scanned the pathology logbook attached to the closed vaults. Specific instructions "your eyes only" a notation had been left to notify Lt. Tatum if anyone inquired about the remains of CDR Brewer.

"Corpsman Jones, Lieutenant Tatum asked me to inspect the body and the pathology report. No need to bother him tonight. I will see him in the morning with a full report."

"Aye-aye," responded the corpsman. "I understand and the less reports I have to file, the better. By the way, aren't you Doc Tierney? I believe you took care of my wife while I was on patrol with the SSN *Whale.*"

"Hmm, I'm afraid I don't recall your wife. What was the nature of her problem?" Tierney had trouble remembering names, but not medical problems nor the fast attack SSN *Whale.*

As they talked, the corpsman became more distracted with family concerns. He expressed gratitude for Tierney's care. He also neglected to record Tierney's visit nor to inform Tatum. "The body was shipped to AFIP (Armed Forces Institute of Pathology) in Washington DC where they're doing the autopsy." Pete restrained his surprise. "Isn't that a bit unusual?"

"Not really, sir. They promised to send it back by Monday. I think it's a pretty big case." The Bureau of Medicine and Surgery had expressed a special interest as well, the corpsman volunteered. "That's what these papers show." Jones flourished a handful of signed Directives from higher authority.

Tierney nodded in acknowledgement, "Yes, Lieutenant Tatum said there would be a lot of high visibility. Well, what do you expect? The guy was an important surgeon."

Shit, thought Pete Tierney. *Something very big is going down, and I have no idea what I'm doing here. I better get the hell out.*

"Corpsman Jones, you wouldn't happen to have any pathology reports on CDR Brewer, would you? I feel awful about his wife. She's been up nights, you know, all the turmoil surrounding her husband's death."

"Doc, the only thing I can tell you is the body was shipped back to AFIP, I noticed a minor notation recorded that the left ear lobe had been scratched."

"What!"

"Yes sir, at least that's the scuttlebutt I picked up around here," Jones said with assurance.

"Does the OIC Tatum know about this?"

"Oh yes sir! He signed this form, DD 1300." Jones held it aloft. "Right here, see his signature right here!"

Tierney knew the Armed Forces Institute of Pathology had some gruesome and politically sensitive duties, identifying body parts after mass casualties, DNA tagging, and such. These had been called into play after the Beirut massacre, Grenada, the Panama Canal invasion.

Pete's contact with the AFIP had been limited to some unusual pathology reports. An official review by the professionals there was like having the forensic pathology gods on the hunt.

They suggested foul play, or official interests at higher levels.

Tierney looked at the forms closely. Indeed, the body had been shipped. But not to the AFIP, as Jones had indicated, but rather, to the Armed Forces Institute of Medical Intelligence (AFIMI) at Fort Detrick, in Frederick, Maryland.

Among other things, the form asked the local pathologist to note any unusual findings after inspection of the body.

The local pathology report read "on the body of CDR Charles Brewer, no abnormality detected."

"If part of the ear lobe really was altered, that information seemed to be conveniently missing from an official file". Peter uttered in a low tone,

But he thought, *it might have accidently been missed as is was a very small patch on the back of his ear lobe.*

"Where's the local pathologist?" asked Tierney.

"Been sent to Bethesda Naval Hospital for a refresher course, I'm told. Two weeks of Continuing Medical Education." said the corpsman.

"Shit!" Tierney muttered.

He left the morgue, walking past the hospital quarter deck. Its walls, decorated with chain-of-command and Sailor of the Quarter photos.

He found his Fiat, threw his cover in the back seat, and turned on the radio.

Tierney had stepped into a hornet's nest. He knew better than to get involved. Still, he made a mental note to talk with the pathologist upon his return.

He drove back to Keyport and reported to Nancy. Keyport is home to the USN underwater research studies specializing in retrieving torpedoes launched from submarines.

"I don't know what to tell you. I seem to have found more questions than answers. I didn't get to see Charlie's body. He's been sent to Fort Detrick, Maryland, for an autopsy at least that is the official word. I'm told the local pathologist was reassigned to Bethesda for the next two weeks."

"Peter, something is terribly wrong!" said Nancy. "See, I told you so"!

"Do you know, an investigative officer, a female Lt. from DC legal arrived at our home this afternoon and had the gall to suggest that if I appear less interested in the autopsy, it might reduce any legal impasse to compensation?" Nancy turned back toward Tierney. "I told her No! You bitch. Charles was not gay!"

Peter, "I don't understand? Nancy, Take away your benefits?"

The Lt. said, "Suicide is misconduct. The government will not support the family of a sailor who commits suicide. They lose all indemnity compensation. Losing Charles is bad enough, but playing with his reputation and now the benefits. I will not tolerate it!"

"Will you talk to the pathologist"?

"Peter, I just don't know, but I can't believe Charles would do this to himself! He cared too much, something must have happened in Cuba!"

Tierney heard the conviction in Nancy's voice. He tried to reassure her, but his words seemed hollow.

"Nancy, I wish I knew more. Charlie seems to be getting a lot of attention at high levels, much higher than I've ever seen before,

The AFIP, the AFIMI, (Armed Forces Institute of Medical Intelligence) but none of what I've learned is really concrete. Lt. Tatum has left word at the morgue to be told of all traffic and inquiries into Charlie's death. Security is tight." Pete decided not to mention the denuded ear lob

The Funeral, a wet day:

Charles's funeral was brief and officially ignored by the Naval Hospital Bremerton Command. Neither the (CO) commanding officer nor (XO) executive officer attended the service. No official eulogy.

Nancy out of sheer devotion and appalling annoyance offered a few unrehearsed words for her husband, child and herself. The only representation from the Naval Hospital Command was a second-rate administrator named LCDR Sharon, along with the command chaplain and of course the perpetual shadow of Lt. Tatum. like a wallflower scribe recording everything, Tatum stood on the far side of the closed casket under a rain drenched awning. Lt. Tatum whispered something into the ear of LCDR Sharon, Peter stood adjacent to Nancy and Kristen. The command representatives stood on the other side of the coffin as it was lowered into the grave. Tatum turned his head to whisper into Sharon's ear. From his distance and for an instant, Peter observes a spot behind Tatum's left ear.
What was that dark spot behind Tatum's ear lobe?

Tierney questioned his visual clarity. Peter removed his glasses, rain drops from the black bill of his hat dripped onto his glasses. Peter removed a tissue and wiped his lenses clean. He now had a rainbow sheen on the lens. He pulled out another wipe and his vision returned.
Pete *shrugged it off believing his vision was faulty.*
He turned to Nancy and asked. "Why are we in the rain and the command is under cover'?
Nancy didn't care and did not respond.

45

There was the traditional folded flag for Nancy and lots of unanswered questions. Taps were played from a tape recorder on an emotional day marked by cold tears, the sight of a fatherless child and an anguished wife made the condolences sound like empty platitudes. The chaplain's words were uplifting, but he did not know Charles. There was one surprise,

Lieutenant Kim Kelly; the investigative JAG officer from DC was in attendance. Her investigation had been abbreviated, a mere formality, almost nonexistent. So why was Kelly in attendance? She hadn't known Brewer.

Nancy wiped her tears as the brief graveside ceremony ended. She felt she had buried an empty box rather than her husband.

Her sister had flown in from Norfolk, Virginia. Tierney noticed her as he put an arm about Nancy's slim waist. *At least there is family here on short notice to support Nancy*, thought Peter.

The chaplain left and Kelly approached.

"Lieutenant Kelly, thank you for coming," said Tierney. They shook hands. "What brings you away from your investigation?"

"Well, Commander, I wanted to express my regrets to Mrs. Brewer. Thought it was the right thing to do under the circumstances. You know, it's really hard to get a sense about things when the Bureau of Medicine and Surgery tears me away from a very important case in DC and asks me to conduct a formal inquiry on something that seems so straight forward." "Does something bother you about the investigation?" asked Tierney.

"Well, yes sir, something does trouble me. I was involved in a very sensitive legal matter involving maritime operations in international waters, an OP-Nav-03 level, a heavy, quite critical investigation. To be called to the West Coast for what appears to be a rather ordinary suicide, well, I mean, my orders are from the Bureau of Medicine & Surgery and the Research and Development Center in Bethesda's involved. It's all….well, very unusual!" "Additionally, the Hospital command has local access to do a JAG corps investigation".

Footnote: OP-Nav-03 = Admiralty level Operational Navy command
It is traditional courtesy in the Navy to address a LCDR as a Commander implying that he will make CDR. Same is true of a LTJG addressed as Lt.

Kelly reached for Nancy's hand. "I wanted to speak again with you, Mrs. Brewer, and express my deep and true sorrow for your loss. Death just seems so final. I've wondered, something very important must have happened to your husband for his body to be flown back to AFIMI for examination. I've never seen that done before except in very sensitive political cases. Please accept my sincere apologies."

Tierney was stunned with the change in Kelly. A woman who had arrived with an agenda. Now she seemed to be leaving empty handed, almost shaken. Pete sensed that she felt professionally used.

Tatum strained to pick up this personal conversation.

Nancy turned to Tierney. Her pupils dilated with a searching gaze. She knew Tierney had not told her everything he knew. A deep silence followed. She turned toward the black hearse, took Kristen by the hand, and walked into the cold rain, Tierney followed. Nancy stopped, turned, and placed her hands over the gold stripes of Tierney's dress blue uniform. She searched his eyes. "Peter, please tell me what happened. Charles could not have died this way! Tell me what you have learned, you promised!"

Tierney escorted her the short distance that remained to the waiting black limousine. He opened the rear door halfway, then stopped and spoke in an undertone.

"I don't know what happened. It really did look almost like a staged suicide. I'll keep looking, and I promise to keep you informed. Nancy, I don't know how to tell you this, but part of Charlie's left ear lobe was surgically altered, post mortem."

"Yes! I knew it! I knew he didn't kill himself! I knew he wasn't gay! Thank you, Peter, thank you so much!"

Kristen followed Nancy into the black limousine. Nancy looked back at Tierney, her eyes teary-eyed in questioning.

"I'll stop by in a couple of days. See how you and Kristin are doing, we'll talk more." Tierney said with assurance.

As Tierney watched the black limousine pull away, the finality of Charlie Brewer's life settled into his consciousness. The rain dripped from his brimmed Navy cover, another bone chilling day, a very wet day for a friend's burial.

The limousine eased out of sight and Tierney turned away. He did not know that Nancy would find her own way to answers. For now, there were only questions that demanded answers. Peter did not know that Nancy Brewer had been threatened with removing her survivor benefits as suicide is a criminal offense, not compensable.

CHAPTER 3

Opening Day, Open Wound

Friday Evening, First Weekend in May Entering the Ballard Locks: "No, I need a forty-foot line!" shouted the lock attendant. "Not a piece of twine," he muttered in exasperation. "Lash it to that forward cleat, no, the one at your foot...your left foot!"

The lock masters at the Chittenden Locks had seen it all. The incoming current from the higher Lake Washington water level threatened to pivot a twenty-seven-foot powerboat and send it against the grain of the locks traffic.

The Hiram M. Chittenden Locks, in local parlance, the Ballard Locks, separated the salt water of Puget Sound from the fresh water of Lake Washington. The lake was thirty feet higher, than the parallel man-made channels much like a miniature Panama Canal. It was a scene of chaotic boat traffic bound for the Opening Day.

Tierney skippered *Cricket*, his forty-f o o t yawl. A weekend of celebration awaited him, the official opening of the boating season in Puget Sound. For fifty years Opening Day had taken place the first weekend in May, sponsored by the Seattle Yacht Club.

Attempts to contact Shawn had been futile. She was gone again, this time off to France.

Mosaics of boaters, rarely at their best and often at their worst, were making their way through the locks. Confusion, close calls, the occasional collision made the lock traffic a tourist delight. The anticipation alone accelerated unnecessary fears and trepidation in the hearts of most boaters.

Tierney and close friends, Bill and Judy Weiss had just completed the two-hour sail from Poulsbo, via Agate Passage to Elliott Bay. The brisk south wind made it a pleasant passage. Rounding West Point, off Discovery Park, and losing their wind, they had fired up the diesel engine; traversed half a dozen bridges, and finally arrived at the Seattle Yacht Club in Portage Bay. They were relieved to find a safe moorage and begin an evening of light conversation, dancing, and drinks.

Tierney was introduced to Washington State's 7th District Representative, Fred Dewey, of Magnolia Heights. Dewey sat on the Military Appropriations Committee and the Health Care Planning Commission, two very powerful positions.

Dewey was well on his way to becoming obnoxiously intoxicated. This surprised no one. He was a bloated man and in his boisterous and stumbling manner he lamented the severe defense cuts that would close bases across the nation. Some in Puget Sound had been targeted, including Sand Point Naval Station, a stone's throw from the Seattle Yacht Club.

"You think the guy would stop campaigning, but Dewey loves an audience," remarked a blue-blazered yacht clubber who seemed a knowledgeable but, reluctant participant.

"I personally want to limit the economic damage and be creative with the residual facilities. No sense wasting good government property and your tax dollars," Dewey proclaimed.

The congressman turned to Tierney. "We will disclose the real reasons, son, at the proper time," he said with a blast of his malodorous breath. "Timing is everything. It's got to look good to the voters, eh?"

With a wink of his eye he added, "Name a hot issue and I'll make it look good in the upcoming election! Jobs, the environment, pollution in the Sound, secondary waste disposal, the homeless, health care, these are the hot issues now. Anything that strikes a chord of voter sympathy, we can market it. We can market just about anything, just need to package it right. These voters can be programmed just like a fine-tuned radio station. All you must do is dial the tune you want 'them to hear."

He stumbled and bumped his glass of scotch against the microphone stand with a magnified thump, sending it rocking. His three escorts quickly guided Dewey back to the Flag Gig, moored in front of the Seattle Yacht Club. A well-groomed brunette in a short, tight black skirt appeared and stepped to follow the escorts. *She is probably his hired companion, window dressing*, thought Tierney. This man Dewey didn't seem to know what he valued, except staying in office at any expense.

On his way-out Congressman Dewey leaned over and muttered, "Pete, is it? Yes, Pete. Sand Point Naval Station will be the perfect site for the start of our local social programs."

Drunks come *in many different forms*, thought Tierney. *some get angry, some quiet. Some agree some grandiose and some are sad sacks Dewey must be one grandiose thinker, especially if he's near a podium.* He watched as Dewey was placed aboard the Admiral's gig and quickly sped away for the return voyage from Portage Bay back toward the locks. The transom light faded as the vessel sped away briskly rocking adjacent boats.

Pete had a hunch he would confront Dewey again, but in a different setting when Dewey was sober and adversarial. In the cool night air Tierney returned to *Cricket* and his warm berth. As always, the boat rocked him sound asleep as if he were a baby in a cradle.

Saturday Morning:

The festivities started with the flag pole ceremony and a performance by the University of Washington ROTC Navy Band. After the crew races, in the cut, a huge chaotic swath of boaters paraded through the same narrow waterway. The cut extended from Portage Bay to Lake Washington It was a marvel to note that so many survived this competitive passage, filled with near misses. Tierney and his guests took the plunge and motored *Cricket* through the cut's passage. There were more drunk boaters per capita here than anywhere else in the world, or so he had been warned.

Once in Lake Washington and clear of the clutter of adjacent boats, they set sail on an easterly blow. What a glorious day, Wind and colors flying as they trimmed the main and jenny. *Cricket* came alive on a starboard tack going north-northeast into Lake Washington.

The conversation was as light and frivolous as the day's pageantry. The salty spray of the sound had given way to a freshwater breeze and the soaring of gulls. Tierney's sun warmed face tingled in the gentle wind.

Tierney wondered why Congressman Dewey's words about social changes had brought Charlie Brewer to mind. As *Cricket* tacked past the Sand Point Naval Station it suddenly made perfect sense.

Pete concluded, *why not set up a regional home of support including medical for people with AIDS at this old Naval base? Charlie could have practiced in such a place without risk. What would be so wrong with an area of quarantine for the public interest, and for the public health? It could be humanely designed to meet various Constitutional needs e.g., privacy, freedom, mobility; but, with sexual and behavioral constraints. Such a social contract might slow the epidemic, allowing time for science and medicine to develop realistic answers. Enough time to catch up.*

"Look out! You're heading right into that Bayliner!" Bill shouted.

"Where did he come from? Look at him, all over the water!"

Tierney fell off the wind and yielded to the Bayliner, saluting in apology for encroaching.

He was in and out of conversation with his friends aboard Cricket. He lapsed into problem solving mode as others chattered. The idea had been planted; *Sand Point could be used as a regional quarantine center, voluntary and humane. What would the voters think?*

The mayor of Seattle had indicated he wanted part of the Navy facility at Sand Point to be used for housing. He also wanted an extension of nearby Magnuson Park to protect public access to the shoreline which was now occupied by the Sand Point Navy facility, an old naval air field that was decommissioned. Tierney was also unaware that the General Services Administration had requested buildings to use as a detention facility for the Immigration and Naturalization Service. Several governmental agencies were already at work behind the scenes, setting the stage for some big change. There was in fact a political movement with an ultimate plan to house, a controlled local, AIDS epidemic. He did not realize he was skirting the subtle edges of a political minefield. However, no one wanted to publicly use the word quarantine.

Slowly, the ideas began to gel. *I need information from the CDC and the gay movement. I need a much better command of sexually transmitted and communicable diseases. I've got to get up to speed quickly. A fellowship in infectious disease might be enough,* he thought.

Tierney recalled the insights of a close associate, Dr. Priscilla Carpet. Her words embedded in his memory, "I do not understand the use of AZT (the only antiviral drug then available) to reduce the infectious state of those with AIDS. It makes no sense. 'Safe sex' is a hoax by comparison, someone's idea of deliberately infecting more people. Why? Fear of retaliation from the gay community?" Tierney made the connection with the documentary film *Panama Connection.* It was about federal money stimulating drug traffic. While at the same time the government was waging a public relations war on drugs. What was the purpose of imposing a National Health Scheme? "I've never seen an infectious disease treated with such a caviler approach." Carpet concluded. "It did not become an epidemic until it became political."

It was an ideological/ political mess and Tierney knew it. He wanted to steer clear. He wanted to ignore the observations of so many of his colleagues. None had ever seen an epidemic handled so ineptly. What had happened to the idea of applied medical strategy for the sake of public health? It was replaced with applied politics.

Tierney returned to the Seattle Yacht Club for a roast beef dinner, followed by dancing. It was a full celebration of hope for the new season of warm weather, gentle seas arriving for boaters.

Sally Palme arrived from Olympia to join Tierney. She worked in managerial support for the Army Air Force Exchange System at Fort Lewis, south of Tacoma, helping to supply goods and services to bases throughout the Pacific Rim. Tierney found her attractive. Still Sally had no chance as Shawn's ghost hovered in the shadows, haunting Tierney. Shawn had attended this event the year before.

Shawn's absence had created a gash in his heart that seemed incapable of healing.

So, began Tierney's journey for answers. Little did he know that he was embarking on a race with time?

June 1992

Tierney received his final orders for the Leadership Management Effectiveness Training course at the Bethesda Naval Hospital campus in Maryland.

He would arrive there in mid-July. Then in early August, he was to report to GITMO for a six-week tropical disease course. In Bethesda, he would be berthed at the Colony Inn on the outskirts of the beltway, almost at the end of the Metro Yellow Line.

Tatum objected vehemently to the "unnecessary" absence of Lieutenant Commander Tierney from the clinic. In his way of thinking, such courses were frivolous. Teaching a physician anything, other than patient care, was a complete waste of time and money. "Keep them out of admin" was his philosophy.

Tierney felt lucky to have a bit of exposure to the administrative side. It was as if a door might open, allowing some sense of control over developments in medicine. He knew Tatum was protecting his turf and hungering for his own little empire.

Tierney was not looking forward to the midsummer heat and humidity of Washington, especially while in dress blues. The Navy had its ways of testing one's tolerance. Tierney though, was in acute need of punching the right tickets for advancement. He felt the need for that elusive fellowship in infectious disease. He had a number of weaknesses, and he knew heat and humidity were just two more on the list.

He had to plan wisely. One week of leave on the waters of Puget Sound aboard *Cricket* would mentally prepare him for the tasks ahead. It would allow him time to relax and sort things out. Shawn was never far from his mind, though fond memories weren't enough. Still he was haunted by Charlie's death and Nancy's lingering plea for help.

The loss of those two had made Tierney confused and indecisive. This was never clearer than on his sailing journey north to the

Canadian Gulf Islands. This troubled passage became not only
a search for a safe port, but it became a soul search.

"Securit-ae, Securit-ae, Victoria Station, Victoria Station,
calling all stations, calling all stations: reporting full gale winds
developing in the straits, expected to build to forty knots with eight-
foot seas." Tierney was already in the Straits, bound for Victoria
BC. He had rounded the last departure point off Port Townsend and
had progressed only seven nautical miles. His ground speed, he
noted, was a sluggish 3.5 knots. It would soon get worse with the
wind and flood tide coming his way. The thirty miles to Victoria
would take twelve hours.

"This is ridiculous!" he muttered as he turned back toward Port
Townsend. Within half an hour he had lost all the ground he had
gained.

"No, I'm not going to spend another day in Port Townsend
riding out a vicious storm!" he said aloud to himself and the
building winds. Tierney turned the boat back toward Victoria.

An hour later, realizing it was futile, he reversed course a third
time. Thoroughly indecisive by now, he proceeded to change his
mind twice more. Finally, the reality of the cold, penetrating sheets
of rain and sleet awoke him. This was no longer a pleasure cruise
he was on the edge. With the wind to his port side, he changed
course to due north and luckily recognize the flatness of Smith
Island. He took a bearing just as the rain condensed to hail and the
storm hit. He had never seen hail in June or visibility restricted to
150 feet. He couldn't leave the helm, so he strapped himself to a
jack line and rode it out. He had the need to urinate and observed
with an odd satisfaction, that the cockpit was filled with sea water
anyway. The problem was; he could barely manage the zippers to
his weather gear and his jeans underneath. All this turmoil and
indecisiveness paralleled his relationship and Shawn's departure.
He had lost his sense of direction. Peter was lost. So, he peed in the
cockpit joining the salt water sloshing about his boots.

The forward lines fell overboard. He watched in exasperation,
not daring to go forward on the wet, pounding deck. His log, had
he been able to update it, would have read, "Can't see a thing! Am
totally depending on the boat. Trying to steady the helm and look
for navigational aids." He recognized nothing as he passed two
buoys. He was lost at sea and he had lost Shawn.

By a stroke of good luck Tierney found his way to Cattle Pass, between rocky Lopez and San Juan Islands. *I shouldn't be so hard on powerboats,* he thought. *If that power boater hadn't found the pass, I wouldn't have had someone to follow. And I shouldn't be so hard on myself, either.*

Finally, he found protection in Friday Harbor on San Juan Island. By now, a full gale was blowing from the west. Tierney's luck had changed; he found moorage on the outside bulkhead of the main floats in a twenty-knot wind blowing off the lee shore. Miraculously *Cricket* was intact, except she clipped the stern flagpole of the boat in front of him, startling its skipper. The man helped Tierney secure the lines to *Cricket.*

"I'm really sorry. I've never hit anyone before. Is your boat okay?"

"Don't worry, man, it's a rental." They both laughed at the wind, The rain and the fragility of luck.

With *Cricket* properly secured Tierney treated himself to a glass of wine, and then another. He allowed his mind to drift to the comfort and softness of Shawn Carole.

If ever God had put a soft angel on earth, it was her! She personified the loveliest features of her Irish Catholic ancestry. Her lush auburn hair framed the delicate features of her face, high cheek bones, a wide mouth, and deliciously inviting lips. For strange reasons, she professed displeasure with these features, making Tierney wonder if she simply needed his verbal approval.

Despite her delicate appearance, Shawn was determined, intelligent, and willful. Her eyes were soft, hinting at vulnerability, and yet she abandoned herself to Tierney with utter confidence. She wanted to please him. Her soft touch invited him to explore and excite her. And so, it was with Shawn a balance of strength and beauty, of toughness and tenderness, of competence and innocence. Tierney had never known a more compelling and complex woman. He had never responded to anyone more completely. There was no part of himself that he could hold back from her. They received each other totally. She knew him without asking questions. Even their silences were rich.

Tierney's reveries were interrupted by the gusts of wind howling and whistling through the rigging, by the torrents of rain. The wind-speed indicator showed a steady twenty-five knots, gusting to forty.

He stuck his head out the hatch to check the lines, and then returned to his single quarter berth. He climbed under the down quilts, turned off the lights except for the glow of a kerosene lantern, and allowed his mind to drift back to the loving times he had shared with Shawn. He poured another glass of rosé and tried to dream of Shawn and the feelings between them. The words they had spoken seemed a distant memory.

Tierney thought back to a day in April of the previous year. He was in his Fiat, on his way to see Shawn. She was waiting for him at her cottage along the Swinomish Slough in La Conner. This was a town of artisans, fishermen, loggers, and tourist shops. She relished weekend breaks from her studio apartment on Queen Anne Hill in Seattle. Here in this wind-swept valley, also known for its spring tulip display, she could regain her focus and return refreshed to face the hectic demands of her career as a free-lance journalist. She loved the quiet, private times she spent with Tierney at the cottage.

The slough was an unusually flat marshy area that radiated some twelve miles from the town. It was in the lee of Fidalgo Island, a protected passage for boaters wishing to avoid Deception Pass, but still confronted by the adjacent Rosario Straits. Both were potentially rough trips if the weather was nasty. The calm beauty of the marshy shoreline and tulip filled valley made a stark geologic contrast with the glorious ruggedness of the Cascade Range to the east and the Olympics to the west. La Conner was a safe haven for boaters as well as for Peter and Shawn.

Shawn's cottage was rather staid compared with some of the elaborate homes that lined the slough. Its simplicity offered a wonderful source of peace, rest, and creativity. It suited her artistic needs. The cushioned settees in the dormer windows were ideal for reading. A covered back porch faced the river traffic. It was a perfect place to spend a wet Pacific Northwest day.

Tierney remember playing with the radio dial as stations faded the further north he drove from Seattle. The antenna had broken and the jury-rigged coat hanger was almost useless. He pushed his glasses back up the bridge of his nose. He was anxious to be alone again with Shawn. He loved having her all to himself.

He remembered ringing the doorbell, walking inside, hearing the screen door slam behind his duffel bag. Shawn had been expecting him, but still her eyes lit up with hungry surprise. They embraced without words. Her kiss was salty, delicious, exploring, and playful. He caressed her back, waist, buttocks, slowly and searchingly, reassuring himself that nothing had changed since they last touched. She was still a tactile feast. He laughed quietly with pleasure, a pleasure she felt.

She was wearing one of his shirts, open at the collar and tied at the waist. She told him that they made her feel close to him when they were apart. Except for baggy sweat pants she wore nothing else a sure sign that she expected him.

Shawn kept the Queen Anne apartment immaculate. In sharp contrast, the cottage was cluttered and messy. Here she was free to paint with creative energy and free to do as she pleased with Tierney. Here canvases, tubes of paint, brushes stuck in cans, and rags smelling of turpentine were strewn everywhere. Here too, their lovemaking was reckless, uninhibited, and creative.

Tierney poured himself a glass of sherry and settled into the oversized chair that dominated the small living room. Shawn had been painting, and Tierney loved to watch her work. Hair tied back, brush poised in her long, delicate fingers, she herself could have been the subject of a compelling portrait, he thought. He particularly loved to watch her when she forgot herself and grew absorbed in the flow of her work. Cubism, she called it. Whatever it was, Tierney found it abstract and not much to his taste.

Tierney watched the light from outside cast ever richer hues across her face and hair. First orange, then salmon, then red, He smiled. An artist would know more descriptive words for these colors. Shawn would know. She had brought such colors into his life.

Not wanting to disturb her concentration, he waited, watched, and admired her. She held the palette in her right hand, painted with her left. His old striped shirt, stained with a variety of colors, flowed from her shoulders down her chest, silhouetting her bosom against the sun's falling light. The suspenders she wore underneath to hold up the floppy sweat pants accented her firm, unsupported breasts. Tierney delighted in her presence and silently applauded her work and her form.

Shawn's fluffy gray cat bounded from the bedroom and onto the fireplace hearth near the easel, startling her.

"Poochie!" she laughed. "You spoiled thing, I suppose you'll want some canned tuna?"

"Shawn," Tierney said with mock seriousness, "tell me why you named that cat Poochie."

"Well, when I got Poochie I was living at home. My father prefers dogs to cats. He wanted to get me a puppy. I suggested a compromise. I'd get a kitten but give it a canine name."

Tierney smiled. No compromise at all. Shawn got what Shawn wanted. The trouble her father must have had trying to say no to her.

Tierney rose and walked behind her, pretending to judge her artistry. She smiled knowingly. He placed the chilled sherry glass against her waist and drew it up under her shirt and against her breast.

"What color do you want here?" she asked.

"Soft flesh." He responded pressing himself and his pelvis against her buttocks.

She lifted the shirt over her head, tossed it toward the fireplace, turned to him, and untied the sweat pants. Tierney cupped her waist and teased the pants from her hips. She dropped the paint brush and explored his waiting mouth, pressing her pelvis into him.

There wasn't a room in the cottage they hadn't made love in. Tonight, it was the living room as the cat napped.

Shawn had a sensual, earthy skill with Tierney, exploring and exciting him, responding to him. Wetness was part of their bond. Theirs was a penetrating love, difficult to distinguish from raw sex.

Shawn sighed, pulled the stained transparent shirt over her torso, and rose from the rug in front of the fireplace. She perched herself on a high wooden stool supported with wire spokes as he examined her painting.

"I think I'll call it quits. I've put in enough effort for one day. You know what, Pete? You've given me an appetite. What do you say we feed Poochie and then go down to the waterfront for pizza? Or else we could have some brought in?"

"It's a nice night--let's walk into town."

Shawn gathered up her brushes, cleaned them in turpentine, then plastic-wrapped the palette. She shook her hair loose, and as it tumbled to her shoulders she removed Tierney's shirt in favor of a black turtleneck. She turned away from him, feeling his gaze explore her body.

"No way, would I leave you hungry." Tierney smiled, slipped an arm about her waist, gave her a squeeze. Shawn turned to him, laughed, and hugged him back.

Those were the moments, the small moments....

After dinner at the wharf side restaurant, they walked home by way of the boatyards lining the slough. Clouds had developed, bringing a light drizzle and a cool, misty breeze from the west, so typical of Puget Sound. The soft air, the sea breeze, the life-giving moisture, Tierney loved the northwest climate. He had never understood why people cursed, rather than celebrated the rain. It was not oppressive, but soothing. As was making love to Shawn.

At times Tierney feared that in the throes of his passion, he might hurt her. Even now as he pulled off his shirt and eased himself onto her he wondered if he was too heavy for her slight frame. But Shawn had never retreated from their lovemaking, ever. Once she had told Tierney as she wrapped her legs around him that she had never felt safer than when she felt him in and all around her.

"Shawn," he whispered softly against her breast, "I would kill to protect you. I love you, Shawn. Much more than even I understand. Such words did not come easily to Tierney. He had loved before but had never been able to say those words with such feeling. With Shawn, he was powerless to hold them back. Everything seemed so Perfectly natural.

"I love you," he whispered again as he gently pulled her pastel dress over her shoulders.

He shivered with emotion and a tear came to his eye, falling to her now bare breast. Shawn was always receptive, and if she had ever resisted, she hadn't made it felt to Tierney. She asked only that he be gentle.

The memories were very clear. Tierney had felt no lack of direction during his time with Shawn. He had been totally focused, supremely confident. No decision had been too difficult. And now this last crossing of the straits--it was so embarrassing. It appalled him, it was so unlike him. His confidence and vision had been shaken so badly it was now painfully obvious. His wounds were open and brutally exposed.

Tierney wondered if any two people could have been happier. His heart had swelled to bursting. Something's gotten into me and I think its terminal, he had joked to himself, bemused by such unscientific feelings. Thank God I didn't learn everything in medical school.

My own private cardiologist, she had teased him.

I feel like I'm part of a damned Harlequin romance novel, Tierney thought, or a Hallmark card. And since falling in love with Shawn, he found himself saying things to her that out of context sounded, well, foolish. Yet, holding her, loving her, he came to think that such comparisons were full of profound truths. Words grew inadequate. That's why lovers spoke their own language, poetic syrupy and sweet. It doesn't matter, he told himself. I want her to know what's in my heart, syrupy or not. Those were glorious times and not for a moment did he doubt they would last.

Shawn's assignments sent her abroad, far too often for Tierney's taste. They sometimes met midway between their respective locations for a weekend of food, fun, and lovemaking. The brief separations only seemed to enhance the pleasure of their time together. They had never let more than a month go by without seeing each other.

Until the change which had something to do with a strange illness in France? Tierney questioned her. She had remained vague, but reassuring. Then gradually she had stopped seeing him. He pressed her for a reason, but she refused to answer. A sense of foreboding came over Tierney. Despite their closeness, Shawn was a very private person in many ways. Instinct told him to give her distance or risk further loss.

For ten months, there was nothing but an occasional impersonal card. No longer would she respond to his letters or phone calls. She was overseas on business, or out of town.

And then it happened. She took four months to make it final, stretching Tierney's nerves. A letter arrived: "I need to terminate our relationship as it began, in the form of a letter."

Damn poetic, he thought.

Was she ill? Tierney could handle that, but then a searing fear. She'd found someone else! No, she wouldn't deceive me, he thought. They had shared an intense, impassioned love for four years. Now something was profoundly different. He grew fearful.

Why had Shawn shut him out?

The last trickle of notes, pale and flat, had closed with a futile attempt at restraint and yet an awful sense of finality:

With warm memories and a hug,
Shawn

Tierney awoke to the howling of elements. He climbed out of his quarter berth, poked his head through the hatch, and saw that the mooring lines were securely attached to the breakwater. In no time, he was soaked. He quickly descended the companionway ladder to the dry warmth radiating from the diesel stove in the cabin.

They had been steamy and brazen lovers, profoundly close and rhythmically in concert, finding delight in a love that felt newfound, even after four years in the making.

The pangs of her absence were close to the surface. Never had Tierney invested so much energy in controlling the need to grieve. He had prided himself for his restraint--except where she was concerned. Self-control was impossible in the face of such raw, complex beauty. Even her flaws held an attraction e.g., her pale skin that wouldn't tan. Then again there we no flaws; her high waist, her hair, too fine, but taking on a reddish hue when the light was just right, the mole on her left breast. "Full and symmetrical" the doctor in him would have said, but the language of medicine lacked poetry. It was dispassionate and distant.

God, how he missed her, all of her. She was passing from his touch, and he found himself powerless, and frustrated.

A change, she had said, a change in her feelings. And then it was over. Still, it took four anguished months for her to decide.

A change! He shook his head. *Bullshit!*

Was this the best she could do? He deserved more, much more. He would have accepted most any excuse--his aftershave made her gag, he was insensitive, or something more tangible. To Tierney's mind a more plausible thought was another man.

A change! Sure, things change. The tide changes, the sky the moon, the seasons, you name it. But you're not the tide. You're the woman I love. I need a reason.

When he had pressed her for one, all she had said was, "I can't give you a reason. You want too much! You're a scientist and you want answers I can't provide. It's too painful! I'm not a test tube."

"A scientist! Tierney spat. How the hell could she talk like that? He was more than a doctor and so the scientific method is not the only way of viewing the world? "A scientist." He repeated disdainfully.

And so it went. Months of agony, self-doubt and attempts to find solace where there was none. "Warm memories indeed!"

Tierney remembered the warm salt breeze that swept the island of Oahu, where they had met and first made love. Since then, they shared love in so many different ways, but a leeward shore on a moonlit night in Hawaii seemed perfect. He remembered the strolls where physical exchanges were energized by caressing, exploring touches. The sandy shores and reef walks ripened with opportunity to probe bodice, body and crevice. A benign search for sea life gave way to a raw craving to generate new and vital life.

Stranded on an outgoing tide, Tierney gained a sense of his mortality. No explanation to him would be exempt from such a staggering loss.

Did the dying feel this way? Tierney had seen his share of death, but witnessing it is vastly different from feeling it. A cold, raw hand had gripped him, chilling him to the bone and the far reaches of his soul.

"With warm memories and a hug, Shawn"

He paused over her choice of words. They offered no emotional invitation to the present. The now is what counts; he had always tried to convince himself. "A hug." *A single solitary embrace. Was this the extent of her feelings for him?*

Tierney retreated to memories of a different time, several years earlier. When they had met in a hotel in Seattle, it was a marginal hotel, but certainly not cheap or sleazy. A chill, damp wind was blowing in from the west, punctuated by long horn blasts announcing the arrival and departure of the green and white ferry boats of Washington.

Another opportunity for their rendezvous presented itself as a medical conference on infectious disease at the Four Seasons Hotel. The meeting had something to do with an insidious disease called AIDS. At the time, the details of this disease seemed a distraction.

Their passion was more important.

Tierney remembered her sitting astride the open windowsill, back against the jamb, safe despite the drop to the street and the noise percolating up and in. It must have been the seventh floor, or was it the eleventh? He had given up trying to remember the rooms they had shared. He remembered only their love making.

The brisk salty air caressed her long flowery skirt and set her auburn hair dancing. With one leg on the windowsill, she gazed toward the water. Her calf and thigh were bare. And higher up …nothing. She was prepared for him. She was provocative with Tierney and yet, delicate, even lady like.

Their mating dance never became a ritual; it was always different, always exciting. Aroused, Tierney passed his fingertips along her inner thigh, tracing ever smaller circles. She was wet by time he reached her.

She was a stunning woman. Even the artificial light of the hotel room brought out reddish highlights of her fine hair. Her light sweater clung to and defined her breasts. Her hands moved with inviting command and rhythmic control. Tierney felt all too mortal in comparison. She had a broad smile and her eyes penetrated him in a teasing delight. She was a beacon radiating from this perch above the city. Like a light house warning of a foul shore yet inviting like a Greek Siren. No, she was better!

"With warm memories". Tierney had tossed the letter into a chart drawer, adding it to a pile that lay dormant awaiting some hope of resurrection.

Tierney attempted every rationalization imaginable for her actions, none held true. He couldn't discount her, couldn't belittle her and couldn't play the chauvinist. He was stuck with the reality of her rejection and had no explanation for it.

What can you do with a single "hug" anyway? He shook his head. I need to find a way to explain her loss, some way to reduce the hurt, and allow the memories to fade; I'm more than a detached nerdy scientist.

Her remark felt like a cheap shot. It stole his humanity. Being a physician was not easy at a time when doctor bashing was socially and politically fashionable. There were too many labels, too many expectations, too many demands and too many malpractice suits. Pete had witnessed dramatic change in the public perception of his profession. Every outside critic now seemed armed with a definition of medicines proper role, yet none seemed to understand it. It had become a profession layered with critics claiming expertise as well as answers. Tierney felt himself relegated to a technician whose success was managed by consumer satisfaction. Medicine, it seemed had become a political pawn. Physicians were no longer allowed to *practice.* Rather they had been pressed into role of puppet, vendor and provider.

Tierney heard himself growing bitter and he didn't like it. My man, you are becoming unpleasant and cynical. You don't like cynics so stop being one.

He sensed that something important remained unsaid. He had a haunting fear that another man had come into Shawn's life. Had he been deceived? How could he ever let his guard down again?

The mooring lines straightened and creaked against the surging of the boat. Warm and dry in the storm, Tierney recalled one last time the vivid sensation of holding Shawn close. He was secure for the moment as he slipped from memories into the dreams of sleep.

CHAPTER 4

More Than Meets the Eye

The day brought sunshine, calm seas and light winds. The weather channel broadcast a high moving in rapidly to replace the cold front, and gale force winds of the previous day.

66

By late morning Pete motored through Cattle Pass and into Haro Straits toward Discovery Island rounding the corner toward Victoria, BC. By comparison this passage was incredibly easy and became an eight-knot transit with the ebb tide in Pete's favor. What a great feeling to moving with ease when yesterday every inch was a struggle. *Amazing how this stretch of water can be so calm one day and the next stirred with frothy emotion and anger, he thought.* It was like a carnivorous sea dragon from the fathoms below. Respect was required to deal with such forces. Pete had no way of knowing the powers that would soon confront him.

It took three hours to make a passage to Victoria. The harbor stood beautiful, highlighting the center of all that happens on Vancouver Island. Tierney made secure his vessel at the pier in front of the Empress Hotel. The Empress is known for its elegant high tea. But, after five days at sea, the simple reality of doing laundry became serious. The laundromat is a convenient walk from the Empress Hotel moorage. There Pete met an engaging couple, Carla and Dave Locket. Exchanging US quarters for loonies to access the washing machines and soap, opened a light conversation. The three briskly covered the local tourist attractions as they ignored the noisy dryers. Carla suggested dinner and drinks aboard their 36-foot sloop. Pete agreed following an ole Navy adage of never turning down an invitation.

The evening was initially of light conversation and multiple topics. Dave and Carla seemed a perfect match balancing each other's strengths, and their conversation with Pete was open and lively. Pete learned of a doctor who, five years ago, had left the Center for Disease Control (CDC) and moved to North D a k o t a .

"No, he had moved to the Milwaukee near Chicago area. Something went wrong; it caused him to leave in an ethical huff. Something to do with biologic warfare, I think," said Carla. "Oh, his name, I remember something like Rice or Price."

Dave prematurely retired as a computer biostatistician from Georgetown University where he had been personally responsible for tracking community acquired diseases on a national scale. He had been instrumental in the early tracking of Legionnaire's Disease.

Carla was a charmer in her late 50's. Slim with a vibrant smile, streaks of grey hair, and was an avid and athletic biker. She loved to cook Guatemalan dishes that she had learned while in the Peace

Corps. They had spent a career of traveling, mostly through Europe and South America. Dave's specialty of biostatistics had culminated in retirement at Georgetown University in Washington D.C.

Pete found they had gravitated toward the northwest after learning about the great sailboat cruising available. They had grown fatigued with the politics of the Potomac and the shallow brackish waters of the Chesapeake a literal swamp and moved west.

Dave spoke freely of the CDC, National Institute of Health (NIH), Health and Human Services (HHS) and the disharmonious, professional rift between the famous Dr. Gallo and the Pasteur Institute in Paris. This eruption of claims came over who first discovered the virus that caused AIDS.

"It had everything to do with big egos and as well as royalties and of course, national pride entered the formula," explained Dave.

"I recall very clearly overhearing Dr. Gallo in his office at the National Institute of Health bragging about discovering the Human T-Lymphocyte virus (HTLV) almost two years before the etiology of the retrovirus was found."

"Can you imagine the AIDS virus discovered years before the onset of an epidemic?" Dave asked.

"They had it isolated in the laboratory years before it ever hit the street." He paused. There was a loud pause.

"Well, I suppose... it's possible. At least it was probably safe if closely guarded in the laboratory, in the right hands." Pete encouraged Dave to continue.

"Nothing sounded safe, then I heard the famed Dr. Gallo interviewed. He admitted to viral contamination across many laboratories. He knew that contamination had occurred in Robin Weiss's Lab, Mario-Stevenson's Lab in Nebraska and a viral laboratory at Duke University. I could not believe he concluded so dispassionately as if these contaminates were expected outcomes. "It had to be a Freudian slip."

Dave glanced over his shoulder toward the passage way of their Sailboat. He feared being overheard.

"Gallo then said the same contamination occurred at the Laboratory in Ft. Detrick, Maryland," Adding, "the one where they produced the viruses."

"Shit," he paused; "Ft. Detrick, MD is the site of the U.S. Armed Forces Institute of Medical Intelligence. It's the same location of USAMRIID, the U.S. Army Medical Research Institute of Infectious Disease. They pronounce it U-Sam-Rid, almost with a sense of controlled authority. More importantly, Ft. Detrick historically has been a center for biologic- warfare from 1943-1969."

"Yes, I've heard of it," Pete responded.

"Yeah, the same place. Same damn neighborhood. Dr. Gallo had admitted it Dave had been privy to the data surrounding AIDS and the political players who were labeled with code names that were difficult to trace.

"What can you tell me?" asked Pete. "I've lost a very close friend in the Navy to a suspicious suicide. He supposedly was HIV positive and was going to get AIDS."

"Come on, Dave, explain. I'm not clairvoyant."

"All I can tell you is that this guy, Price, resigned some five or six years ago midpoint in the statistical AIDS epidemic. It breached his ethical code. Someone had created the AIDS virus at Fort Detrick. Price was so pissed that his name is associated with this deception"!

Dave continued, "I've become aware of these events because the leading argument for Gallo's defense, against the Pasteur Institute, was the clear and certain identity of the viral particle. There was a big to do about shipping vials of AIDS viruses between France and the United States. Price controlled the exact retroviral coded sequence. Startling information! From nowhere Price had retrieved this information from his earlier viral experiments at Fort Detrick. You see, Price also worked at the AFMIC (Armed Forces Medical Information Center)."

"So, go on!" Pete prodded.

"For certain, I know, a perfect genetic viral match was made, precisely made. The odds against that spontaneously happening are incredible, on the order of a trillion to one. It surprised us all. It's very suspicious to have someone precisely identify a viral genetic code while seemingly searching for an unknown. It suggested the obvious, that the unknown was not unknown. Maybe that's why Price resigned? Shit, they had the virus in the lab before it ever hit the street."

Dave paused, "For all I know, Price could be the fall guy."

"Politics and numbers are very powerful and influential tools.

Numbers don't lie, but a lot of liars play the numbers."

"Price was well respected," Carla continued, "but rumor had it that he couldn't handle the stress of working for a government organization. You know lots of back-stabbing, internal stuff, I was told he may have become an alcoholic."

Now, Carla!" Dave interrupted. "They may have found it easier to defame the man rather than deal with him!"

"Yes, it was Raymond Price, a Ph.D. in genetic stuff and virus things," said Carla. Her husband nodded and had another shot of brandy. So did Pete.

The conversation continued until the wee hours. Pete finally excused himself at 2 a.m. and walked back to Cricket. Friday nights on the stone bulkhead surrounding the inner harbor was usually raucous; a perfect stage for entertainers and tourists. But this night was quiet and Pete needed a respite.

He slept well and awakening late, treated himself to bacon, eggs and a latte. He invested the rest of the day to Cricket's upkeep. That evening Pete decided to have dinner at the Irish Rover, a sporty little pub across from Market Square. It had been named in honor of a roving Irishman who established the pub with his last dollar. After finding success he again returned to roving. The walls were covered with international flags and pennants of the United Kingdom, Ireland and Scotland.

It was an early dinner, before the evening crowd and the harsh, tone-deaf band arrived. Pete met an anthropologist, a Dr. Stephen Anderson, from the Cultural Association of Greater Victoria. Anderson was well-informed on native cultures. Pete was unsure how they struck up a conversation, however it had continued into the wee hours of morning. After several bowls of a steaming Gaelic stew and several Irish Harps, they settled down to the discussion of AIDS in Canada.

Anderson had some very unusual views, but he was willing to share those insights with the right audience. All it took was a little encouragement.

"Most infectious diseases that affect man in epidemic form, you know, like, influenza, plague, leprosy, and legionnaires, all die out naturally," he said, "Especially if the disease is virulent and deadly. The infectious process literally kills its host. Then the agent dies and can no longer infect others. This has been true of every epidemic known to man. Many are characterized by a natural

70

extinction coefficient."

"I've never heard of such a term before, extinction coefficient," Peter. Anderson stopped, bent over the table leaning on his elbows as mused "Historically no epidemic has behaved like this. HIV and AIDS, are the exception and all the others of a natural evolutionary origin that were not, well, developed elsewhere."

"Developed elsewhere? What are you talking about?" Pete asked.

"I mean, not man-made," he stated without flinching.

"What, have you had too many beers, man?" asked Pete.

This was the second time in two days Pete had encountered the suggestion of the epidemic being man-made. He didn't like it and felt it was the beer talking. Still, it was not beyond the scope of imagination.

A birthday song began and drew Pete's attention to the happy crowd sitting at a long wooden table. They were celebrating the birthdays of half a dozen young ladies. Pete felt suddenly lonely in the crowd. It was a private party, and he would have enjoyed being part of it and meeting these young women.

The joys of living surely surpass the turmoil of our troubled times of epidemics, he thought. Pete chose not to speak of Price, the CDC, AFMIC and Fort Detrick, or the death of his friend, Charles.

They stopped talking and watched the celebration.

Pete noted the names of the women whose birthdays were being celebrated posted on the wall adjacent to the pennants. Three was, Michelle, Nancy, Joanne, Tricia, Francesca and Allison. He was taken with Allison. She had a sparkle in her eye and wore a form fitting sweater that hugged her nicely. He wanted to approach her, but it was impossible with such a crowd. The loneliness soaked into his bones like Arctic waters into a dry sponge. He felt out of place. He wrote a note for her and gave it to the bar tender and watched him deliver it. She read the note and tossed it aside with a cruel laugh. He was in the wrong place. He walked back home through the harbor to find his warm quarter berth awaiting.

Soon again he would be underway on Cricket, and his voyage would carry him away from the loneliness he felt among strangers. He wondered why such social animals found it so hard to find meaningful relationships. *Why are we all very fragile? Being human sometimes is not always good!*

After the few days in Victoria, Pete continued his journey north to Nanaimo, on the east side of Vancouver Island. Time now demanded, he must return to his rented maid's quarters at Keyport, WA in anticipation for his schedule flight to Washington D.C.

He must plan enough time for a return passage, with enough slack for a layover in anticipation of bad weather.

Peter did not anticipate getting caught in a fog bank while crossing Rosario Straits. Bird Rocks, is clearly labeled as a navigational hazard and became symbolic of the maze he would soon encounter. Navigating a fog bank was much less dangerous than finding his way through the viper pitted swamp of Washington, D.C.

CHAPTER 5

Cuban Experiment: Quarantine

WASHINGTON D.C.

Pete struggled with his two bags as he checked in at the Colonial Inn. He in a heavy stride, threw his luggage on the bed as he intercepted a phone call. It was a real surprise to hear Shawn's voice from 3000 miles away.

"How are you, Peter?" she asked.

"I'm fine but very surprised to hear from you. How did you know where to find me?" asked Pete.

"Well, you know me. I pretended I was the secretary of a fictitious CDR Brogan from the Bureau of Naval Personnel. Your office clerk told me where to find you. They don't know much about security at your clinic, do they?"

"It's not my clinic and they don't know much about the Navy," he said with irritation. "How are you Shawn? I've missed you!"

"I've just returned from Paris."

"On a story?" asked Pete.

"Yes and no. There was some personal business involved. I also was covering the political developments of the Mitterrand position regarding a unified European currency."

"When will I see you again? It's been a very long time, almost a year. I want to talk to you."

"Maybe, when you get back home? By the way, Pete, why are you going to Cuba?"

"Who told you that?" he asked in amazement.

"The secretary at your clinic."

"I told you it's not my clinic. I guess we'll have to do something about the security." Pete shook his head in disgust. *He wondered, why am I dealing with this issue of the clinic's security, the real issue is Shawn's disappearance.*

"I'll be gone about six to seven weeks. Maybe we can talk when I get back."

"Yes, we need to talk!" he repeated.

"OK, Peter. That would probably be all right. It depends on how I feel. They want me at a conference in Paris, but first I must talk with my editor at the Boston Globe. Then I catch the Concord out of La Guardia."

"Why, are you ill?" he asked.

"I haven't been myself, and I can't explain, Peter."

"Call me when you get a chance. I shouldn't have any added traveling for at least another three months."

"Take care of yourself. Good-b-y-e," she closed with a lilt in her voice "Love yah" and hung up.

He'd learned that she was not feeling well, still caring, but emotionally aloof. Peter was puzzled as he hung his uniform in the closet and turned the air conditioner on. It roared aloud, and he shook his head, *I'll not sleep tonight, but it's quieter than a Carrier berth and it is good not to be haze grey and away.*

There was *something to do with more medical tests. She didn't really say it but Pete felt it.*

Pete reflected with insecurity, I'll never really understand women and few men will. That surgery she had ten months ago seemed to screw her up, he thought. *I wish she hadn't become ill in France. There's no good place to become ill, but at least I might have been able to help if at home.*

Pete wondered if he should blame himself. The night before she left for Paris, they had made love with great passion. *He worried that a sudden pain she had experienced was caused by him.* Unknown to him, she had ruptured an ovarian cyst. It had slowly begun to bleed. Time had carried her to Paris before it was discovered.

He left the small motel room looking for a sports bar, a cool draft, and the Washington Herald.

The Headlines: **Indifference to AIDS Spells Doom to Millions**...as reported by the National Commission. The commission had formally reported its findings to the President under the direction of Dr. David Rogers. In two more years, 350,000 were expected to die in the U.S. alone. They recommended a "national plan" for combating the dreaded disease. They Proposed a Universal Health Care Insurance to cover all citizens. There were some twenty-five other proposals of smaller degree and lots of financial influence. *None of the proposals seemed to deal with the real issue of an epidemic.*

Where are people's heads these days? Why can't they see through this empty rhetoric? Pete pondered.

Louis W. Sullivan, Secretary of Health and Human Services, had rejected the idea. He announced a summit with insurance industry representatives to discuss health care reform. Sullivan had made it clear that creating a government-run national insurance plan would not be embraced and was not a solution. Rather, it was a distraction from a real solution.

The only recommendation that made any sense was a central plan to control the disease, at least until the magic cure arrived, if ever there was one that came along.

In an adjacent article Pete read with interest of the Pueblo Development in New Mexico. It was an experiment in adaptation to life in a confined biologic environment. All facets were self-contained and reportedly financed by private money. Half a dozen scientific types from anthropologists to geneticists committed the next three years to being in isolation from the rest of the world. It

75

was to be placed somewhere near Taos or Albuquerque.

If I ever get to New Mexico, I'll look up this bio-cosmic experiment! Thought Pete.

Still nursing his beer and the Washington Herald, he read that David Barr, Assistant Director of Policy for the Gay Men's Health Crisis in New York, was angry. He publicly scorned Kimberly Bergalis for focusing her anger in the wrong direction. Bergalis was a 23-year-old woman who was dying of AIDS and was attempting to move the Congressional hearings to mandate testing of all physicians and dentists who did invasive procedures. She had been infected by her dentist in Florida. Her tragedy was the first case known of such a transmittal. This was later determined to be an intentional infection by a desperate dentist who wanted to prove AIDS was more than a homosexual disease. He infected half a dozen patients by injecting tainted blood from carriers of HIV, into patients hoping to prove it was also a heterosexual disease.

"I did nothing wrong," she said, "yet Kimberly stated, I'm being made to suffer like this. My life has been taken away." She quoted to the news media.

The gay movement chastised her for such a remark, feeling it was self-serving, almost as if such a cause were unworthy. "We who are dying with AIDS are not the enemy, even though we are presented as such. We are dying from the same neglect." Pete felt that such criticism rang hollow!

It's a hard thing to die, and quite enough without someone using your death for political purposes, thought Peter. It took another year before the dentist's gay lover publicly disclosed the motive. The dentist wanted heterosexuals to get the message that AIDS was their disease as well. He injected tainted blood into the gums of his patients. It took Barbara Walters to extract the truth. This was never a heterosexual disease excepting tainted blood transfusions, accidents with needles and shared needles in addicts.

NAVAL HOSPITAL, BETHESDA, MARYLAND:

Leadership Management Effectiveness Training was an exercise in patience, but it allowed Pete a very nice break from his routine of clinic care. During off times, he explored the vastness of the Bethesda Naval Campus, where admirals were a dime a dozen.

One afternoon he stumbled upon the Research and Development Laboratory under the directorship of Rear Admiral Hays. It was a few blocks from the classrooms and seemed to offer an open-door policy. Pete was escorted to the basement where experiments were being conducted in battlefield recovery. The experiments included rapid bone healing using electrical stimulation and prolonged red cell survival studies. The information derived from such studies is critical in combat environments.

Several hematology studies were under investigation. Pete was captured by the technology and the open visibility of these experiments. This contrasted with one laboratory in the basement with a cipher lock securing the contents behind a door labeled "QA". *What could possibly be secretive about QA, except for who got hung,* wondered Pete. Of course, everybody in Navy medicine knew that QA meant Quality Assurance. Even the Surgeon General considered it a potential witch hunt that followed the Billig case.

Billig was a surgeon who supposedly bungled open-heart surgery and was court-martialed, but finally acquitted. Naturally, QA took on a whole new dimension and did not have an admirable track record. It had become a poorly tolerated system of internal abuse. The political correctness of QA had become a re- born form of McCarthyism.

While at Bethesda, Pete scheduled an interview at the Navy Hospital in preparation for an Infectious Disease Fellowship. He arranged the interview to follow his return trip from Cuba, where he would take a Tropical Disease/ Infectious Disease course.

FIRST OF AUGUST:

Pete flew aboard a C-12 out of Andrews Air Force Base in Washington D.C. to GITMO, Cuba. It was a smooth flight, but a tough cross wind landing. The hangars were separated by empty spaces which made a cross wind landing very difficult. At one moment, the wind was there and the next was gone. Prevailing easterlies and a complicated runway made for an exciting arrival to Discovery Island, Guantánamo Bay.

He looked out the window and saw fences separating the U.S. presence from the Cuban nationals. The weather was balmy, and the tropical waters a deep coral blue, reminded Pete of the three-year tour he completed in Hawaii as a flight surgeon.

Pete held the flexible aluminum railing as he descended the ladder from the plane and felt the warm tropical sun caress his body. He opened his palms as if to absorb a winter's deprivation in one moment. He walked slowly across the tarmac to the Naval Air Terminal but waited outside in the tropical air. There was no one to greet him. The warm easterly winds caressed his pale skin. Palm trees broke the wind with feathered reeds, they were planted to surround the air terminal.

Pete took in a few slow deep breaths absorbing the warm air. His glasses fogged in the humidity. He cleaned the lens and proceeded to baggage claim, waiting for the conveyer to discharge his luggage. *Pretty hard to lose your gear on a little twin engine like the C-12.* GITMO had a rolling terrain best appreciated from a hill side.

The tropical setting of the Caribbean and the beautifully protected harbor reinforced Pete's admiration of the Navy. They knew the value of a good harbor. He boarded a shuttle for the BOQ and as the open-air diesel bus climbed the hill he could see across the bay. There across the water, was a vast expansive city of tents. Hundreds, lined up in rows, on the distant peninsula occupying an old airstrip. The shuttle stopped at the BOQ. As he registered Pete asked the third class, "What are all those tents over on the eastern peninsula?" "Well, it's the Haitian refugee camp. We call it Tent City among Other things."

"Tent City," Pete repeated. "Haitians, oh yes, of course." He had forgotten. It had been in the news lately. Some military coup in Haiti and then all those boat people came here. "How many are down there anyway?"

"Doc, are you here for a visit, or on orders?" asked the third class.

"I'm on orders for a tropical disease conference." Pete handed his orders, marked Original, to the clerk.

The clerk examined the orders, stamped the back side, signed it and looked inquisitively at the doctor.

"Lt. Commander, sir, the whole damn west side of Haiti lives down there. We can't figure out who is who. Some got diseases I've never heard of, others are criminals, and some are just survivors of leaky boat trips. We call it Camp Buckley, Sir." He continued. "I don't know the whole story, but it is the Haitian Refugee Camp we call Tent City."

Pete completed the formality of checking in, stowed his luggage in the room, changed into Bermuda's, a salty shirt and left in search of the Officer's Club.

Over a brew at the club, the bartender updated Pete on the

exercise.

"The Joint Task Force was overseeing this officially dubbed, humanitarian effort, caring for the refugees until it could be determined if they were truly migrants or refugees. This was an important distinction politically. Refugees were valuable and politically exploitable. Migrants were liabilities and of no value."

Amazing, thought Pete, *the wisdom and insights of bartenders, some become a periscope to the motive and quagmire in the beltway and the Whitehouse.*

"Tell me more," Pete encouraged.

Lynne Smith, a Navy nurse, interrupted and introduced herself. Pete welcomed her company, shook hands and smiled. She was unassuming, a small blond with penetrating blue eyes.

"I overheard," she interrupted. "I've worked here for two years. I know GITMO well. I've breathed it. It's no mystery. Buy me a drink. I'll tell you what I know"

Pete nodded to the bartender who became silent and delivered a brandy to the lady. He withdrew, and Lynne proceeded to expose two years' worth of a frustrating effort.

"It was the obligation of the US Immigration and Naturalization Service (INS) to determine the political status of the tens of thousands of migrants that flowed through Camp Buckley. INS became the time delayed bottle neck for disposition and repatriation. Migrants became the operative word," she said. "INS determined if the Haitians were truly refugees seeking political asylum or if they were really migrants requiring repatriation back to Haiti."

Pete listened carefully.

"It's politically pretty sensitive stuff," she added.

"We get a lot of congressmen and news reporters down here, looking for stories or causes. Guys like Jesse Jackson, Al Sharpton looking for issues of mistreatment of Haitians and discrimination."

Pete nodded understanding.

Lynne continued. "The internment started in November of 1991; the internment started on what was an unused landing strip, McCullom Air Field, where the tents were built. A year later we had Tent City. It reached an all-time high of 12,500 migrants. Initially the Haitians, I mean migrants, were separated by interview stations. The communicable diseases went into separate quarters in an effort to protect the rest of the population."

"Do you mean they were quarantined?" asked Pete.

"Well, yes of course. The interview stations determined if the migrants sounded infectious. If they had a fever, night sweats, open sores, you know. Then they were all sent to the delicing showers. It, reminds me, of WW II in Germany.

Anyway, the people with tuberculosis and malaria went into a separate Quonset hut. We had to seal up the holes in the aluminum walls to keep the mosquitoes out. Otherwise we might have an internal spread of disease."

"What happened to those with AIDS?" Pete asked.

"They were further separated into an area that we were not allowed to visit. They were sent to a special encampment, with the yellow tents. They used the yellow liners from the tents. All the Haitians were given color coded wrist bands: green bands were clear of disease; red, required close observation within the next 24hours; and blue. Well blue represented immediate isolation for HIV or for TB, Malaria, or Dengue virus."

"I need to see this," Pete asked.

"Don't worry, I'll show you around tomorrow. Besides if you're here for the tropical disease course, you'll get first-hand experience. You're going to work in the trenches, my friend."

Lucky me, thought Pete.

They parted company, and Pete returned to the isolation of his room at the BOQ.

The next day Pete awoke to the sound of reveille. He quickly dressed in a khaki uniform, grabbed some coffee and headed for the Naval Hospital atop the barren hill overlooking Guantánamo Bay. He reported to the quarter deck of the hospital and was given a brief tour, then introduced to the X.O., Tim Reilly, a medical service corps officer.

From his second-floor office overlooking the harbor, Reilly pointed in the distance to Tent City.

"That LCDR Tierney is the greatest infectious disease experiment you'll ever see in your lifetime. Nowhere else in the world is such an exercise in progress. That will be your home for the next ten weeks, except of course, you will be covering the emergency room of the hospital, in your off time."

"Yes sir. I understand," Pete reacted.

Over the next weeks Pete lived and breathed tropical disease medicine in Tent City. The seven percent who were HIV positive had indeed been further isolated as Lynne had said. No one spoke of this group as they represented an embarrassment, a political embarrassment. Whatever was to be done with this group of about 100 Haitians, nobody knew. None of us would dare talk to the news media or the numerous visiting congressmen.

Despite social and language barriers the average migrant required about 48 hours to figure out the rituals of the system. Filarial worm disease with elephantiasis of legs and scrotum were common. Affected men arched their backs to support scrotums that drooped like water balloons to knee height. It became dubbed the "GITMO gait". The disease could be diagnosed from 100 yards away.

The Joint Task Force resided in relative splendor and isolation up on the hill above in a large, white, three story building. The Immigration and Naturalization Service also called this home and kept civil hours. Eight to five with no exceptions made.

Traditional infectious diseases were treated at a make shift hospital, a converted cafeteria called the Blue Caribe. Immediately adjacent to the Blue Caribe was Tent City, it was located on the air field. Further west was the fence separating communist Cuba. HIV was not treated in the Blue Caribe. We were told the yellow Tents in the distance were for unusual diseases. *Pete thought about the yellow tents. He wondered if Charles had known more than he should about the yellow tent. What was he doing down here?*

Pete ran into Lynne and she continued to tell him of the history.

"We had riots in early April of 1991. The young healthy males turned the honey bucket port-a-potties over atop the barbed wire fence and climbed over into freedom, but it was an empty escape"

"There was nowhere to go on the abandoned air strip, except outside the fence, which was enclosed by another fence. Despite the language barrier, they all seemed to know there was nothing to gain by breaking into Cuban territory. Instead they just milled around in indecision and a short-lived freedom. They all seemed quite willing to return to the confines of the tented city in time for dinner."

Pete probed about the yellow tents, but Lynne could not add any information, only that it was off limits to the medical community. It was a closely guarded secret. All that was known was that the migrant population reached an all-time high of 12,500 Haitians.

Those that were truly seeking refugee status were screened for eligibility and given asylum in the US as deemed politically correct. The Joint Task Force Headquarters stood above the cafeteria converted into the inpatient hospital the Blue Caribe.

The overflow of infectious diseases spilled over into eight make shift yellow tents. They were told the yellow was neither significant nor symbolic, but rather was just the color of a tent liner. It sufficed for both purposes.

Pete recalled the visit to the leper colony that was on the wet windward side of Molokai. The tales of Kalliapappa, Father Damien,and Michener's Hawaii, told descriptive stories explaining the horrors of quarantine. *But,* **it did save the Polynesian culture!** Pete felt *that success must stand for something!*

Academically it was a terrific exposure to tropical medicine an unusual experiment of medical/political internment. It was the chance of a life time according to the X.O. of the hospital.

Fellowship training in tropical disease or not, Pete still ended up covering the emergency room. It was called an efficient administrative oversight. While on duty for the emergency room, Pete was called to take care of a Cuban national who had just been shot in the right leg. He had tried to escape under the fence and was in full stride as a Cuban guard spotted him and brought him down. An internist normally would not take care of gunshot wounds, but this was the Navy. Your level of comfort was no excuse nor of any major concern. The Cuban spoke fractured English. His name, Carlos Sanches, was printed on the metal tag strapped about his wrist. It also listed the sanitarium, Santiago de Las Vegas, attention Dr. J. Perez Filipio. "Carlos, what does this mean? Do you have an infection like? Tuberculosis?" asked Pete.

The Cuban answered cautiously and in slow English.

"No, no, I am in detention. They cut off my privileges to visit my wife and family. I have to see them! Once the guards found me I had to turn south. The fence was so close to freedom."

"Why are you in prison?"

"I'm not in prison, I'm in a quarantino."

"OK, then why are you in quarantino?"

"I have AIDS and everybody that has the virus is there."

"You're in quarantine!?" Pete echoed in amazement. "For how long, and who knows about this?"

"For the past five years, and you know the Navy knows." "The Cuban Navy?"

"No, Your Navy, the U.S. Navy. Isn't that where I'm at?" Carlos suddenly started looking around with apprehension. "My leg hurts. Please do something besides talk!" Pete cut his pant leg away and

82

exposed the wound. It was a significant wound, probably from an AK-47, which blows big holes. There had been little bleeding, but a big entry hole and a bigger exit wound at the calf. Carlos would never walk normally again. Pete gave him a shot of morphine and began probing the wound after a local anesthetic. His healing without opportunistic infection was a very real issue, especially in a host compromised with AIDS.

Further examination revealed peculiar, violations, purple, circular eruption behind his left ear.

"What is this Carlos?" asked Pete.

"It's the mark they gave me when we entered the sanitarium. We all got one. It brands us for life to the walls within the Santiago." It was an "A" subtly inscribed within a "Q".

I've never seen this before, thought Pete. *But, maybe...,* He rubbed his forehead.

Damn! It was on the cipher lock at Bethesda's Research and Development, and It looked like an "A" superimposed upon a "Q". This might have been the lesion removed from Charles's ear lobe as it was surgically denuded?

"What the hell's going on here"! Exclaimed Pete. *Quality Assurance. What the hell is the Navy doing in Cuba?! WHAT WAS CHARLES DOING DOWN HERE!? You had better WAKE UP FELLA; YOU'RE BEING USED LIKE A SACRIFICAL PAWN! Who was that Admiral Hays at R&D anyway? What were Carla and Dave telling me about that doctor who went to North Dakota?* He opened his briefcase and tossed unorganized papers aside looking for a pen.

This whole QA business must have been cleared at a high level, a very high level. With the Haitian Tent City, it sounds like some snarky Carter plan to me. I 'll need to play it real cool, real low profile while I'm down here...pretend to pick up a little tropical disease medicine and learn what I can until I can get back to the States.

"Carlos, I'll call a surgeon in to look at your leg." "Doctor, will you send me back?"

"No, Carlos, I won't send you back to the sanitarium, but I don't know how to get you back to your family."

Pete knew the political attention and high visibility would not allow Carlos to stay in American hands, especially if he represented someone with AIDS and a QA label on his ear. "It doesn't matter, I'm a dead man anyway," he sighed. "Better to have died at the fence," said Carlos. This six-week course in Tropical Disease took on a whole new meaning. Pete considered resigning from the Navy to seek a civilian fellowship where he might be free of the government. Before he submitted a letter of resignation, though, he decided to collect all the information possible, both in Cuba and when he returned to Bethesda, after a stop at the CDC, in Atlanta. The information might protect him. He wrote technically to Shawn, feeling it would make little difference in their relationship. He also wrote describing the warmth of the area; the tropical sun-bleached sand and clear waters. *I bet she would look good in this gentle surf, on this sandy beach. Maybe I should hang loose, cut my losses, and look for civilian options.*

The uncertainty ahead troubled Tierney. He knew Lt. Tatum could not be trusted. *He may be privy to what's going on. He's probably an official snoop for the Naval Command,* thought Pete. *How will I ever get orders cleared through that guy?*

Pete's letter of resignation from the Navy was drafted but held for later reflection. It would have to be sent at the proper time through the correct chain of command. For the moment, he would sleep on the idea. Knife and fork school taught him that the U.S. Navy religiously thrived on protocol. One simply did not bypass a limited superior with important information. The beauty of a very large bureaucracy was that nobody knew what anybody else might be doing. Hence, the delays in action were often opportunities and advantageous to those who planned.

Pete figured he might have enough time to interview at Bethesda and snoop around the belt-way.

I need some clear answers! I can't get them without investigating in the right places. A top- secret security clearance would really help at a time like this. So, would getting out of GITMO.

I couldn't get out of this black hole even if I wanted, he thought. *I'll just have to play it as the cards fall!*

It was late September, on a Tuesday and Pete had until tomorrow afternoon to sort out his response to what was happening in GITMO. His flight aboard the C-12 was scheduled. He was on the manifest. *What will I be able to learn with so little time left in Cuba?*

Pete was vividly aware of the damage and wondered who was behind the effort to support quarantine in Cuba. He began asking himself a ton of questions. *Why was it veiled in enough mystery to kill Charles? Why was Charles a threat? Was it that he knew too much?* There was ample evidence that the Cuban experiment was endorsed by the US Government, but only a select few knew. Pete wondered, *is Representative Dewey aware? Of course, he must be. After, that" social planning comment" at the Seattle Yacht Club, and I'm certain Rear Admiral Hays also is involved, especially with his R &D, QA cipher lock. I suspect much higher levels are involved. It could extend even up to the surgeon general...It's impossible to have a grip on who are the power players? The Navy was such a large bureaucracy that it's not even a question of the left hand not knowing what the right hand is doing. Rather, it's a question of the left not even knowing the right exists.*

If this is all above board, and everybody knows, then why is it veiled in secrecy and mystery? If quarantine makes sense to the US Navy, the US Army, a few select legislators, then why the elusive clandestine activities surrounding the experiment in Cuba?

Of course, there is a very real and great political movement that is in opposition to quarantine. There is fear and deep anger over such an approach. The gay community historically has feared quarantine over the past decade. All the efforts to close the San Francisco gay bath houses were met with strident political resistance. Individual rights were pitted in a clash with public responsibility. We all know that sympathetic political powers will only publicly support a more visible and politically correct "Humane" approach. They would not publicly object despite the undisputed progression of this disease and its evident threat to the entire population. Their indecision was killing America. What could possibly be their motive? Who could possibly be behind this and as systematic distortion of truth?

These issues involved proper timing, until there was such public outcry accepting the ideas of quarantine. When many deaths reached a critical level of public discontent, then angry demands will be for any solution irrespective of a humane solution. Pete hesitated in thought. *Maybe there's more than meets the eye! Maybe something much more important is at stake and must be kept quiet?*

Carlos spoke of the massive Cuban AIDS quarantine program. "All of us with AIDs are given a cot and housed are free to move about, work and are paid a salary for their confinement. Everything else was free, even cigarettes. The responsible Quarantino allowed freedoms and privileges but there were rules to follow. The initial isolation began in an old estate, Fina Los Cocos on the outskirts of Havana".

"So, how did the Navy get involved?" Pete asked.

"I do not know, Amigo, it is a mystery to me. I don't like waiting to die even with liberties." "We're lucky to have some Catholic priests and seminarians. So mass and confession is for us as Cuba is largely catholic"

"Why are Catholic priests in prison"? Pete asked.

"Well they have AIDS as many are polished palomo." "We've seminarians, but is a problem" He added. "What can the church do with them except give them to a prison ministry?"

"A few years ago, there were so many in the sanitarium, the government was forced to make more prisons in other provinces. They replaced the military guards with medical doctors and nurses. Instead of a criminal, I became a patient."

"What were the rules?" asked Pete.

"No sex without a rubber. It is a crime. No sex outside the sanitarium. Sex without a condom and with an uninfected person is murder and you are punished. Some shot. No questions asked, no courts, no defense. It isn't a complete life but is better than none. We do well for our country by protecting our countrymen from our infections."

"Does a rubber make a difference?" asked Peter.

Carlos paused, "Doctor, don't you know, quarantine works, and rubbers make the government happy."

What a fool I am, felt Pete, *like so many others.*

Pete reflected on the meaning of Salah,...don't ask so many questions...rather be still and listen.

Pete at GITMO expected to learn about tropical diseases, and awoke to discover a world of conflict, contrast, and coercion

Pete knew he might never learn if Charles was bisexual, but it appears the issue was a planned distracter. This was no suicide. Charles was killed, and it seemed unlikely he met his death in Cuba. Shipping his body back to Washington State would have been sure folly. Too many would know about it. Someone in the local command had to be the designated hit man. Could have been doped then flown to the Bremerton air field where he entered the BOQ drugged or drunk, then killed, too many details to cover up. *Charles, an astute clinician, must have discovered something critically important or he knew too much.*

Pete felt the peril surrounding himself, he was endangered, *if they discover I know about Charles's death, the R&D laboratory experiments at Bethesda, and now their naval experiments with quarantine, he thought.* 86

The surgeon that will look after his wounded leg will do so with some sense of technical achievement. This surgeon will probably not notice the branding on his ear lobe because he will be too focused on the leg wound. The hospital administrator will not arrive until the morning and will not discover Carlos is from Havana until, maybe late

that same afternoon. The nursing supervisor will undoubtedly become distracted by quality assurance protocols and not have the slightest idea of the impact of Carlos 'escape from the sanitarium. No one will know for at least one or two days and my flight out of GITMO is tomorrow for Washington D.C. via Atlanta. The most likely pressures would come from the hospital administrator.

Pete decided a low profile was critical. He needed to research Navy information data sources not available to civilians. Such info could save his life. He realized that he would need to be prepared to quickly depart the Navy when timing was right. As Pete awaited his departure from GITMO, he must plan escape options. But, for the moment, he must stay inside this simmering pot. The heat of a kitchen would be a relief by comparison.

His mind leaped with options, while sorting out connections. *Was the Sand Point, Seattle quarantine effort an example of a nation-wide effort based on the results learned from the experiment with Quarantine in the Sanitariums of Cuba?* It might take months for the Navy to realize Tierney knew more than he should, much less allow him to depart the Navy once they had realized what he knows. The advantage of being a reservist was finally starting to pay off. Regular Navy types only departed with direct presidential and congressional approval. Only timing and preparations might protect his life and reputation.

Reservists are treated differently than regular Navy types.Reservist have a sunset law, if their contract is not renewed, it lapses and the reservist can exit the service at a predetermined time. Pete might not have to call special attention to resigning if he times it right, *that's good, he* thought, *I must maintain a low profile.* He drafted a letter of resignation to BUPERS (Bureau of Personnel) via BUMED (Bureau of Medicine) and to his local command anticipating timing events to his advantage but, held back from submitting it just yet. *I will first need to snoop around the beltway!*

Pete reinforced the need to be particularly cautious and alert in all his future dealings with Lt. Tatum once back at the Bangor Subbase. *Tatum will try to consume my attention with unnecessary tasking, a typical strategy by service corps administrators.*

That evening, he wrote an updated letter to Shawn describing his discoveries. If she recorded the events and perhaps used her writing talents to make public the events he had uncovered, if he was suddenly found dead, or missing, at least someone important to him would know. The void of communications between them had disappeared over the past year. She had finally allowed him near her again in correspondence, but not physically or emotionally. Still there was a sense that the relationship was not completely over, at least not yet. Pete felt it not yet a hopeless endeavor as there still was meaning between them. Their closure was not finalized. There are more than memories between these once intense lovers. He wrote her with urgency.

As he returned to the BOQ at GITMO and packed for the next day's departure. He was emotionally and physically exhausted.

That evening on the delayed newscast piped into the BOQ, Peter Jennings reported on AIDS in France. Between, 1980-85, transfusions were not tested for the AIDS virus although, the test was available in the US market place. Officials in France were under investigation and indictments as 50 to 100 citizens per week were infected with the AIDS virus, when it could easily have been prevented. Not unlike America this epidemic had been allowed to happen. Blood banks in France refused to test their blood supply. Jennings reported it was a question of national pride, and a question of royalties. It had imploded upon itself in this mosaic of confused human conflicts. Thousands of Frenchmen were intentionally infected, and it was totally preventable.

France prideful and arrogant did not want to use US screening methods. Jennings also reported that the Pasteur Institute had rumored that the hepatitis B vaccination transmitted the AIDS virus. There was no elaboration on this rumor other than it being reported as "speculation".

Pete slept restless, tossing about and sweating. By early morning he was packed and ready for departure. He returned to the Naval Hospital on the arid treeless hill overlooking the windswept bay. The hospital was located within one half mile of the fence guarded by the Marines that separated GITMO from communist Cuba. Tent City was across the bay below. He needed to check up on Carlos and his progress after surgery for the gunshot wound.

Carlos was found on the surgical ward, in the screened open-air lanai, sitting in an old squeaky wooden wheel chair. His leg elevated on a raised support. He had undergone a wide debridement of the wound to his left leg. The wound was packed wide open with iodine impregnated dressings to allow a prolonged secondary healing process. He was in good spirits and surprisingly little discomfort.

"Gracias, Doctor. I wish I knew what to do next," he said with a searching dark brown eyed gaze.

"Wish I knew how to help you Carlos. I'm not sure what to do myself," Pete admitted. "I'll be heading back to the states today I wish you well in your recovery."

"Gracias, Senior Doctor. You have helped me more than you know."

"No, Carlos, you have helped me more than you know! Promise me not to tell anyone about that branding on your ear and its meaning. We wouldn't want them to know of the Quarantino."

Carlos nodded, knowing the importance of this secret and smiled a very wide toothless grin, gestured to Pete his agreement. They shook hands, and Pete departed the ward. He walked along the green tiled floor to the quarter-deck at the main entrance of the hospital. It faced toward the east, and his gaze scanned the harbor below. The submarine tender, Spear, the Virginia class guided missile cruiser CGN South Carolina plus a fast frigate that he did not recognize were all in port.

As he rode in the shuttle to the airfield, he marveled again at the warm caress of the air mass and the texture of tropical environment. It reminded Peter of Hawaii without the Aloha spirit. His thoughts wandered to that idyllic setting as he boarded the twin turbo propped C-12. He loved to fly in this aircraft. It was a smooth takeoff, and the pilot with an open cockpit seat was happy to see a flight surgeon aboard and invited him forward. Pete entered the cockpit and was welcomed into the right seat as they made a standard rate left turn to bear on a due north magnetic heading. The islands of the Caribbean fell away as they gained altitude. There is beauty below. The light coral blue made it lazy and inviting. The coral shone through the shallow waters and looked like flat white mushrooms or clouds beneath the sea. It reminded Pete of flying over the atolls of the Western Pacific. His pilot, a Lt. Shane Workman loved his job and what could be better?

Pete secured by a seat belt, allowed his thoughts to drift to Hawaii and then to Kalaupapa on Molokai. He had been enthralled with the writings of Michener's "Hawaii", and under such influence made a visit to the Leper colony of Kalaupapa, the site of a mass involuntary quarantine for those suffering from leprosy in the 1860's. It was located on the windward, wet side of the island held captive in isolation so desolate that tales persist to this day of inhumanities beyond the darkest of description.

There was a switch back donkey trail that descended the shear slopes to the flat and luscious peninsula below that was Kalaupapa. In the age of modern medicine treatment was one of sulfones and early detection. Today, isolation and quarantine have no place in the treatment of leprosy.

However, circumstances were quite different in Kalaupapa during a different era. At that time leprosy threatened the survival of the entire Polynesian culture within the Hawaiian Islands. This was a time when such medicines as sulfones were not yet heard of, much less available. There was no cure; there was only separation, isolation and a demonic death from a disfiguring illness.

Father Damien died here, like so many other lepers and with only the hope they gave each other. Today the leper island tells a tale of sorrow that is real and palpably felt by those who pass through.

It is now a quiet place with the summer trade winds warming the flat unprotected land mass. Father Damien's small white church remains with a spire and a singular bell in the loft. A graveyard is on either side of the reddish volcanic dirt road that leads a sense of being personally touched forever to the church's front door. Pete remembered feeling a bit contaminated by visiting this land of isolated anguish. It was not a bad sense of contamination, but of being personally touched.

He glanced out the window of the aircraft. He could see the Florida Keys dotting the shore that lined and buffeted the land mass. *It's surprising how close Cuba is to the US,* he thought. *Maybe some form of quarantine is equally as close.*

His thoughts returned to Molokai and how the winter cold winds and the Mauka showers, kept the land and those held in quarantine always in dampness. Most died during the winter months of pneumonia, tuberculosis, exposure, broken spirits and infections associated with self-amputations in neuropathic extremities. These were neurologically insensitive extremities that lost sensations and at least, mercifully, limited the physical pain.

These were human beings that did not look human. They hobbled on limbs without toes and stared vacantly from faces that lacked noses and lips. These people were herded on sailing vessels like cattle and cast into the sea to swim ashore to Kalaupapa. It was an epidemic called Mai' Ali'i. There was no cure. Quarantine was the only hope. It would take another seventy years for a real scientific cure to become available. It is well known that the Polynesian culture could not have survived seventy years simply waiting for a modern cure. Isolation via quarantine was indeed mandatory to maintain their civilization.

It may have appeared by modern standards as inhumane, thought Pete, *to be shunned by your fellow man and thrown into an exile of an uncaring and certain death.* Leprosy had a history that spanned four millenniums, and little had changed in how people treated each other. Although AIDS was different there was as well a parallel. It remained an inhumane practice until social caring and purposeful order developed on its own within the leper colony. Order and caring made it humane .*Had mankind become the victim of rhetoric and conflict so unwieldy that values Became confused as if of equal value and therefore of no distinct value? Or had the rhetoric become so gilded with political correctness that history and logic were no longer part of the solution? Pete* pondered. Would society catch up with what was learned at Kalaupapa? Pete did not know, but Quarantine was being tested in Cuba, and it was the only place in the world where it was statistically successful. Some would say this were only possible because of Castro and communism. A free society would never allow this to happen. Pete knew he could not sort out the answers by himself. He also believed that allowing a certain predictable death rate was unacceptable. There was no argument that could justify it. The QA symbol was not Quality Assurance but code for **Quarantine Access**. The Research and Development Lab at Bethesda under Admiral Hays was keyed with the QA code. Who else knew besides Tierney?

Pete concluded, Charles must have known, that's why he was killed!

ANNAPOLIS, MARYLAND

Nancy Brewer felt the empty hole in her heart with the cavernous unexplained loss of Charles. She would awake alone in the rain filled air of Annapolis. It was a muggy chill. She rolled over, reached to the left side of the bed and rediscovered Charles was not there. She knew he would never be there again. Her heart could grasp this darkened awareness only in small bits. Her throat wailed in empty sobs into the still night air. She knew she could only let the sorrow and grief out in the privacy of her bedroom. She would worry like so many mothers. She worried that Kristen would not develop properly without her father. She worried that her daughter would do poorly in school. She knew that Kristen would need more, and that one parent was not enough. Nancy could not be father and mother. Buy it was of no counsel.She was alone and that was personal.

Despite her emotional turmoil she was not one to let Charles' death remain unanswered. At times, she fixated on revenge. It was the suspicious tampering of Charles ear and official distance of the Navy that gave rage its focus. However, she had also felt gratitude and great fortune to have found a mentor. This took the form of a cranky old lady who learned the power of writing letters to politicians and anybody else who might be within ear shot.

Mildred Canter was a cantankerous, elderly woman who learned to keep her eyes open and write letters. She wrote lots of letters, most often to congressmen and newspapers. She created immeasurable grief for the Air Force from her ranch just south near Nellis, AFB. She had lived on a mountainside in the military operating airspace (MOA). The Air Force had a way of doing low level high-speed training flights right over her secluded ranch. She became an expert in identification of aircraft types with tail numbers. Even the international fly-ins of operation Red Flag did not dispel her, the Air Force learned the hard way

They, with a chuckle under their breath, respected her political clout. Then when her son died in the Beirut bombing she moved to the hills of West Virginia, so she could be in contact with the information clearing stations. Her research disclosed major flaws in the security system of the Marine barracks; her trade name became "Granny C". If there was a legal way to get information, she would find it.

Nancy discovered a close trusting friendship with Mrs. Canter. Granny redirected the turmoil and energy boiling within Nancy toward asking the right questions in the right places. Granny had become an inspiring mentor.

Nancy with her prior research skills, learned to apply the Freedom of Information Act obtaining the Uganda briefs and the reports from the Viral Research Institute in Entebbe. By contrast, AIDS made deposed General Idi Amin look saintly. Amin alone had slaughtered 300,000 in Uganda. While HIV had killed half a million, and a million more were infected.

Nancy from her kitchen computer obtained briefs between the International AIDS foundation, the World Health Organization and the Armed Forces Institute of Pathology. It took her months to understand the global scale of the epidemic. Being black, female and the wife of a service man killed while on active duty carried a lot of weight and opened doors of information normally closed. Nancy knew what she was doing but did not know which direction to take. She was driven to find out who killed her husband and she knew enough to not take it personal. She vowed not to be victimized again.

"It was bad enough they killed my husband, but they mutilated his body and ruined his reputation. I will not forgive them for that!"

"And you said you weren't going to take it personal." Granny said.

"I thought you had learned something from me. How soon you forget, child. What else have you done?" asked Granny.

"I've located the data on the polio vaccination in Central Africa and the reports from Cuba and Haiti."

"Did you see this report of the Anthrax leak that killed 300 people in the Soviet city of Sverdlovsk in April of 1979?"

"No, child, how did you learn that?"

"From the intelligence brief to the CIA two weeks after the leak," she said. "You can bet that put pressure on the military to develop; a response to biologic testing in Russia."

"I've got to find Peter. Where is he? I've left notes and messages. Granny he could be dead like Charles. He went to GITMO as well." "Be careful Nancy, you worry too much. And you must not worry Aloud!"

CHAPTER 6

C:\Password-(NIH-QA-CDC)

Early September: Washington D.C.

National Institute of Health

The brief stopover in Atlanta allowed an abbreviated phone call to Shawn. Pete was disappointed. He did not want to speak to her voice mail. But, he recorded his message; he had arrived back in the U.S. and dashed back to the awaiting C-12 for the flight to D.C. Traveling in dress blues was inconvenient but required while on Navy business.

"Nice to see the Potomac River again," he mentioned to the civilian passenger in the aisle seat next to him as the aircraft was on final approach. The guy grunted an acknowledgment but had been engrossed in his paperwork and business spreadsheets. Peter expected a restrained response. Must be a DOD technical rep he thought.

Pete studied the Metro directory with color coded rail lines dissecting the beltway. The blue line from Bethesda connected with the yellow to arrive at the Pentagon. *That could wait for another day.* Pete wanted the elevated Metro Yellow Train toward Rockville, where the National Institute of Health was located toward the end of the line. He was familiar with the area, felt well-traveled, smug, a bit cocky about it. Arriving on Wednesday granted him time to check out the National Institute of Health as well as a satellite building across the train tracks from Bethesda. Still, he needed to make Monday afternoon's fellowship interview at Bethesda Naval Hospital.

He had learned a lot more in GITMO than the academics of tropical diseases! Now he needed to understand who was behind the quarantine experiment.

Pete left the Colonial Inn early in search of the library at the NIH. The huge white forty story structure was in easy walking distance. He discovered a special access code was required for entry. The archives were secured by a cipher lock and what appeared to be a very inattentive uniformed guard. The guard's pendulous belly placed visible tension against the strained buttons of his uniform. It seemed this ponderous habitus was one of the job requirements as was his firm grip on the ever-present coffee mug.

The Freedom of Information act may apply to every American Citizen, but the "need to know" dictates what is learned by a Naval Officer. Peter knew he was not authorized access to the top-secret information in these archives.

He prided himself for being an observant student of people. If he wore the gold chain of an attaché, carried a legal briefcase, a clipboard and had the cipher code, he might just be successful at breaching the security.

He might pose as on official business for some admiral. The right questions, properly phrased, might open the guarded door. With a hastily developed strategy, he departed the library, returned on the yellow train back to Bethesda. There he found the uniform store and purchased an attaché's gold chain for his shoulder and a clipboard. He hopped back aboard the elevated train for the return trip to the NIH Library.

NIH was a huge complex chartered under the direction of President Franklin Roosevelt as the country struggled to stay out of

World War II. His words at the dedication were, "We cannot be a strong nation unless we are a healthy nation."

With 50,000 researchers, it was the center of information and part of the Public Health Service, owned by DHSS. It was so large a bureaucracy that its budget exceeds six-cabinet level departments. It has the largest advisory system in the entire government.

Pete entered the elevator and punched basement. He placed his briefcase down and wiped the sweat from his forehead. He felt the air stream from the air-conditioning and was appreciative. The stainless-steel doors opened to a long passageway. A sign pointed to the archives, labeled Research Archives, Viral. The hallway was busy, mostly civilian traffic.

He found a young medical service corps officer wandering the library hallways. "Excuse me, Lt. J.G. Brown, I left my code back in the admiral's car, could you spare me the embarrassment, so I don't hold him up unnecessarily? I need the code to the Viral Archives."

"Of, course, Commander, it's CQR-30979," he offered.

"Thanks Lt., You've been a great help!"

Peter shaking his head and mumbling to himself, *stupid man probably doesn't know what security means nor understands what burn bags are for.* Damn service corps! He needs operational ship board time to cure him of that lame hospital manager's mindset. Pete walked down the hall, ignoring the security guard who had turned away from his desk to fill his coffee cup from an urn in an enclosed alcove.

Pete punched in the CQR code and glanced over his shoulder. The security guard was adding sugar and cream.

Click, the locked door released its latch. Pete was inside as the security guard turned to see a closed door.

Pete scanned the library and noted a series of computer files. He typed in AIDS and found a huge section on the epidemic. With a sense of urgency, he sought out collateral data on the computer log system supporting the theme of biologic leaks, biologic warfare, chemical warfare, and radiation leaks. None of these topic categories led anywhere.

He entered the side computer systems dealing with viral data and epidemics. Here he retried all the themes again. No luck. He tried

Strategic and tactical without success. The subject "Cuba" led to a quick blind alley. "Vaccines" led nowhere. "Flu" didn't help either.

"PIG", hit the jackpot, like silver dollars cascading out of a slot machine at Vegas. Pete looked over his shoulder to ensure no one noticed his excitement. His excitement was like a silent earthquake, but nobody else was shaking. Within minutes Peter had a complete printout referencing the biologic warfare leak that characterized the "SWINE FLU EPIDEMIC" of the mid 1970's.

More died of the vaccination or complications than ever suffered from the so called "epidemic". More people were stricken with the ascending paralysis of Guillian-Barré Syndrome, a complication of the vaccination, than ever got swine flu. This was "The Epidemic" that affected a mere five Army personnel out of Fort Dix, New Jersey, and within a mere four months the entire United States population was dutifully undergoing a mass immunization program. Nowhere in the history of the world has a public policy been so quickly enforced and like sheep, the public accepted it. Nor had a vaccine so rapidly become available and actively used when only five Army soldiers became ill. Only one died, and that was because he refused medical attention, Rather, he had decided to go on a required physical readiness test running 1.5 miles.

Ah, yes, Pete read, it was a Private Lewis who was on record as the only known death of the epidemic.

A Colonel Bartley speculated that Lewis would never have died if it were not for the required physical testing. None of the other four ever became ill nor had any complications, only two were ill for more than ten days. Even the sergeant who attempted mouth to mouth resuscitation on Private Lewis did not get ill.

That surely doesn't sound very contagious, thought Tierney, *and it surely would explain why this "epidemic" miraculously never crossed the border into Canada.*

Shaking his head in disbelief, he wished he had access to the records of political communications that must have occurred between Canada and the United States. How would you reassure a neighboring country that there is no concern for an epidemic that threatens the entire adult population of the United States, but miraculously stops at a shared border?

He read further. Hundreds of people developed the neurologic paralysis that ascended their legs to chest level. Some became paraplegics during the aftermath of this 1976-77 vaccination program. Some became quadriplegics. No one knows why 500 people developed permanent paralysis or neurologic complications from this vaccination many with Guillian-Barre Syndrome (GBS). Nor has the rate of GBS been associated with any other mass vaccination programs.

It seemed clear from these documents, that the Swine Flu Epidemic was a biologic warfare virus created in the Army laboratory that accidentally leaked within the confines of a small group working with the virus at Fort Dix, New Jersey. This is a respected biologic research laboratory.

Pete felt it was probably designed for use against a future adversary to temporarily compromise their fighting ability. The target in the late 1970's was likely the Soviet Union. Meanwhile, the Center for Disease Control and a Dr. David Sencer, recommended stockpiling a vaccine for a potential swine flu epidemic. This vaccine was hastily recommended to the American population under the pre-election political pressures of President Ford. He of course was the president who often stumbled and needed to appear decisive in handling a national crisis. Rather, the crisis appeared to be pre-election posturing.

Or was it really, he thought, *a fear that a virus made for biologic warfare had escaped from its glass vials and threatened an unplanned epidemic.*

Dr. R. Price was noted as a co-author of this and subsequent papers on the subject.

Was this the virologist Price, the guy that Dave and Carla from Victoria BC had described? Yeah, it was Raymond Price whom they mentioned. He was a virologist and immunologist who had left the Center for Disease Control for ignominy in Milwaukee, Wisconsin. Something had to do with an ethical dispute. I'm sure he was the man they spoke of. He had quit work and a career with the National Institute of Health because of some ethical conflicts, alcoholism, or political issues as I recall. Where was he located when he wrote this? OK, the CDC in Atlanta, will have to be my next stop!

Pete explored the files, studied cross references and invented associations all to no avail. He decided unnecessary time was being spent at risk of exposure. He jotted down the needed references, placed it in his coat pocket, stood at the computer terminal, closed the files and hastily walked to the exit of the archives. He was quietly pleased but surprised that no one questioned his presence in the library nor intercepted his exit. It must have looked routine for an admiral's aide. He smugly applauded himself, but still was unsure. It felt too easy.

There was no time to relay this information to Shawn and her editor. He had time only to arrange a rental car, cancel his present hotel reservation, close his unpacked bags, and fly back to Atlanta. If he could stretch his luck, he might gain access to the CDC files without unnecessary attention. After the CDC, his next appointment window was Bethesda Monday afternoon with Dr. Ambose, head of the Department of Infectious Diseases.

Atlanta, Georgia

Tierney sat next to a petite blond college student returning to Emory University on Delta flight 307. She graduated from Bellarmine High School in Tacoma, Washington. They seemed to speak freely. Pete asked about Atlanta, she spoke with enthusiasm and held back nothing.

"Atlanta is not a one-horse town," she explained. "It was controlled by several families but owned by Coca Cola."

"Not Pepsi, but Coke", she emphasized. "A waitress might say... Sorry we only serve coke, is that ok?"

There was no deep message here as Pete cared little of turf wars, but was intrigued with the power of influence.

"Atlanta is not just Coke country; it is also CNN, Ted Turner, and Atlanta Brave Country. It is the home of Delta Airlines with its north terminal consuming the entire ramp. All others go to the south terminal." She paused, tossed her hair, and pulled her leg under her butt, easy for a flexible young college student.

"Atlanta is Jimmy Carter country and home to the Carter Center at Emory University where annually he speaks to the students."

"Besides the Carters, there are the Woodruff's and the Dobb's associated with business, law and the school of public health. There is the Candler School of Theology initially established at Oxford, Georgia and is a direct pipeline to Emory University."

Pete admired her enthusiasm and felt he was with a tour guide in the eyes of a young woman.

"There is the Rolling's Research Center and the Yerkes Primate Research Center, one of the largest primate centers in the world."

"You're kidding me. What do they do there?" Pete asked.

"No idea, secret stuff for all I know, maybe viral studies with monkeys."

The flight attendant momentarily interrupted by offering soft drinks and peanuts.

"They do research into diseases of third world countries she continued. It is pivotal to Emory University's role and the Center for Disease Control. It's all part of the 2000 Project under DuPont among others, with efforts to rid Africa of Guinea worm river disease and kuru, a viral neurologic disease from monkeys." She explained.

"Atlanta is a Mecca for change, from the midtown artistry and center of homosexuality to the intellectual avant-garde. This is the cultural and commercial center of the neo-south." She proudly exclaimed.

Pete never learned her name.

Center for Disease Control

Tierney stepped out of the rented silver Honda, adjusted his uniform, adjusted his cover, locked the door and paused as he studied the entrance to the C D C .

The sidewalk led to four tall, white columns marking the entrance to a colonial, brick, three-story building. This Williamsburg style of southern regality stood on groomed acreage donated by Emory University dating back to the early 1940's.

Despite being a federal agency since the early 1970's, it maintained an air of medical academia about it. The gray vinyl tile floors perfectly matched the institutional green painted walls. Pete entered the foyer, paused in study of an office directory. It had highlighted letters on a black background with a reflective glass. He noted the location of the epidemiologic archives.

Surely it too would be locked and guarded, he thought. *If only I could get past the security into the Intelligence Library.*

The glass reader board reflected the background entrance. He studied the hallway traffic. There were no military uniforms. He worried that he would stick out like a sore thumb. He studied the reception desk. An elderly woman with a frilly blouse was on the telephone, and there was a registration log. He did not want a record of his visit. He must avoid registering in the log. He remembered the attaché's gold shoulder ring stowed in his briefcase as he lifted it from the floor. There was no other civilian garb that might appear authoritative. He decided to play the same hand with his Navy uniform and see if it worked again.

He turned from the directory and walked with shallow confidence toward the reception desk. A name plate read 'MRS. WAKEFIELD'. She was still on the phone. He noticed the men's room to the left, nodded to Mrs. Wakefield and veered off toward the restroom. There he regrouped and studied his appearance in the mirror, cooled his face splashing water and secured an attaché's gold loop to his shoulder. With a deep breath, he cautiously left the restroom and again studied the main hallway. An elderly lady of slight stature caught his eye; she appeared to be a librarian. She had soft, hazel eyes and a quick smile.

Pete stopped her. "Excuse me, would you help me and spare me the embarrassment of bothering my admiral?"

Her eyes widened, and with a glow in her cheeks, she paused in whimsical remembrance.

"Oh, you're a Naval aviator," she said with surprised recognition. Her feeling for the Navy dress blue uniform was instantly readable and heartfelt.

"No, I'm a Navy flight surgeon. The wings sort of look alike," he said as she examined them. "I need help in finding the archives. I'm afraid I've misplace the code and the admiral is waiting in the car, for the notes we forgot."

"Oh yes," she said. "I understand. An admiral when kept waiting could become very upset for any delay. I had a friend who was a Navy pilot, with a long pause, she held back a tear!"He well, …..we were in Pensacola together". She recaptured her composure and asked, "How can I help, you, I mean the admiral?"

"The admiral asked me to get his lecture notes and references from the library and I've misplaced the cipher code. Ma'am, your help would be much appreciated." Pete shifted his weight and the briefcase to the left hand.

"We have a meeting at 1400," Pete added with pause and glanced at his watch. It was 0955.

"Yes, of course, the admiral."

Without further hesitation, the woman gave the code to Tierney. *Must be the luck of the Irish,* thought Peter, *or maybe it's the influence of any Navy Wings of gold. They seem to have broken many a lady's heart. Only a Navy Pilot could pull this shit off.* He felt admiration but hoped that some of that luck and charm might rub off on him. The last time he was down memory lane was at The Mustin Beach Officers Club in Pensacola. There was mostly a lighthearted debonair atmosphere there, such that kicking tires, and burning holes in the sky was very much alive. The gardens and entrance to the Mustin Beach Oak Club remained lined with inverted tail hooks symbolic of more than carrier landings. It all made sense. It was the scene of generations past, a scene born of tradition in the heart of naval aviation.

Peter gained ready access to the archives. The cool temperature of the room was healthy for documents and computer discs. The files were in the west corner in a small room with four cubicles each with access to the computerized filing system. This archive was very old, but there was a new section that had the latest in research publications and potential projects. Everything conceivable was cross referenced, by topic, by author and by association or projects.

It became a matter of pick and choose, retrieve and exit. He wandered through data on Hepatitis B, vaccinations, quarantines, Swine flu and Cuba. Occasionally behind him, the door opened and he would have company for a while. During these interruptions, Pete would change the screen and scribble meaningless notes on a yellow legal pad. When the intruder left he extended his neck and rolled his shoulders to ease the tension. There now was an annoying knot in his neck. He wiped his damp palms on his white shirt and retrieved the desired computer screen.

Somewhere within the chips of the terminal, the link he sought was hidden, but where? With the San Francisco connection, he learned that Australia's first twenty AIDS cases were linked to the US. The "Sky train" took him to France where AIDS was the charter disease connecting to New York and San Francisco. Blood transfusions were a legalistic mess, but the files were incomplete. Someone had put a clamp on the information.

Although he had no trouble finding documents that the blood banks had arranged blood drives in the gay Castro District of San Francisco, despite knowing there would be certain contamination of the general blood supply.

In the hall outside the door, footsteps paused, and then moved on. Pete looked at the door and then to his watch. He had been searching the computer system for over two hours. At any moment, he expected Mrs. Wakefield to walk in. He rubbed his palms on his pant legs and tried "Special Forces".

Pete believed in following his instincts. It may have been the rumor from the Pasteur Institute that pointed him in the direction of Hepatitis-B vaccinations.

The San Francisco connection was critically important. It may have explained why international cases were linked to the United States.

Special task forces, he found, had been sent to Africa by the World Health Organization to vaccinate the population, especially in South Africa, and Zaire. The CDC sent a task force to San Francisco in the mid 1970's to selectively vaccinate the gay population with Hepatitis B. The vaccination in this early stage of development was derived from human sera from the homosexual community, not synthetically derived from genetically spliced viral replications as it is today. That of course, meant it was not pure by comparison. Physicians tacitly avoided this vaccination and waited for the technology to develop a synthetic pure vaccine. Today these viruses are used for genetic manipulation of diseases.

Genetic splicing was becoming an awesome, frightening science, thought Peter. *We simply are not prepared to deal with such ethical problems.*

Pure is one of those words that makes everyone shudder, he thought, and rightfully so, for much speculation had historically occurred regarding this entire immunization program.

It's crazy to believe anyone might contaminate the vaccination serum; he reminded himself, *just paranoid craziness!*

He reminded himself that there were some very talented and very good people trying their level best to solve this terrible epidemic. They simply could not all be on the dark side.

He advanced the cursor and noticed: *the first accelerated rate of AIDS cases appeared*

Shortly after this selective gay male mass vaccination effort in San Francisco. These separate vaccination programs coincided in time with the national Swine Flu mass vaccination program. Where was the connection? Was there a connection? Proving a connection might be impossible although he knew the original blood samples from the gay population of San Francisco were locked away in a refrigerated safe at the CDC.

Pete's thoughts raced, the homosexual population has been with humanity from the dawn of ages, why suddenly would they become the primary host of a new and terrifying disease? It made no sense for something to suddenly erupt in a select population of homosexuals and IV drug users.

For lack of any other ideas, Pete typed in "Stats."

The latest 1992 data from the CDC confirmed 93% of all AIDS cases in the US were still in homosexuals, bisexual males, IV drug users, those who received blood from these groups, or women sexually involved with bisexual males. Nothing had changed in over 12 years except for political rhetoric.

"Heterosexual explosion indeed," Pete mumbled with sarcasm. The millenniums of time had never seen such a disease. He looked at the wall clock again. He had been there nearly four hours.

Pete realized that continuing this train of research might end in another dead-end street. Before leaving the archives, in a final gesture he typed "c:R.Price", then "c:Dr-Price", then "c:Dr.Price", into the computer's eight figure file.

Bingo! He hit pay dirt. Suddenly there were matches, by topic, by authorship in mass vaccinations of polyvalent live and attenuated T-Cell immune responses! Dr. Price was a key link.

There was the link between the Hepatitis B vaccinations and the AIDS epidemic in San Francisco.

Pete looked at the clock, wiped the sweat from his brow to the rolled up long sleeve white shirt. He had no time to digest the historical impact. This was political dynamite. Anyone remotely associated with this project was tainted like sick, decaying meat.

This is Hot! I better make a few cross- referencing notes and get the hell out of here!

Facts accumulated from gay bars and bath houses. He typed in: print command, exit, directory, and retrieve, print. Change drive, directory, retrieve, print, function key, library. Print. Pete pounded the computer keys, looked at the clock, five hours. The door, still closed, no noise outside.

The doorknob turned as the door opened. It was the janitor in gray coveralls. The janitor did not speak; he just picked up a waste basket and a box of recycled paper.

Pete took off his glasses, wiped the sweat from the lenses and rubbed his forehead. It was a cold sweat.

Print! When the last sheet rolled off the printer, Pete exited the computer and tripped the off switch. It had taken five hours, forty-five minutes.

I'll be out of here in five minutes.

He collected the sheets of paper and tossed them in his briefcase. He tucked his shirt in. It was damp to the touch. Rolled his shirt sleeves down and replaced the blue, uniformed jacket.

Where is Mrs. Wakefield? He thought.

He slowly opened the door and departed the archives trying to control his pace. He must not appear hurried. He felt his palm sweaty against the leather briefcase handle. He switched hands just as he entered the hallway. He looked for the information desk.

Mrs. Wakefield had been replaced at the reception desk. A middle aged black man, with grey receding hair gave Pete a cool, seemingly uninterested, glance. He never stood but nodded. With hesitation, Pete acknowledged with a brief nod as he pushed open the large, walnut doors into fresh, cool air and the Georgia late summer sun. He inhaled deeply.

I must find this guy, Price! I've no hope, unless I find Price! I hope no one stops or notices me, how could they not notice, he thought. *I'm sweating like a pig, I'm lucky it's late on Friday when everyone wants off work with a sunny afternoon and a good weekend to enjoy.* He resolved, *if I'm stopped I'll say the admiral is upset and anxious to catch a flight to a meeting at the Pentagon.*

He passed several men in white jackets, carrying clipboards and breast pockets stuffed with pens. Another passed with his head down, wearing trifocals fixated on the sidewalk and wearing a poorly kept suit. All wore badges. Pete stuck out like a boil.

Finally, he found his Avis rental car. His pace was calmer, but he shuddered with the chill of discovery.

This has got to be another biologic warfare experiment! The AIDS virus must have been co-mingled with Hepatitis B vaccinations in the homosexual community of San Francisco. I better get out of here fast!

He tossed his jacket into the back seat, backed out of the parking lot and headed for any exit going north. Pete signaled and eased into traffic.

Was there any wonder why 88% of the gay males in San Francisco with AIDS were also positive for Hepatitis B? The CDC publicly claimed that only 8% of the gays who were vaccinated with Hep-B got AIDS. The CDC was now trapped in their own lie. Why would anyone do this? What could possibly justify this misuse of power and the public trust? Who would do this? Why? The CDC, NIH or some unknown group with an agenda, played with biologic warfare in an experiment that got out of hand? All or none the ideas were possible, but none made sense as to explain a motive. The Hep B vaccine was first developed from the blood of homosexual males in Castro district as it was a co-inhabitant of both diseases. This vaccine was discontinued a few years later and replaced with recombinant Hep-B which was much safer. He turned on the radio. Country and Western, he switched, more C&W, he punched seek and switched again only to find Michael Bolton whining. That was enough, his mind raced.

It seemed impossible to control the disease in San Francisco. The futility of "safe sex" in the gay population was well known. Mayor Feinstein wouldn't close the bath houses which festered with every known venereal disease. They became the perfect breeding ground for a disease that experimentally might appear confined. But, this was confined to a select population at a critical moment in the mid 1970's, a population that seemed unable to wield political clout. How wrong they were. Then the gay movement was more of an oddity, and San Francisco was a city of incredible tolerance.

106

The IV drug user however had no political clout and was an oddity, How wrong they were. Then the gay movement was more than an oddity, and yet San Francisco was a city of incredible tolerance.

Pete drove in silence as he fidgeted with the air conditioner. He decided not to try the radio until up the road a bit and free of Atlanta.

As he drove in silence he thought of his last trip to San Francisco.

He smiled in recall of an episode near where the cable car reversed direction in the heart of the business district, near the Hyatt.

A young man with wild eyes and matted hair postured in a threatening fashion vaulted off a park bench shouting threatening nonsensical utterances. He was crazed. His chants were warrior like with wild gestures and flailing arms. Everyone including Pete cautiously moved away from this man and uncomfortably waited for the cable car to arrive. Finally, after what felt like an eternity the cable car arrived. Pete found a seat between two women. The lady to the left said, "He sure is getting agitated, I haven't seen him so bad."

"How long have been watching this guy?" Peter asked.

"About seven months," she said matter of fact.

"Seven months," Pete repeated with alarm and amazement!

He knew no other city would have protectively watched over such a strange and threatening man.

"He comes down here three or four times a week and acts out a ritualistic fantasy no one understands. He's from a prominent family in Sausalito, across the bay," the woman added.

From that moment, Peter had the greatest of respect for the tolerance of San Franciscans, a city that cared with interest but from a distance.

He drove aimlessly for an hour, then headed north on Interstate 85. As he left the outskirts of Atlanta, he tried the radio again, still country and western. He turned it off and slowed the air-conditioner fan down.

He arrived in Charlotte, North Carolina pulled off the highway near a road side Colonel Sanders. A remodeled motel was across the street.

Peter signed the register, paying cash.

I want no record of my whereabouts, no credit card trail.
Amazing that I could enter such a high-level secret archive
leaving no trail, applauding himself in silence.

He smiled as he entered the motel room. He threw his bag on the single bed, and relaxed with a long, pounding cool shower. He walked across the street to the Col. Sanders Restaurant and sat in a narrow booth with two pieces of chicken, a scoop of mashed potatoes, coleslaw and a crumbly biscuit that wouldn't hold butter. It landed in his growling, anxious stomach like a cold brick. Maybe Charles knew about the vaccinations, maybe he knew about QA? Where did he fit in? Why was he killed?

The fried chicken had turned cold and was no longer palatable. It lay in his gut like a restless volcano unable to vent. He tossed the remaining breast into the paper sack and walked across the street to his motel room.

"I must find Price!"

"He's got to be the key."

It must have been top secret information that got Charles killed, maybe he had joined the dark side?

Tierney forgot the risks as fatigue wrapped around him. *I'll leave for Norfolk, Va. in the morning, find a place and write an updated brief for Shawn's file.*

His senses wandered to Shawn. He placed his hands behind his neck noticing the knotted muscle had unwound. He smiled with cockiness. The computer archive break in went so well. He was getting better as a thief and feeling a bit smug about it. Not cocky just proud to become a better thief. He fell asleep before he got his shoes off, still sticky with sweat as the air conditioner droned away.

One hour after Tierney had exited the CDC Intel Library, a black security hire locked the doors for the night. He dutifully followed procedural rituals in the security Intelligence Library. He rewound a tape of the monitoring cameras which recorded every move made in the archives coding it with the computer information base. He placed the tape in a tray, storing it in a safe for the next weekly review. Peter was unaware that he was surveilled. It would take time to for security to determine the identity of this navy doctor.

His reflection on the computer screen was recorded and cross referencing with the data researched.

108

CHAPTER 7

Bethesda Naval to Wauwatosa
Last Week in September

Being near the Atlantic seaboard and the Chesapeake Bay rejuvenated Tierney's spirit, as the ocean did this for Pete. He had joked with Shawn that it was his only Darwinian connection. Pete drove all morning, arriving in Norfolk and continuing to D.C. It was another three hours on the interstate via Richmond. He arrived Monday afternoon, in time for the fellowship interview at Bethesda Naval Hospital. Despite his physical fatigue, he was emotionally energized.

Dr. Ambrose, the faculty representative, was hurried, factual, and distantly preoccupied. Pete's appointment for an interview was on the agenda, but was not a pressing issue nor of interest to Ambrose. Pete learned that he was one of many that had applied for this very competitive fellowship.

It's not nice being constantly humbled, he felt. It reminded him of when he first joined the Navy. They assured him that he would find it necessary to get used to eating crow occasionally. He just never expected black feathers in his mouth all the time.

"Dr. Ambrose, I've a special interest in the AIDS epidemic, I'd like to study the Navy plans for managing this epidemic?" asked Peter. "LCDR, hum...yes, Tierney". He fumbled with a stack of loose papers in a folder. "You're being interviewed for a fellowship in infectious disease. Managing the epidemic is not a resident's concern. You're here to learn the entire spectrum of infectious diseases. AIDS is but one of many. You will need to know how to treat it appropriately i.e., according to protocols, according to standards, and procedures. Do you understand? There really is no room for, shall we say, individual creativity. We have no room nor interests for creative thinkers here! This, after all, is not an art class. It is medicine by protocols! Tierney, Bethesda is THE Teaching Hospital of the US Navy!" "Well, Yes, Sir! I understand. I would like you to also understand that I'm especially interested in the big picture. How society deals with such a threat to humanity. The entire world has a contagious epidemic on its hands where 14 million are infected. I want to be part of the solution."

"Doctor Tierney! As I've already indicated to you, this is Bethesda Naval Hospital, The flagship hospital of the US Navy!" Ambrose was now hostile as he continued this pointed lecture. He continued to press the message and with growing academic distance.

"Your job, DOCTOR, will be to learn. See all you can within the brief and exhausting time you have with us. Dealing with complicated diseases like AIDS will only be a small part of your training. I might add there are many well qualified competitors seeking this position! Ambrose stood from behind his Navy grey metal desk, motioned toward the door. I'm sorry, that is all the time I have to give you in this discussion." He glanced down at the beeper strapped to his left hip, punched a button and noted the number.

The good Dr. Ambrose then dropped Pete's folder on the desk, grabbed his stethoscope and paraded out of the room without so much as, "Have a nice day."

"Yes, Sir, thank you, Sir!" Tierney projected to the departing man's back.

What the hell happened?!

Tierney, you lame nut. You pissed the guy off in less than two minutes. Stick to being a nice guy!

In disgust, Pete departed the third-floor office of Bethesda Naval Hospital, with a bitter taste in his mouth.

The bastard seems to think he can manage behavior by role definition and dangling a carrot. You dangle it, and I bite. Damn these ivory tower types! They're demeaning, pompous demigods, and I didn't learn a damn thing about the Navy's role in the epidemic.

I'd better start looking elsewhere, like at a civilian fellowship. Since I'm already here, I might just as well see if Ican find the infamous Dr. Raymond Price, Pete thought.

Had it not been for Dave and Carla on his trip to Victoria BC, he would have never known where to begin the computer search for Price in the CDC and NIH libraries. He had already confirmed Price's research and involvement in the Swine Flu, Hepatitis B and AIDS vaccination projects.

Yes, Price had departed because of ethical and political differences, and I believe they said he had moved to Milwaukee, Wisconsin. Pete had to find Raymond Price.

Pete decided to return the rental car, fly to Milwaukee where he knew his way around, having trained as an intern at Milwaukee County Hospital. He dropped off the rental car and hurried to the ticket counter.

His flight departure was delayed so he had time. Pete found a small pub with a large screen video. He selected a small corner table, arranged his briefcase between the wall and his left leg. A well angulated waitress, middle aged with red hair was singing under her breath. With a genuine smile, she recorded his order.

Pete scanned the room. Whitney Houston was singing on a big screen. The waitress appealed dutifully involved in collecting fees. A mixed couple sat nearby, *probably a teacher*, Pete thought. She wore a wedding band and ordered a chardonnay. Whitney Houston finished her song, "I get so emotional."

Tierney returned to the lobby of gate B-4 and found a plastic cushioned lobby chair overlooking a Brazilian commuter aircraft. He watched the aircraft as it was attended on the tarmac. Sitting across from Pete, was a chinless thin man with bottle thick glasses studying what appeared a technical manual. The man meticulously highlighted as he read. Everything about him was organized, from the chapters read, to his hand full of colored highlighters. This was a man who never looked up with a stray thought. He could be a perfect plant, Pete thought.

Boarding was announced, and Pete gathered his briefcase, tossed his jacket over the same arm and boarded. He got an aisle seat toward the tail of the plane. A gray-haired woman with a white cane was escorted down the aisle. A name tag was pinned to her thick sweater. She clutched her hand bag with both hands and her lips were constantly moving as if in silent vespers. The pinned name tag read, "I need wheel-chair assistance", Myrtle Blake. The chinless man sat in an adjacent seat to Peter's right. He continued highlighting the manual.

Pete felt blind like Myrtle and studied by a strange man.

Billy Mitchell Field, Milwaukee:

Pete stepped off the commuter jet, passed quickly through the crowd, caught the escalator down to the baggage claim, and found a telephone portal and directory. He ran his finger down the forty some listings of Price's. He narrowed the list to six. Telephone assistance for Dr. Price was not helpful. Titles of MD, Ph.D., were not helpful, but a simple listing of R. N. Price caught his eye. It looked like the best option. Pete dialed the number.

"Is this Dr. Price from the CDC? There was a long pause. Pete added. "I'm Pete Tierney, a Navy doctor who has just been to GITMO. I need to speak with you!"

There followed another long pause. Pete did not believe the adage that whoever speaks first loses. "Dr. Price did you hear me?"

"Yes, but I have nothing to say."

"My friends, Dave and Carla, mentioned you to me. They sail a boat out of Fox Island. They said you would be straight with me about the vaccinations!"

"Where are you now?"

"At Billy Mitchell field, could we meet somewhere?" Pete asked.

"What makes you think I have anything to say?" "Sir, I've read your works from the CDC". Pete paused, "I can read between the lines.".

"I don't go out much, OK!" Price's reluctance made Pete wondered if the line was tapped." "Be at Anthony's cellar in Wauwatosa by 9:00 p.m." Price instructed. The phone clicked dead.

Pete glanced at his watch. It was 7:25 PM, He glanced around the room. The highlighting specialist was gone. He couldn't believe his luck. Price had nothing to gain by meeting with him. You never know what goes through another man's mind. Peter searched through the yellow pages looking for restaurants and lounges. He found the address and phone number of Anthony's cellar and made a reservation. If Price was open to a long discussion, they might be up very late. Price said he was scrawny, no, he said wiry and would wear a buttoned-down Brewer sweater. There was no way Peter could miss him. He sensed he knew this man without having ever seen him.

THE MEETING:

Pete felt awkward and uneasy meeting someone he had only read about, but suspected Price was a key player in an epidemic out of control. He was tired from the f light. The rum he had on the flight didn't help. Only personal contacts could make the puzzle piece fit. He could learn only so much in a library.

He hired a cab and found Price at Anthony's in the Wauwatosa restaurant recognizing him without a description. Lean, bedraggled, feisty, inquisitive, be speckled, he was. He found Price not without social skills belying his appearance. Price had shaggy hair, wore a Brewer sweater, and was the clear image of an intellectual.

"How did you find me?" Price asked after introducing himself. He was sitting in a corner chair with his back to the wall. The sweater made him look fuller, but it did not fill out his face which was hollowed, deeply lined, bony, reserved and weathered.

"It wasn't. easy! Dr. Price, the odds were against me, like finding the right pebble on the beach. I found your articles in the secured archives of the CDC and the NIH.

"You must have known where to look," Price studied Tierney as he answered. "Sort of, and it was with a bit of luck, you might say. I ran into friends of yours, the Lieber's who were passing through Victoria, B.C. They gave me some leads. I had to invent an Admiral to gain entrance into the libraries. Price studied Tierney. After a long pause he asked, "Was it Pasechnik?" "Pasechnik?" Tierney tried to log into memory of the foreign name. He was horrid with foreign names. Russian names made it even harder to remember. "I don't recall a Pasechnik. What's his full name?"

"Never mind, have a seat. With such a Herculean Effort Commander, you have earned my attention. I'm surprised you've found me. I'm more interested in what you've learned! What do you know about me?" Price asked. The restaurant busied itself with waitresses carrying trays of food and drinks. There was an annoying background of rock music. The clientele seemed to need every moment filled with sensory stimuli.

"Is this a safe place?" asked Tierney looking around. "As good as any, what's on your mind, Commander?" "I read your secret publications on the Swine Flu Vaccinations and the Hepatitis B vaccination in San Francisco."

"What exactly do you want of me, Tierney? I'm out of the business. Retired you might say, no longer interested. I'm living in isolation; actually, I'm being monitored by a few men and don't know who hired them, but, they keep showing up at various places. Maybe FBI or the residuals of a supposedly defunct (CONIELPRO), group. Seems, it was disbanded for using illegal tactics until an Executive Order put them back in business. Could have been President Carter."

"Are we ok talking here?" Tierney asked.

"I snuck out the back door, left the lights and television on loud. The watch dogs are monitoring me, I believe they have become bored following me for the past five years. You're my first arrangement. I doubt their marginally aware."

"Doctor Price, I believe the government started the AIDS epidemic. My guess is it started as an experiment in the gay community and now they're trying to cover it up. I need to understand your role.

"I don't know what right you have to come waltzing into my life like this, asking such questions. Let me see your I.D., for all I know you're a reporter."

Tierney opened his wallet and produced his military I.D.

"All right, Lt. Commander. Let me be direct. Someone misused my research. I was trying to help the Department of Defense and the Armed Forces Medical Intelligence Center. We were in a race with the Soviet Union for the strategic edge in the biologic weapon system arena. We were successful, mostly. Yes, technically successful, but we failed in many ways." Price lowered his head. Pete respected Price's need for reflection and felt an admiration for this stranger, whom he suspected of being used for his scientific knowledge.

He continued, "The swine flu epidemic was never an epidemic at all. It was a biologic weapon developed from the bio-lab at Fort Dix, New Jersey. I'm afraid it leaked from the lab." "I thought as much.

Pete nodded and encouraged Price to continue. Pete could see it weighed heavily on Price. "Vladimir got to you didn't he?" "Vladimir?" Pete probed. "Yeah, Vladimir Pasechnik, a Soviet from the Biopreparat in Obolensk."

"The Obolensk facility was picked up by U.S. Intelligence for covert offensive biologic research in violation of the 1972 treaty. Vladimir Pasechnik defected to the west seventeen years later." Peter nodded encouragement, as if he knew. Price continued.

"The swine flu project was a biologic designed for viral warfare. We had prepared it as an airborne delivery, but also in a testing vaccination formula to protect our troops or the public at large. There was a leak within the laboratory technicians, and we were forced to hurriedly develop a vaccination once a half dozen army technical people were involved. The CDC was called in too early. We could have suppressed the information you know, kept it quiet long enough. Long enough for the dust to settle, but the press got a hold of it. We didn't know how far the virus might spread. We didn't have time to run controlled tests. We weren't any better than the Soviets, just trying to look squeaky clean."

"Shit." Price lowered his eyes and he paused while toying with his beer.

"Were it not for five military lab techs directed to the local military hospital with the CDC suddenly arriving to control the event's visibility, we might have been able to keep it quiet.

"President Ford stumbled on this one like he always seemed to do. Ford stumbled a lot. There was the germ-warfare researcher who was killed by the CIA because he knew too much. Ford apologized to the family in 1975 and paid the family $750,000. It was messy business.

"It became a cover-up, a cover-up of catastrophic proportions."

"So, there never was a swine flu epidemic?" Pete probed. " No. There was never an epidemic. It was a biologic leak designed for viral warfare prepared as a new vaccine for our troops, but we were forced to mass produce it for the entire US civilian population. We were afraid of an uncontrolled epidemic. If the leak had not occurred, the Soviets would have never guessed nor stood a chance. We miscalculated, badly!"

Pete understood Price's urgency to tell everything. He felt like a priest in the confessional.
"Yes, you got it right, Tierney."
"So how did you get to Pasechnic?" Price asked.
Tierney tried to ignore the question. Pete had to sound authentic and still was of unclear of Pasechnik's role.
"There is a physician/ attorney, Cyril Wecht, who accurately describe the political setting at the time. How the Ford administration used this vaccination program for all the wrong reasons. He considered the event "Political Folly". This was well recorded in the literature from the American Society of Law and Medicine but gathered little attention. It however was never in Wecht's realm of considerations had it been a weapon system.

This would never have become an epidemic had not five lab techs gotten exposed to the virus and became ill. Not a single swine flu case occurred in the six months after the death of Private Lewis." Said Price. "Lewis was the young man who refused to be hospitalized like the other lab techs and ran his 1.5 mile physical readiness test. He had a cardiac arrest. Can you imagine, mouth to mouth resuscitation efforts by a staff sergeant never infected the sergeant? "
"Pretty strange, I'd say", Price continued. "It's absolutely amazing why nobody in America asked what was going on?" "Did you ever wonder why no one in Canada was immunized against this swine flu?" "We have an open border, five lab techs form Fort Dix are exposed, one dies, our whole nation is encouraged to get vaccinated and the Canadian government isn't worried, excited not demand the same vaccination program?" "Canada didn't even limit border crossings from the US." Price nodded. "Presidents and Prime Ministers talk"!

That is why it never crossed the border."

"So, Tierney, tell me, how did you guess, and how did you guess right?"

"Look, Price, I lost a friend. Several for all I know. I want to know why! Maybe I'm lucky; then again maybe I'm cursed. I don't want to feel like a secret agent afraid of my shadow. Like the rest of America, maybe I'd be better off not knowing," Pete snapped.

"So, tell me, Price, why did you leave the NIH & CDC?" Pete asked.

"I'm a scientist. I've a Ph.D., in immunology and virology. I know a great deal about molecular splicing especially with retrovirus. I wanted to help prevent disease, especially infectious diseases as it could affect so many people. My professional interests and my vaccines were misused."

"You didn't know what they were doing with your vaccines? How could you not have known?" "I don't have an answer, naiveté?

I suppose. There were so many political pressures and time tables to meet. Whoever used the vaccines used it on a population that I didn't have control over. I just developed the vaccine, first the Swine flu, then had some limited involvement with the HIV virus. Another colleague developed Hepatitis B. I guess using the two in a controlled select population to prevent hepatitis, seemed OK. I didn't like it when I heard what they were doing. I still don't like it, that's why I resigned, was never asked nor informed of this human experiment in San Francisco. It seemed to make sense to reduce the human response to Hepatitis B, by blunting the immune reaction, after all it is a live, although, attenuated virus. Hell, I was told it was just the process. I did not know what process they were talking about."

"The immune response became confused and overwhelming, when multiple vaccines are introduced, but a real lasting protection is developed, at least to the Hepatitis B vaccine. Both HIV and Hepatitis B, as you know, are transmitted by the same methods, e.g., sexual transmission and blood exchanges." "Vladimir Pasechnik, spilled his guts, didn't he? "Pete nodded.

Price went on, "We were all under incredible pressures, especially with the known biologic anthrax leak in April 1979 in the Russian city of Sverdlovsk. The Soviet's called it a result of bad meat, but our intelligence sources had it pegged as a biologic weapon leak directed toward Western Europe and the US. The Sverdlovsk epidemic killed 100 to 300 of their own citizens in six weeks. NIH and the CDC felt the pressures. They had an intelligence directive to develop prompt countermeasures of the viral warfare type. By comparison, to have only five of our own soldiers at Fort Dix come down with the swine flu, was, well, a small miracle by comparison".

"We had our orders to catch up with the Russians, and to be creative about how we did Pasechnik genetically engineered a dry form of a super plaque, resistant to antibiotics. Medical intelligence knew of the Obolensk Facility 60 miles south of Moscow and the Soviet violation of the 1972 Biologic Warfare Treaty. Somebody knew about it as we were constantly pressured for a better bug, a better germ-warfare threat. Biopreparat was the secret of the century. U.S intelligence knew about it but Gorbachev denied it existed. Bush and Thatcher put public disclosure pressures on Gorbachev. Still he denied it."

"Shit, they had a fifty-foot steel cube where animals were tethered to the floor and died horrid deaths. We worried about terrorists getting their hand on these bugs. The pressure was constant."

Tierney nodded understanding and searched Prices darken eyes. He wanted to understand this man as a focal point in history and in his own life.

Price couldn't stop, brushing his hair aside. "We, not me, linked Hepatitis B vaccine to the AIDS virus, before recombinant, pure Hep-B was available. Some say it had first been linked to Polio vaccines in the WHO (World Health Organization) immunization of third world nations. Africa became a problem, a very real and visible problem. I think the association with the green monkey was a deliberate distraction, rather than a virus jumping between species. I'm not sure what is really true in Africa, but the viruses are very similar, similar with evolutionary roots between man and monkey." "Damn, this monkey connection keeps coming up. In Japan a similar virus STLV infects the macaque monkey. News Week magazine just released an article linking the evolutionary monkey theory, but they of course did not have the inside story. Rolling Stone magazine touched on the same issue." Peter added.

"Shit, everybody is screwing with biologics and American's are too busy looking in the mirror, they miss the big picture. I think they're simply preoccupied with the good things in life, like making a living and raising a family."

Price rubbed his arms, seeming to get a grip on himself. "We're no better than the Soviets. We have Fort Detrick, Maryland, just a Sunday afternoon drive from Washington D.C. It's been the bio-warfare research think tank headquarters since World War II."

Tierney remembered Dr. Gallows Freudian slip, "The AIDS virus was produced at Fort Detrick."

"All I know for sure is that the AIDS epidemic occurred near vaccination time lines. The similarities are more than casual and are clearly not vague. One would have to be blind not to see the relationship. One should wonder why the highest global rates are in the Central Africa and the San Francisco, New York area. European, Australian, and Pacific Rim cases all seem to trace back to the US. The so called Gay Flight Path of global travel!"

"Is it safe to talk about this here?" asked Tierney as he scanned the room.

Price, no longer certain of anything, shrugged his shoulder. Pete ignored his own question and continued, "Do you know about the quarantine experiments in Cuba?"

Price's face became a ghostly white. "No! What is going on there?" Price asked leaning forward on his chair. "You mentioned this in your phone call."

"An illegal segment of the Navy is actively involved, supporting the Cuban government's use of human experiments in quarantine of HIV. The Haitian Leprosarium is now visibly in the news. It's becoming a real hot bed of political embarrassment. What to do with these people? How to cover it up? Over 150 Haitians with AIDS have been held at GITMO. It has become a political fiasco."

" I had no idea! That means the Agency is setting the stage for a nationally controlled program. Meaning they finally recognized it as beyond control."

"What Agency?" asked Pete?

Price ignored the question. "How long has this experiment in Cuba, been going on?" he asked.

The waitress interrupted. "You want another beer?"

Pete held up two fingers. Price waited until she was out of hearing range.

"At least five years. I think they're waiting for enough statistical deaths in the US that would create public outrage to politically demand the use of Regional Quarantine Centers. What is this AGENCY Stuff?"

"They have names, no location, but some are high level governmental officials, some military, some elected congressional leaders, some at the high level, but no flunkies. It's an inner network. Faceless, I don't know much about it except that they seem to know everything. Some reference it as T.A.N. meaning The Agency Network. Some of us are used without knowing our work is being misused. There are a lot of people in government whose life's work is misused. If only I had access to MIPS!"

"MIPS?" asked Pete.

"The Medical Intelligence Processing System, an on-line computerized system tracking all infectious diseases on a global scale. We know daily what's going on with the simple movement of a mouse that produces a schematic global summary. We even know what research is going on and if it will have any merit. My guess is experiments in Regional Quarantine are displayed graphically throughout the world. This tracking system is as good as any incoming missile launch sequence. For instance, we know that AIDS is the number two killer of young Parisian males. It represents 40% of the deaths of males in Paris between the ages of 25 to 40."

"At least 300 of almost 600 in this age group of young Parisians are known to have died of the tainted blood derived from AIDS infected homosexual males in 1991. Almost 12,000 have died in France over the past 10 years. Only traffic accidents kill more males in Paris," Price gestured with his hand and knocked his water glass over. "Sons of bitches, they targeted the Castro District of San <u>Fran</u> for blood donations. You would think they wanted to contaminate the blood supply of the whole damn country."

The waitress arrived with the new beer mugs and wiped up the spilled water.

They waited for her to finish and find some distance.

"It will not take them long to find you Pete! They will find you! You had better find a way to save your neck. There's no place to run."

"Why haven't they already killed you, Price? "

"There's no need to kill me, they've already ruined my reputation. They've misused my research. I'm a marked man and I'm dying, so I'm no threat to anyone."

"I don't gain anything if I tell; there is nothing in it for me." "You're dying?"

"We're all dying; I just am going out with AIDS. I became careless. I was distracted, jammed a broken pipette of contaminated blood into my hand while doing research." He looked at the scar in his left palm showing Peter. Looked like an ordinary scar, not a death mark. "I literally gave myself a disease I'd helped create. Maybe I had a deat h wi sh . " He added. "We were all wrong in our planning. We expected sexual transmission. You know, get them in the bedroom. We discovered after the fact it stayed rigidly within the homosexual and IV drug culture like a leach. Peter, you must believe me. Only a select number of officials know what I do and they constantly monitor my whereabouts!"

Price turned away and wiped the sweat from his neck with a table napkin.

"Pete, you're not safe being around me! I'm highly visible and always monitored. You will know when they suspect you...!"

"So why are you telling me all this?" asked Tierney.

"No one else has asked for the truth. Everyone wants to blame someone. They all have some empty cause like social equity or social justice. No one wants the truth."

"Is there anyone that keeps close track of your whereabouts, your movements?" Price asked.

Tierney immediately thought of Lt. Tatum. *Do you suppose he knew about Charles before he was killed?*

This doesn't make sense. Tatum wouldn't know how to administer tetanus shot much less place IV's and give the right dose of surgical anesthetics in a Kevorkian dose. Tatum couldn't have killed him, but he surely knows how to keep tabs on us. Somebody else at the hospital must have done it. Maybe some hospital- based anesthesiologist? A hired gun.

"You better find a way to tell the world what's happening here, Tierney, otherwise you'll be just another casualty. The Navy will go out of its way to help you disappear!"

"Yeah, just great, Price. Now you tell me! How would you control the epidemic, if you could?" Pete asked.

"For the moment, selective regional quarantine might be the only answer to slowing the epidemic, even though it may be well past the window of opportunity. The vaccinations under investigation offer some hope. Even though years away from even testing. The drug AZT and DDI although both anti-virals, won't do any more than simply allow those with the disease to live a little longer, in a sexually active infectious state. Right now, it is only used after AIDS has clinically become active at an end stage of the disease. They have not considered using it immediately after, say a high risk sexual encounter. That's early in the infectious stage. Presumably that's when it might conceivably be m o s t effective. I cannot imagine why it's taken over 10 years to consider using it early in the disease, unless, of course, it has all been for a political social cleansing purpose."

"You're right, Price. My medical friends feel the same," admitted Tierney, and continued, "Yeah, it's fool hardy. It is a stupid way to handle an epidemic! I mean give people with the disease drugs that allow them to pass on the disease while in an infectious state and not really trying to control the epidemic. It's just platitudes of indifference, like approaching a volcano with a blow torch. You just can't fight this fire with fire."

"Controlling this epidemic is the real crucial issue The Agency will attempt to emotionally move people to adopt any plan that suggests a solution, e.g. A National Health Plan," Price added.

"It really suggests control. We must talk more, but it's not safe being together. We're too visible."

"Where can we meet?" Pete asked.

"Write me or call this friend's number. I have a PO Box under a different name. It allows me a little freedom."

Tierney hailed the waitress for a bill. Both he and Price waited in silence. Their table was in a windowless corner, across from a gas fireplace with artificial logs. They both glanced away and scanned the room. It was empty and late. The bar still held a few stragglers. The information Price and Tierney had shared was too complex and sensitive to digest at once. Both were strangers yet touched the core of an epidemic that threatened the world. There was a sense of anguish, futility with precious time already lost. Two men could not possibly change the outcome of this epidemic. One was dying of the disease he helped create and the other was trying to explain the loss of those he loved, neither had the powers of connections. They had only truth, and there was danger in knowing such a truth.

Both rose from the table and walked into the night air stepping outside the restaurant. A Burlington Northern train shuddered through the intersection, its horn faded in passing, and the ground trembled.

"Should be easy to move the world," Pete shouted over the thundering noise. "All I need is power, mass, and momentum, and a little truth. You got any of that stuff, Raymond Price?"

Ray smiled, pulled his collar up around his neck buttoned the jacket, and nodded yes. "Let me think on it, Pete!"

They shook hands and departed on different paths into the night. Pete shivered with the coldness of death surrounding him as the damp night air rose off Lake Michigan. This rogue wave of an uncontrolled man-made epidemic rolled across America. Power politics in a biologic war might consume more than just Peter in a fight he could not escape. He was in over his head and water survival training would not help.

He must speak with Shawn.

She had changed so dramatically in the past nine months. It occurred after that close call with the emergency surgery for a ruptured ovarian cyst.

It was probably my fault, he thought, *for being too passionate sexually that last time we were together. It was just before she left for Paris. Maybe I hurt her,* he hesitated with fear.

Peter beat a hasty return to the airport to catch a standby vacancy on the next flight. He would have never guessed a red-eye flight existed from Billy Mitchell Field to Sea-Tac Airport. Even in a crowd he felt hunted. Hard to find anonymity when he felt stalked. Time was at a premium and seemed just another enemy.

Tierney searched the crowd. He saw no one that appeared suspicious. The chinless corporate man was nowhere in sight. He boarded the plane convinced his imagination had gotten the best of him.

He found an aisle seat amidships. Pete pulled out pad and pen and began to write: My Dear Shawn...

I'm glad they serve scotch on the red-eye run, he thought. He asked the flight attendant for another and the stewardess seemed to realize he was under pressure. She was thin as a rail, her uniform draped with long flowing lines. She had caring blue eyes. Pete felt the warmth of the Scotch fill his belly, then his head. They were somewhere over Montana at Flight level 340 when the stewardess again passed in the aisle an offered a fluffed pillow and shut off the reading light. Her dress brushed his right arm and her light perfume rested in his memory. Pete felt drowsiness coming and promised himself he would not snore. An hour and forty-five minutes later he awoke to the familiar alarm announcing to fasten seat belts as they approached Sea-Tac Airport. It was 4:15 AM local time and another forty-five minutes before Pete finally located his car in the Budget parking lot. He still had a two-hour drive ahead.

Pete was exhausted by the time he arrived back at Keyport. The apartment was cold and damp. He dropped his bags on the kitchen floor and noticed the flashing light on the answering machine. He ignored it. He sat on the side of the hide-a-bed and pulled a wool Navy blanket across his lap. He crawled under the sheets.

He didn't remember dreaming but felt warm and refreshed when next he recalled the familiar sound of seagulls crying. He rolled over and the digital clock-radio read 5:07 pm. He would make it to work on time by tomorrow.

The morning's mail included the New England Journal of Medicine offering a position at the University of Washington in AIDS Research. He would apply.

Journals to review:
Hastings Center on Bioethics
Babel and Beyond: among the topics:
ARE THERE TOO MANY PEOPLE IN THE LIFEBOAT?
WHO DECIDES FOR WHOM?
WHAT SHOULD AFFIRMATIVE ACTION AFFIRM?
PLURALISM: IS IT A VALUE TO BE CHERISHED OR A
PROBLEM TO BE SOLVED?

This was sponsored by the Starkoff Institute of Ethics, whose goal was to identify sources of moral conflict and to explore the value frameworks guiding decision making capabilities.

Pete wondered aloud, "Have any of these scholars dealt with the reality of a man made epidemic?" Now there was a real ethical dilemma to deal with

A Letter from Shawn:

He tore the envelope open; it was very short and quite distantly impersonal.

She was ill; apparently from the transfusion that was required during her surgery she now wanted to see him. "With Warm Memories and a Hug" Shawn

What the hell is "this warm memory and a hug", shit! he thought while alone in his cold empty cottage.

"What is she doing, trying to kill me with platitudes?"

There was an official Naval Hospital manila envelope, from the QA department from Captain Johnson, acting chairman.

Pete scanned the letter. The (QA) Quality Assurance Committee has raised the question of his competence and continued privileges at the hospital. They requested Tierney's appearance to explain to the surgical department the mishandling and adverse outcome of a patient with a gunshot wound to the elbow.

Nurse Rutherford had collected all the documentation and Capt. Johnson would preside.

Lt. Tatum also had a second case that required "scrutiny, a case of a native Cuban with a gunshot wound to the leg."

"Shit." Pete muttered. "They are on to me."

He tore open the next envelope, also from the Hospital but from the Professional Disciplinary Board. He scanned the letter. It was a questionnaire dealing with secret clearances to National Libraries. He scanned the list and the archives of the CDC and NIH were included.

The box was getting tighter. It was a setup. He needed time and he didn't have it. He was in a corner. He had to get back to Price. He had to get to Shawn. He had to avoid Tatum.

He had dreaded coming back to the office. It was predictable to be greeted by bad news. But being tracked was another matter. Somehow, they, whoever they were, discovered Pete knew too much. Who are these people in TAN? Shit, they're faceless, their nameless. They kill from distant cover and under a thin veil of altruism.

Pete believed he had learned as much as he could while in the Service. There was too much turmoil surrounding him to make any decisions about the Navy except to hold tight for the moment. *The fellowship position at Bethesda will most certainly will collapses, then, well, I'll wait. It might be better to wait and see which way the wind blows. Some answers will surely come when the fellowship committee makes its decision in the next six weeks.*

He again noticed the blinking light on the answering machine. Although he expected messages after a long trip he had an inexplicable sense of urgency and foreboding. He pushed the playback button and momentarily heard what he had hoped and yet feared to hear. It was Shawn's voice; she wanted to talk and left her beach cottage number in La Conner.

As Pete began to dial the number, he felt the approach of a darkening fear that centered in his heart. He hung up the phone and paused, walked to the kitchen door and stepped onto the outside porch, took a few deep breaths and wondered how he would ever control the emotion in his voice.

Had she found someone else?

He chastised himself for being so shallow, another man with Shawn? He could not stand to think of it. Surely, she would have told him if that were the case. *She would not deceive me. She could not deceive me!*

Pete returned to the phone and dialed her number.

"Hello." Her voice was quiet and soft.

"Shawn, it's me, Peter."

"Oh, Peter, I need to see you, I must see you!"

Something in her voice sent a chill down Pete's spine. "What's wrong?" he asked, trying to control the sound of his voice. He knew he wouldn't get an answer and that he shouldn't have asked.

"Pete, I just need to see you and, talk with you...Please!"

"Shawn, I'll be there as soon as I can, I've got to make a few phone calls first, check back in on duty at the clinic, but I'll catch the next ferry. I should be able to get there in, say about nine hours. Is that OK?"

"Yes, dear, but be careful," she admonished.

She sounds so very weak and her voice is rocky, thought Pete. *Something is terribly wrong. She called me "Dear". Maybe this isn't over with yet.*

Pete dashed off a letter to Dr. Price, asking if they could meet, suggesting a rendezvous near Taos, at the Bio-Cosmic development in New Mexico. He addressed it to his PO Box in

Milwaukee, Wisconsin.

Ray, 'he wrote,' the biggest risk I have is convincing the OIC, Lieutenant Tatum, my boss that I need to go on leave with such short notice. For all I know he is part of The Agency Network. It may seem hard to believe, but I must have his approval to go on leave, or I'm in deep trouble.

See you in Taos,
Peter

Pete then gave his old tennis and attorney friend Phillip Lege' a call. He got his answering machine and left a message.

"Need to see you. It is important, legal stuff. Hope your leg is better and we can hit some tennis balls around."

Next, he called the clinic and checked back in on duty, but asked for new leave papers to be placed at the front office.

"I'll stop by to pick them up."

The duty corpsman who answered the phone said, "Good to have you back Doc! Things are a mess here. Lieutenant Tatum is on the rampage again and he wants to see you ASAP. Something to do with a gunshot wound in Cuba."

Without other interruptions, Pete hauled the same bags back to the car and headed to the Winslow ferry terminal. It was likely to be a long wait since it was Friday afternoon. He hoped Shawn was not too impatient.

His mind ran wild with worry. *Is she sick or is someone in her family dying? Is she with someone else who treated her badly?* All he knew was that she sounded frightened, alone and in need.

Pete checked the ferry schedule from Winslow to Seattle, locked up the apartment and hopped in the Fiat for the ferry terminal. The Fiat responded to his needs handling smartly on the country roads. He passed over the Agate pass bridge and noticed the fog rolling in like a carpet. Winslow was only fifteen minutes away.

Bangor Clinic:

The phone rang. Lt Tatum at the Bangor Clinic picked it up. It was the X.O. of the Naval Hospital. "Tatum, how is the family?"

"Fine sir, but I don't have a family." Oh, sorry "added the X.O. and changing subjects. "It's about LCDR Tierney. I have an urgent message from the Naval Investigative Service. There is reason to believe Tierney was reviewing secret files at NIH."

"You're kidding?"

"No, a surveillance camera seems to have a reflective image on the computer screen that appears like Tierney. They know the figure on the screen is a flight surgeon, a LCDR and photos from personnel seems to match. They cannot decipher why he is an attaché'. Do you know anything about this Tatum?"

"No, sir. Nothing personal if that's what you mean.

He has been troubled by the death of his friend CDR.

Charles Brewer.

Knowing how close they were, I suppose that's normal."

"Well, Lt. Tatum, what are your feelings about this Doctor Tierney, professionally, as a naval officer?"

"X.O., if I may be candid sir, I don't trust him. I don't believe he is a team player. He thinks on his own. He doesn't seem to follow the usual protocols, questions processes. I think he's potentially dangerous, a trouble maker."

"We'll need to keep a close eye on him. Do you understand Lt?" "Yes, sir. I understand. Of course, I'll keep close tabs on him. "What about the NIH?"

"We're working on a positive identity. Naval Investigative Service has rerun the computer information file to determine what he is looking for. Searching for information on AIDS and immunizations seems the most likely."

"Yes, Sir, He was supposed to be in GITMO and Bethesda, not the NIH."

"I understand," said the X.O., "Keep an eye on him, a close eye." "Yes, sir. I'll talk to him as soon as he gets back from Cuba." "Give my best to your wife, Lt."

"Yes, sir, thank you," Tatum answered, "but I don't have a wife sir!"

As they spoke of Peter, he had arrived at the ferry terminal on Bainbridge Island, in the quaint village of Winslow.

The Washington Ferry System is like the state's adopted aquatic bird, closely tied in with the western Washington atmosphere. The Ferries are painted a deep green on white.

With a throaty blast of its horn, the Willapa lunged sluggishly from the dolphin pier at Winslow for Seattle. The twin screws threw up a wash as mass became momentum and she got underway. The wash then became subdued as she pulled away to a silenced rush that was better felt by a passing vessel crossing the swells.

The sky had been overcast all day, and the temperatures began to fall with the setting sun. The dense fog kept rolling in from the north. The ferry seemed in a race against the sweeping blanket of dew. He had been in this situation aboard his sailboat, and without navigational aids the fog became very dangerous and frightening.

The fog enveloped the ferry like a thick white veil of a ghost. Visibility fell to less than 2 00 yards and the penetrating dampness changed the watery world into a search for visual clues. Listening carefully gave only a false sense of control. A sudden collision with anything floating out there seemed imminent. You felt your way like a blind man on a street corner.

Not a lot different than searching for hidden motives, thought Pete. Motives shrouded in the secret hands of politicians. Why was this epidemic unexplained? It was unsafe to ask questions. It clearly was dangerous to ask indiscriminately. The ferry turned sharply to port. Blakely Rocks, Pete thought as the fog horn droned.

At least my feet are anchored securely to this steel deck. But I'm worse than blind, he told himself as he struggled to make sense out of it all.

He told himself that the blind was better off as they at least knew they could not rely on visual clues.

Pulling low the brim of his wool cap Pete felt his hand pass through the moist air.

There was no shoreline to guide the ferry except by radar. It slowed to a crawl, feeling its way. He was sure the ship's pilot was pinging surface contacts with radar. The fog horn played its hollowed tone.

Pete felt certain the helmsman used an updated Loran system. Still he felt it necessary to help by trying to see through the foggy mist, searching into the fog. The ferry came to a dead slow and turned to port. He guessed they must now be entering the winding narrowed stretch of shallows off Blakely Rock. A lot of boats have scored that shore, thought Pete.

Where was Shawn in all this mess? He felt as completely lost as he searched for clues to her disappearance. Her reasons for departing were as vacant and vacuous as a black hole.

He was lost in a global epidemic. He was lost in the fog surrounding Shawn. He needed God's radar and hand to get through this mess unlike this ferry. He must find some answers.

CHAPTER 8

What Went Wrong

Keyport to New Mexico:

Pete drove off the ferry on the Seattle side and immediately phoned Phillip Lege'. He had hoped to garner quick legal advice and to schedule a time that was not conflicted.

Lege' scheduled a tennis game for Sunday afternoon. They had agreed to meet after his game at the Seattle Lawn and Tennis Club located on the western edge of Lake Washington. The fog disappeared as the ferry approached the warming landmass of the mainland.

"No, I can't do it now. I've got to meet this girlfriend. She has stretched me out for the past year or so! Now she wants to see me. I must resolve this. How about sticking to the Sunday plan of just meeting?" "OK, that'll be fine. She must be important to take precedent over epidemics and experiments. Sounds like a lot is on the line," Lege' added.

Pete didn't enjoy Lege' sarcasm, still he knew that he was right. "I know, Phil, it doesn't make sense, emotional stuff never does, but it's important to me. I must see her first. I've got to go, she's expecting me and, I've got to get on the road and avoid the traffic on Interstate-5. See you in a few days. OK?! I'll call you since I'm not sure how long this will take."

With the traffic snarls and commuters trying to get out of town on a late Friday afternoon, it took Pete over two hours to get up to Shawn's cottage in La Conner.

He knocked on the screen door and waited for her to answer. There were no lights in the cottage. Then a light came on and after what seemed an eternity of waiting, the door opened, and it was Shawn.

She was much thinner, and she really had no weight to lose. It was very apparent that she had been ill. She appeared tired and although her eyes continued to show a spark, they were drawn with concern. There was a degree of pallor in her face and he guessed she had lost almost 10 pounds.

They embraced for a very long time, tears came to each other's eyes and they kissed.

"Shawn, what is it? What has happened to you?" Pete felt himself bracing for what would come next and he knew it was not good news.

"Oh, Peter," Shawn's voice broke and tears flowed down her cheeks. "Oh, Peter," she wept.

"I almost died once, and it took me months to recover so I felt I could not handle this again. I've never been afraid of dying as much as I've been afraid of losing you. If I could just be close to you, I know I could stand just about anything, but, not this. Why must this be happening to us?"

"What, Shawn, what are you talking about, tell me!"

Pete had taken Shawn into his arms again. She had made a faint gesture at resisting, but she had neither the strength nor the interest.

Between sobs, Shawn's words became, thin and wrought with suffering.

"Peter, I have AIDS! And, I'm dying. That transfusion I had, in France, my surgery several years ago." She cleared the emotion from her voice for a moment and continued "for the ruptured cyst of my ovary, they gave me a bad batch of blood. It had not been tested. I'm told they didn't do any testing prior to 1987, because the Pasteur Institute in France wanted to use their own proprietary testing. The test was available from the US for several years and it wasn't used. I'm not the only one. There are thousands of people in France who were transfused with tainted blood. I'm so sad, so very sad that I cannot be with you as we were before. I want so much to love you completely". She sobbed and could speak no more. Her slight frame quaked with emotion. As Pete held her, she cried, as if she had been holding back tears for the years apart and could contain them no more. "Shawn, Oh, Shawn, my precious love."

At first the tears would not come for Pete. The shock was too great. He felt an immediate need to comfort her. What to do? What to say? What to feel?

Shawn struggled to regain her composure, but the tears kept welling up. Pete saw that she was shivering. He got a wool blanket from the closet and wrapped her. Then cradled her in his arms like a baby and rocked her gently, for as long as needed.

He whispered, "It'll be all right. I'm here now, it will be all right." He said the words over and over like a mantra as the night grew deeper.

Slowly, but finally, the sobbing ebbed. Peter laid her gently on the bed. As he softly stroked her hair, Shawn fell into a peaceful sleep.

Seeing that she would rest for a while, Pete began to be aware of his own emotion. A fury built within him and a rage that frightened even him. He paced near the fire place, looking out the sliding glass door into the darkness. He opened the glass door of the veranda and stepped outside. The air was cool now as the overcast veiled a full moon.

He started to walk with a quickened pace into the waist-high grass. It slapped his arms and thighs. He did not know what to do. He felt his heart well up with tears and feared the flood would sweep him away. He started to run through the grass faster and faster. The blades of tall grass were slapping his legs as he ran he was only vaguely aware of any discomfort. Still he ran until his heart and legs ignored the sorrow and the ache. His lungs burned with the cool air. His heart felt it would burst like a dam and yet he still ran. He stumbled in the unpredictable footing of uneven terrain. He felt he might explode and he wished for the oblivion that it might bring.

He stumbled again and again. His feet and legs no longer belonged to him. He finally could carry himself no longer and crumbled in a heap, on the edge of the marsh his knees sunk into the moist sod. There he let out a wail, a torrential and tormented cry. He was a mortally wounded animal. He had no breath left to ask why? He could only cry aloud into the mooned sky.

"No, not Shawn, not Shawn, No, not Shawn. Please, dear God, not Shawn! You've no right to her! You have no right!"

He slumped to the ground and wept, uncontrollably. Nothing would ever be the same again. Nothing could ever be the same.

Shawn would not have found him in the tall marshy grass were it not for the brilliance of the moon and Pete's sobs. He was in a heap, a cold wet mound of exhausted drained human flesh.

She knelt beside him and placed her arm around his head and shoulder drawing him close. Finally, Pete rose to his knees. He advanced to a half crouch and then they held each other, the empty shells that they were.

To the unknowing, it appeared a sorry mess. This young couple held each other and staggered back toward the cottage, through the deep grass by the slough. It was already near day break; the cheerful birds began to sing of the morning light.

At the cottage, Pete turned away from Shawn for a moment. Through the window, he reflected on the passing river to the sea. There was an empty glaze in his eyes, with the sorrow and the vacant loss of his search. There was nowhere left to turn except back toward Shawn.

She put the same wool blanket around his chilled body and guided him to the bathroom for a warm shower. Afterwards she placed him in her bed and wrapped her body about him. Neither was certain who was dying.

It was dusk by the time they both awoke and now discovered their hunger. They ate warmed leftovers in silence but, with the same small touches that once invited enticement and zest. There had been in the past much soft foot play under the dining table. This time he just crossed his ankles and she rested her ankles between his. In the past these touches would have ignited a night of lusty passion, but not today. No one could fire Pete's basic instincts as completely as she. He could still love her by being close and intertwined.

Shawn would not let him stay. She feared it would excite their mutual passions.

"I will not give you this disease," she vowed.

The night air was frosty and crisp. The smell of a wood fire came from a neighbor's home. Pete stood on the porch shifting his weight and feeling the cold begin to penetrate his sweater and green parka. Pete tested the air with his breath. It condensed in vapor as he waited for her to see him off.

He mused, *my best friend is dead, and my lover is dying. My own government experimented with a biologic that threatens the world and only a few of us alive know of it. Likely, I too will be killed. I stand here marveling at the condensation of air coming from the breath that is my life. A life I wanted only to share with Shawn. Who is it that dares to deny me such life?*

Her parting kiss was brief and business like. He drove to the south in search of that dark country road that led back to the ferry.

The drive gave Pete time to organize his thoughts and feelings. Without noticing the passing time and what had transpired in-route, he was surprised to find himself on the boarding ramp leading to the ferry bound for Eagle Harbor. The ferry's long throaty horn signaled its departure and spelled the end to their physical closeness, but not their love. It was a long empty night.

Pete was suddenly and rudely forced back into reality. The ship's intercom announced repeatedly, a green Fiat blocked the port side exit in the second row. An attendant shook Pete from his trance.

"He wasn't hard to find," the attendant told a colleague, "he was the only one left on the ferry, so he must have owned the Fiat."

With this awakening, Pete decided he had nothing to lose. There is nothing more dangerous than a man on a mission with nothing to lose. He lost everything and everybody of value, except Peter had not lost himself.

Pete arrived back home in Keyport and fell into a deep sleep.

The next morning, he showered, had breakfast and tried to sort out what happened. He decided it was time to tell Nancy Brewer what he believed had happened to Charles. After nearly three months on the road, he barely noticed the changes in the neighborhood. He walked seven houses down the block to find Nancy.

Their home looked abandoned, the grass uncut, car gone, even the drapes were gone. Sam, their neighbor to the left was in the yard tending his rhododendrons.

"What happened to Mrs. Brewer?" asked Pete.

"Two weeks after the funeral, a Mayflower sixteen-wheeler arrived. They were packed and gone within days."

"Did Nancy say where they were going?" "Back to their family in Annapolis Maryland, I think. She left her mother's phone number." Sam gave what limited information he had, and Peter slowly walked with his head held low in thought. *I suppose it makes sense, if there is no family here and the Navy is no longer a part of your husband's life. It just seems that two weeks is an awfully rapid exit. I wonder if the Navy pressured Nancy in some way. Why bury your husband in Washington State and then move back to Maryland? Usually it takes months of planning for such a move. He felt he knew Charles well enough, but he also recognized in his widow Nancy, a very determined. He knew she would not let his death lie unanswered! He admired her as much as he did Charles.*

SUNDAY
MEETING WITH COUNSEL:

The fog lifted again as the ferry made its mooring at the Seattle terminal, exposing a beautifully sunny day with a warming easterly breeze. *A perfect day Pete felt, for tennis with Phillip Legé, perfect for adding spin to his service delivery. The wind had an even greater effect of adding extra action to new tennis balls. Phillip would likely have great fun destroying me he thought.*

Tennis could be a cut-throat game and was good training for an attorney in a court room, especially one that might save my life, thought Tierney. *Besides I badly need his help.*

Pete arrived at the tennis courts as Phillip was about to finish his earlier game. Legé had now fully recovered from his knee surgery and appeared to play with a new sense of security. He was striding with ease for those deep cross court shots. Pete raised his right arm to capture his attention. Phillip raised his racquet in recognition. They found an awning that shaded a table. Both ordered a Tacoma Brew. "Not everyone drinks lattés." Phillip said as their glasses met. "You sounded pressured on the phone Pete. What is going on?" asked Lege'. "I need a lawyer." Pete paused and looked over his shoulder.

"Phil, I've got some serious problems. You were an attorney in the Navy and I hope you can give me some advice."

"What sort of problems?" "Have you ever dealt with the death of a fellow sailor that was officially covered up to look like a suicide?" asked Tierney. Phillip took a sip of his beer, looked out toward the lake paused a moment, gently passed his finger tips to his lips then back again refocusing on Pete's eyes.

"Yeah, I have, there was a new pilot on the carrier, USS Ranger who had a cold-catapult shot. It got ugly and heads rolled, big names, Admirals fell from grace on this one. The Commanding Officer of the carrier was relieved for cause. There was an attempt to cover it up. That's what really caused the troubles. It got ugly. They tried to make it look like pilot error. The young Lt.JG. died. It was his first cat shot off the carrier. He had, in the tradition of naval air, arranged to keep the holdback pin as a souvenir. What they didn't realize was that the father of the pilot was a close friend of a Senator. It does pay to have such connections."

"Well, Phillip, you're not going to believe how much trouble I'm in, but my ass is in deep. It won't be long before I'm a visible target. For all I know, I already have been targeted." "How big is this?" asked Phil.

"I'm certain it has the highest level of awareness, support and political influence! My friend, a Navy surgeon was killed. He knew that there were human experiments going on in Cuba, probably also in New Mexico. Charles, this surgeon, simply knew too much."

"These were social experiments that were designed to use quarantine as a safety valve. If the disease, AIDS became uncontrollable, quarantine would be imposed. They recognized the spread of AIDS was caused by a viral leak from a military biologic weapons laboratory. Pete, let's find a better place to talk. Can you come over to my condo tonight?"

"They will get me one way or another," said Pete with a sense of resignation.

"You mean someone in the government will either kill you or ruin your reputation so badly than nothing you reveal will matter."

"You got it. You've experienced their work before?"

Phil nodded, and took another sip of his beer.

"There's more." Pete added.

"More, you stumbled into the crime of the decade and there's more. How did I ever become your friend?" Phil shook his head and added the rest of the bottle to his mug. "Oh, yeah it was tennis. I better learn to choose partner's better."

"Look there is this lady friend. She is dying of AIDS. She is a journalist and has agreed to keep an active file of everything I've learned. She'll notify her publisher that the story will be released in its entirety if I'm killed or harmed. She'll leave it in her will for publication if she may not be able to complete it before her death."

"So, you've taken her to bed and she's got AIDS. Tierney, you really are trying to get killed! So, are you sero-positive for the virus?"

"No, I'm OK', we haven't been together in over a year. That's why she has avoided me."

"Pete, you're on your own with this woman, but my best advice is that you must force this experiment into the court rooms of Military Justice. That is the only way to make the experimental release of AIDS virus and the quarantine experiment available for public scrutiny. This information is a political nightmare, a threat to the government or the agency, whomever they are. They do not want to look bad in the public eye. They won't stand by idly waiting for you to attack them."

"OK, I'm listening, go on." "You may need to press for a court-martial!" "Are you crazy?" said Tierney.

"Yes and no: If you lose the case, you're a goner, but you're a goner anyway. If the publisher follows through on your lady friend's journalistic skills, they will probably not believe her anyway. She is a dying woman and the world really couldn't care less about what happens to Pete Tierney."

"OK, Phil, you don't have to go out of your way to make me feel good." Pete reacted.

Legé continued, "If you're court-martialed, it will make public the record of your discovery. It will also make public the leak of this experimental viral warfare thing. If it becomes a matter of public record, they would never be allowed to introduce top secret materials, certainly not on a black project. National Security would be jeopardized, and no military court would allow that to occur!"

"Go on, I'm listening." Pete jotted a note on his paper coaster.

"It's a fine point in the military judicial system. The interests and rights of the State are paramount and supersede those of any individual. This conflicts with individual constitutional rights. That's where the rub occurs. A right to know top secret material does not exist. It can not be made public if it's perceived to harm the government or national interests. The Air Force experimented with LSD in World War II, and the Army used it experimentally in Vietnam. This information is harmful in times of conflict to the war effort, but keeping this information classified, supersedes any individual's right to know."

"However, the right of the state to avoid a public debate in the form of a Courts-marshal, when the introduction of security material becomes a matter of public record, would and could not be allowed. They also cannot convict an officer where evidence is lacking. Your defense would require the use of this classified material."

"So, Peter, they cannot afford to make you a public martyr. Under Article Three your case would likely be dismissed. You would be separated with an Administrative Discharge. They just simply cannot afford to publicly prosecute this case for fear of disclosure of such highly classified materials. The high visibility of this trial might mandate your reassignment to a duty that might allow the Navy to frag your ass. It also might make you such a highly visible person, that any attempt at killing you would become immediately suspect. It would invite media attention and they don't like dirty laundry being publicly aired. Pete, if you play your cards right, you might just be able to keep your skin and your reputation." "My Navy career is dead. How would I ever get a job with a dishonorable discharge?" "What the hell do you want Pete? You want your cake, love, success, adventure and to sit on a security pot! My friend, you have no choices left! Anyway, what the hell are you worried about jobs for? You're the one that had to get nosy, expose the death of Charles as a murder and a DOD cover-up. Then you had to disclose to the world that the AIDS epidemic is more than a mistake, but the use of viruses for strategic warfare planning, and you're worrying about a job!"

"OK, OK, -Look Phillip, let me get a grip on all this first. Let me sleep on it and I'll get back to you. OK?"

"Now you want time! Peter wake up! This is real time."

Phillip said with a jarring edge to his voice. He pushed his beer away.

"Alright, just give me some time." Pete nodded and scratched his scalp, a nervous habit that brought no obvious solution.

Peter took his time driving back to Keyport. He took the long way, across the Narrow's bridge and pondered what actionable course to take.

Surely, the government can't be so stupid as to think they can keep this a secret forever. They must have a backup plan in case a regional quarantine system is rejected by public opinion. For their own spineless political necks, they need a better backup plan. I must meet with Price in New Mexico! There must be more to this puzzle. He needed to investigate New Mexico.

CHAPTER 9

New Mexico, Black Project

Pete dreaded returning to work. Certainly, he would be greeted with bad news. Generally, someone had died, or an administrative investigation was underway. All but a few felt overworked, or the administrators were silently irritated because the census was down and being bottom line thinkers, the only thing of importance was a summarized patient count. All the unanswered questions remained as the latest bad news hits first. But Peter knew his ass was on the line with vultures circling.

Pete's strategy was: sort through the pile till you find the good news and massage the bad news.

He noticed Tatum keeping a close eye on his activities, questioning everything. Pete wondered if the extra click on his calls suggested a monitoring system. Tatum had the master phone receiver. All active lines lit upon his telephone board. Tierney's appearance before the credentialing committee was scheduled three weeks away. He must prepare a response to questions about professional competence. It was a QA thing,

Within two weeks Tierney received an official letter of acceptance to the infectious disease fellowship at Bethesda Naval Hospital. He however was not their top candidate, nor were they his first choice. After the interview with Ambrose, Pete had a residual sour taste in his mouth. This letter was a copy of the official Navy message format. It had been routed via the usual channels so God and country and now everybody knew LCDR Tierney was a third alternate.

Although not a flat rejection, he thought, *it's just as good as a slap in the face.* Not only was he tacitly accepted, his nose was publicly rubbed in the impersonal abrasive message. It was part of the irony of the Navy that was built on the tradition of pomp, circumstance and protocol, yet struggled with intrapersonal decorum.

He also discovered a letter hidden in the stack and originating from P.E. Schmick, from Milwaukee, Wisconsin. He nearly tore the letter in half getting through the envelope. It was from Ray Price, taking some small delight in avoiding his surveillance watchdogs who had been cross assigned from the Secret Service. Price was enthused, but not well. He had continued to lose weight, had diarrhea again and was feeling very pressured.

Price felt his life's energy slipping away by the constant surveillance of his home and life. He had developed a sense of urgency and proposed they meet in Albuquerque. This could only be a three-day evolution. A low-profile excursion as he called it. He would depart the house on Thursday evening, through the unguarded alley to his neighbor's home. They would appear to drive him to a hotel in downtown Milwaukee for a business meeting. "The neighbors are just friends - they don't need to know any more," he wrote. "They will actually drive me to Billy Mitchell Field. From there I'll catch the red eye flight on United to Albuquerque.
See you there Friday!"

R. Price, Ph.D.

Pete had grown to enjoy Ray Price and his humor. He loved titles, respected ideas, and achievement despite his disdain for authority. Pete felt they were a good team.

Since Raymond Price rarely went anywhere, his surveillance

crew could be easily distracted. By the time of discovery, he would have flown on the "Friendly Skies' under an assumed name. Price was having fun with this caper and Pete could feel the excitement in his letter.

This left Tierney with, but five days to arrange airfare and use several of his remaining days of leave. It was always difficult to make hasty arrangement in a medical department. Navy medicine was more troublesome than most. Pete had thought it better to fly to Denver and drive to Albuquerque in a rental.

Time would not allow any screwing around, he told himself as he called United. They could not book passage to Denver, so he settled on Albuquerque and told himself it would be all right. *I'll rent an open bed truck when I arrive and consider putting several bales of hay in the back to appear local. No, on second thought, I'll rent a Jeep. Nobody will ever notice, especially with New Mexico plates. Everybody drives a Jeep in these parts, he reassured himself.*

Pete felt secure that everything could fall into place. Surely nothing would go wrong, but still he had to convince Lt. Tatum that his leave application was necessary. Tatum was not to be trusted. If New Mexico was listed as the destination it might excite Tatum's curiosity, he knew he had best not use it. So, he filled out the leave request form for a sailing trip in Puget Sound. I can be reached on Channel 16, call sign Cricket. He knew no one ever left their radio on continuously so a missed call is expected.

The less Tatum knows the better, Pete decided.

Pete drafted a letter to Price suggesting they meet at the 'Library' a local bar near the Radisson Inn close to the University of New Mexico. It was a perfect location as it was only a short distance from the Albuquerque International Airport, a jointly used field by Kirtland AFB. He hoped the message would not be intercepted and would arrive before Price's flight from Milwaukee. As was Tierney's luck, Tatum was consumed with administrative requirements and his underling a JG Swift signed Tierney's leave papers. After all, it was just one day over a weekend departure.

Five days later:

Price and Tierney met at the 'Library'.

The background atmosphere was penetrated by a primitive loud penetrating basal rock. People shouted in each other's ear while billiard players positioned themselves for a good line. The crack of the cue ball being hit as the cue probed into the smoke-filled air. Pendulously bellied men with shined belt buckles, shouted to one another. Heavily flanked women long lost in figure sipped their beers in empty waiting. The sounds were deafening yet few seemed to notice. The ball game was on five unwatched T.V. screens; periodically they added comfort to the lonely.

There seemed an empty security in the burning cigarette in one hand and the golden hue of an unspent beer in the other.

Tierney focused his attention away from the local atmosphere towards his friend Ray Price.

Ray looked physically drained, but paradoxically there seemed to be a new vitality about him. There was a sparkle, of mischief in his eye. There was a sense that Price was now going for the jugular. Tierney recognized this from his experience with the Seals before they went into Granada. It was the eye of a defensive linebacker with a hunter killer instinct. Coming from a research virologist, it was a delight to see Price back in the game.

Pete could see all of this in Price's eyes. Price clearly was a different man from when he was last seen. He was motivated. He wanted to make right what was stolen from his life's most creative work. He had also lost a good deal of weight on an already slight and frail frame.

"What do you suspect is going on here in New Mexico?" asked Price. "Ray, you look worn, are you, all right?"

"I've no time for chit-chat Tierney! What do you know?" "OK, while reading the national newspaper, He was taken by the proximity of stories regarding the plight of Kimberly Begalis who was dying of AIDS, transmitted purposely by her dentist. The dentist used a shared infected syringe in many patients attempting to prove this to be a heterosexual disease. In the same section adjacent to this article was a new anthropologic study of a bio-cosmic experiment where scientists were isolating themselves, putting themselves in quarantine. They were attempting to survive for a long time in an environment excluded from society. This was a form of reverse quarantine protecting self against infectious agents. They were all scientists of different kinds, anthropologist, biologists, physicists, geneticists, all sponsored by the University of New Mexico. They were going to spend the next three years living in a glass bubble isolated from the world in a form of reverse quarantine. They make their own air thus avoiding air transmission of infectious diseases.

"Ray, I'm telling you it is frightening to connect these simultaneous experiments. This association cannot be made by pure chance. The message began with, Begalis, who was dying of a disease we cannot control, and next we discover; we're going to isolate ourselves from the destruction, by Reverse Quarantine."

"The real question is who are **WE?** "How do they know what they know?" asked Peter.

"Tierney, I was wrong. I thought you were on an empty search, morbidly lost in a morass about this woman, Shawn. I was wrong. We have work to do my friend. We have a man-made epidemic to stop and a government to hold accountable."

"Are you all in Peter?"

"Why not, I've nothing else to lose? What could be more dangerous than a man with nothing to lose?"

Peter paused, "You're right. I knew it has everything to do with the AIDS epidemic and some social experiment near Los Alamos. It's highly classified."

"What are you trying to say, Tierney?" Pete replied "I can assure you I become suspicious when I connect the Cuban experiment of quarantine with many federal laboratories like the Sandy Research & Development, Los Alamos Lab, in such cozy proximity to a Bio-cosmic quarantine experiment in New Mexico. I also learned they opened a secret Primate Research laboratory in Albuquerque, dedicated solely to AIDS research. I want to know what is going on in Chaco Canyon and believe it is more than the peyote talking!"

Price nodded, "Now that you mention it, I remember, the CDC had shipped tons of medical equipment, culture tubes and plates to Los Alamos. Every time I went to the shipping office there were stacks of boxes marked Biologic on the loading platform addressed to Chaco Canyon near Los Alamos. This was quite a while ago, I mean years," said Price. "But I recall thinking that the volume of tourism surrounding Bandelier National Monument would make it's too well trafficked for a Black Project. My guess is it's somewhere in the wilderness of Chaco Canyon, or near the D. H. Lawrence Ranch. As you know it's used as a retreat for special faculty members at the University of New Mexico. For all I know it might be a good cover up. I don't know the university but can assure you that I become suspicious when I see that QA label on Biologic boxes awaiting shipment."

Pete paused and added, "I've seen that QA label before on a wounded Cuban in GITMO. I'm fearful we will not find any evidence of what we're looking for. Then again, I'm afraid we will find it and we won't know what to do with the information. Ray, are you with me on this one?"

"I would not miss this for the world. Pete, I've got to tell you, I'm afraid of snakes. Milwaukee is a safe place, but mesas and rocks? I don't like that Pete! There are all sorts of crawly things under rocks or behind them."

"Not to worry, my friend, these snakes rattle! Besides what do you have to worry about? You're the one with AIDS. You'll probably kill the snake!"

"Let's start with the Taos Pueblo Reservation north of here. Then explore the Los Alamos, Chaco Canyon area." "Will the four-wheel jeep work?" asked Price as they headed north on Highway 25 from Albuquerque. "Not to be concerned, I'll drive, you're sick and worry too much." said Peter.

The air conditioning system was turned off and the canvas top opened as dusk approached. It was a cool evening and a good time to be on the road.

"What prompted the Agency to settle on HIV virus?" asked Peter. "I'm not privy to all the viral studies or the strategic planning that went on behind the scenes, but I was told to look for a virus that was selective in the population it infected and similar to the Feline leukemia virus. These retroviruses behave like the AIDS virus." Price paused, wet his lip, and wiped his short mustache with a tissue. He continued, "HIV is like the transmission modes of Hepatitis B. They're more than similar; Hepatitis B and HIV are absolutely identical in their routes of transmission!"

"My department, proposed several possibilities, but the real trouble was coordinating the masking problems with the molecular biologist."

"Plague struck Europe in the middle 14th century and was probably a variant of plague. It's not a clear science".

"Those of us, in the global biologic warfare arena, believed that our military should also be immunized against Anthrax, smallpox and meningococcal meningitis. Such steps have been taken to make this happen."

"So, what are you saying? I mean, come on, Ray, what's the point of this guess work? Is it some double O-7 viral jousting match?" Pete's raised his hands off the steering wheel gesturing as he awaited Price's response.

"Tierney, you can be dense. If the epidemic in Europe was probably caused by let's say a variant of plague and it has taken seven hundred years to figure it out, does that not suggest we are not on our game. Then any technocrat junky virologist can introduce a selectively virulent virus like HIV and then mask its presence by vaccinations with some other viral agent, like Ebola, EB, Polio, or Hepatitis B. The only thing needed is to create a public need to vaccinate and then appear benign and authoritative in giving it. Only a governmental agency tasked with the welfare of a country could project such a fatherly image and then market the damn system as necessary! We need to sound like scientists, get them worried and vaccinate them! We've been turned into social engineers, using bio-molecular science in a brave new world."

"Damn!"

"Exactly, the World Health Organization while vaccinating central Africa with polio or smallpox could easily have contaminates introduced in the form of other viruses or viral particles. The timing could only be traced if the original sera, before and after vaccination is saved and stored for future testing. We would never know who introduced the contaminants. The World Health Organization would not have been able to detect these subtle hidden serologic changes."

"Tierney, do you know about the Dugway Proving Ground?"

"No, I'm just as dumb as everyone else in this country. What's that all about?" Tierney asked. "It was around 1984 or 85, just after we learned of Russia's secret cities. Hundreds died in Sverdlovsk. They renamed the city. Now it 'is called Yekaterinburg. It was a biologic leak that killed everyone. This is part of Russia's dark side. We knew of sixteen secret cities. If R&D plus bio-warfare centers were included it would total eighty-seven hidden cities."

Price reached in his jacket vest pocket and pulled out the soviet map of renamed cities.

Tierney glanced at the photo-copy and returned to concentrate on driving. They hit a bump and Pete placed the map on the bench seat between them. "So, Russia is always toying with us?" "And we mess with them, big time!"

"So, tell me Tierney, why did Casper Weinberger, the Secretary of Defense in 1984 try to justify building a high-containment facility for testing aerosolized lethal pathogens? He tried to finance the project at the Dugway Proving Grounds in Utah? Someone leaked it to the press and because of public outcry, the project was scrubbed?" "We were doing the same thing the Russians were doing?" asked Peter, startled!

"Yeah, you bet your ass!" said Price. "We had to keep up with the Soviets. They at least estimated the dead and take blame like Yeltsin did."

Price glanced over his shoulder forgetting he was alone with Peter in the Jeep. He leaned forward. In a quiet voice, "This viral contamination process was believed to have been followed in San Francisco with the gay community. But, well, the time for diagnostic proof may have passed. The serologic window of opportunity has slipped from our grasp, like soft sand in our hands. It's not a moot point as some would have you believe, especially for those of us who struggled to put out the fires that are now raging throughout the world."

"Have you ever noticed how the leading researchers and authorities avoid the question of: What is the source of the epidemic?! If any question should be answered it is this one!"

"Where did the source come from? It was as if a silent and deceptive virus was cast into a river of life during the spawning season. The only record would have been a sample of the water before the spill downstream. After the spill, the contaminated virus did its job. It was selective in whom it might kill. You can only find that out after the fact by which fish ended belly up. Then you know something killed the fish, and only certain selected fish. The game is to discover, in retrospect, what happened in the moving, changing viral and cultural stream of life, almost an impossible task. Almost!"

"What really did happen up stream?" Peter asked?

"It's difficult to accurately learn the truth when the information is under such close wraps! To this day the official word is that of all the gays immunized in San Francisco with Hepatitis B, only 8% have converted to a positive HIV test. This is over eight years of study. Now do you really believe that?"

"My guess is the figure is closer to 80% and the real serologic evidence is covered up and I don't know where to find it. I cannot imagine an active homosexual male in the Castro District of San Francisco having a mere 8% chance of sero-conversion after eight years of multiple sexual exposures. The CDC must believe we're all idiots. The statistics are so farfetched that it suggests that simply having the Hepatitis B vaccine might protect against AIDS. My guess is an honest figure. It's not 8%, but 88% converted to a positive test for HIV." Hep B vaccine simply does not protect from HIV

"Yeah, I agree 8% seems incredibly low," Pete said. "It's another compounded lie! I don't know where to find the real evidence, maybe serum kept in a CDC freezer veiled in a back room somewhere."

"Their statistics are so far-fetched; they suggest that simply having the Hepatitis B vaccination actually protected the gays against AIDS." "Absurd, nobody is going to believe such crap from the CDC!" said Price. "Nobody!"

"I'm really having trouble believing all this," Peter said with a need to say something, almost as if he needed to publicly object to the inhumanity of it all.

Price was on a roll. "Then there was the Marburg-Ebola Virus, where laboratory workers were in contact with the blood of vervet monkeys from Uganda. Eighty-five percent died. There was a sudden explosion of cases in the Sudan and Zaire. They were all RNA solitary stranded viruses with an envelope like influenza. Lassa virus from Africa, Junin virus from Argentina and the Machupo virus from Bolivia likewise are single stranded RNA viruses with reports of nine separate epidemics in western Africa since 1973. Peter, we haven't even talked about Monkey B-Virus which is a Simian virus that often infects laboratory workers who work with the legendary African green monkey. It was also grown in monkey kidney tissue cultures," Price added.

Peter sensed Price's intense conviction. With such vigor, it was hard to believe Ray was a dying man.

"The famous Dr. Sabin reported that an unidentified monkey virus contaminated Koprowshi's Congo vaccine," Price continued. "There is no question that there are strains of simian immunodeficiency viruses (SIV) that are almost identical to HIV-2. As we speak, this epidemic is active in West Africa."

"Ray, that green monkey stuff, I'm told is just bull shit. It's no more than a racial slur, with evolutionary cluttered logic, left wing fundamentalist stuff. It's all bullshit."

"It's as bad as the mysterious Yellow-Rain hysteria in Viet-Nam or, the defoliant, agent orange which was colorless, but repackaged in orange barrels and drunk as a hazing ritual. A Man's drink, you know, necessarily, required if you wanted to be part of the aggressor pack."

"Keep your eye on the road Tierney! Man, you're off track again. Wild, what did Shawn ever see in you?" Price pointed to the yellow median stripe of the highway to direct Tierney's correction.

"Pete, have you ever considered the power and importance of tactically placed distracters. If the Agency wanted to deflate any argument, it would first find a plausible way to tie it to another intolerable issue, like racism, or other emotionally charged issue. OK, it's linkage which is the politically correct phrase. As far as distracters are concerned, they can be legitimately used. For example, the eating of carrots to improve vision, helped cover up the development of Allied radar for targeting in WW II. But, why did it take 13 years before attenuated vaccination programs were undertaken? Immunity worked for polio, measles, mumps, smallpox - where is the magic?" Price was angered and raised his arms up into the air. "Pete, I believe they used the AIDS virus and hid it in the Hepatitis B vaccination, like a Trojan horse. Now they are simply allowing the epidemic to continue, as with The Band Played ON".

"Respected scientists believe this but are afraid to speak out. I know this with certainty as my laboratory developed the AID's virus and then allowed it to be misused." Price added.

Price turned to glance out the window. "Let's pull over, I need to get out and stretch."

Pete pulled off the road. It was dusk, and the shoulder was not well-marked. They got out and walked to the front of the Jeep. Price was angered, pensive and kicked a sign post. The sign read "No Turn Around". It marked a narrow and deeply rutted trail into the dark toward a mesa in the distance.

"Don't you understand, Pete, the truth is masked by politics, masked by racial conflicts, by the blame game. If I were to design a perfect terrorist virus it would be a retrovirus, recognized only sometime after it was introduced, and its tracks hidden and mired in conflict. It would first be very difficult to trace and second it would eat at the very fabric of a nation's soul. It would need to eat at the very fiber of a nation's ethnic diversity for maximum impact. Then, finally, it would devastate the economic fiber of a country."

"It could not be a quick and dirty kill. That's too simple. The loss is too short. It would have to be like an infectious cancer hidden in a multiplicity of disguises selecting specific groups especially groups that are out of the main stream, e.g. the homosexuals, the perfect victims"

Price continued; "We also learned a great many lessons from the Vietnam War. Among other things, the Viet Cong learned it was better to injure a soldier than to kill him. An injured man requires half a dozen people to care for him. Just to get them off the battle field. This will tie up medical assets including personnel in his care. If he doesn't survive in the short term, then the long-term care is even more fiscally burdensome to a much larger segment of society. To be brutally honest, there is little monetary killing effect in a quick death, compared to the burden of long term suffering. The V.C. wanted to get the most from its killing potential."

"You're saying viral warfare is more onerous and costly if it causes a long-term illness?" asked Tierney.

"Exactly, Peter. The retrovirus of AIDS exerts its most destructive force over a long period of time. In other words, it becomes a timed delayed viral weapon system that lies hidden and dormant. It causes long term losses. That's why it's so effective! There could be no greater financial impact to a society than to have its citizens linger in a long and protracted death spiral."

Pete soberly asked, "Why? How could anyone do the unimaginable?"

"The strategy is; if you can't beat or match them with Star Wars, you break them in the privacy of the bedroom. You beat them in

151

their pocketbook!"

"It also has the advantage, the cultural dimension of divisiveness." Ray continued, "It pits the homosexual against the heterosexual in moral and economic issues. The irony is the players are unknowingly used to stir the pot of continued conflict."

"All of us get so caught up in simply struggling to survive and care for each other. That is the human element. We can miss the reasons behind the question, who did it? If this is all evolutionary stuff, then why have there been nine separate epidemics in western Africa since 1973? What has accelerated the evolutionary process? The social conflicts are not just at home. None of us ever expected this virus to get outside the laboratory," said Price. "We studied it, we strategized with it, we wondered what it might be, but never in our wildest dreams did we think this would happen, even after the Swine Flu fiasco. The virus for AIDS was developed and isolated two years before it hit the streets."

Peter asked, "Is there a way to prove that the original vaccination with Hepatitis B is the immunologic distracter, masking the addition of HIV?"

"Real hard to prove that. There clearly is no obvious paper trail, but my guess is that the serum from the immunized homosexuals in San Francisco is still available. If the trail hasn't been destroyed, hidden or tainted. If we had proper unbiased testing, we would be able to clearly track the historical trail behind HIV." The vaccine for an associated disease of Hepatitis B was developed from the blood of homosexual males. That vaccine was discontinued after several years of encouraging its usage." Price added.

"Is there an epidemic of Hepatitis B?" asked Pete.

"No, there's only an epidemic of interest, and marketing fear plays well yes really very well, with all of the American public!"

"Did you know that the CDC is planning to vaccinate the entire country against Hepatitis B? Universal vaccination is planned for the entire country to prevent a low rate of mortality. AIDS of course by contrast has 99% mortality and already 1 million in the U.S. are infected. Now that is a real epidemic"! Price explained boiling with anger!

"They're vaccinating against Hepatitis-A, which has limited mortality associated with it. Why do you suppose there is such

152

energy, such pressure and enthusiasm to vaccinate? They are also planning to vaccinate against Chickenpox which in large part is a disease of inconvenience."

"OK, you tell me Professor Price! WHY??"

"I believe, to hide the viral markers and confuse the issue even more! Like chaff from an aircraft locked on by an incoming missile."

"That would explain the question of "Why now?"

"What do you mean, Peter?"

"Damn, you're thick too, Price. That explains why after thousands of years of people on this earth no such virus had ever developed almost exclusively in homosexuals. Homosexuals have been with us since the beginning of time. Why now did they develop AIDS?"

"Good question! Why now?"

"What ever happened to the concept of Viral Mutations?" Pete asked.

"Reasonable question, usually it takes years for viruses to change character. This one is all over the place in different genetic strains, in different parts of the world. We're the scientists who applaud ourselves because we think we can predict which Flu vaccination will be in vogue next year."

"Look, Price it's not your fault. You can't blame yourself for what the government or the Agency does with your research."

Price ignored the suggestion and continued as if he was in a lecture hall.

"It's also important to know that certain cofactors stimulate the virus to behave differently in different groups. I mean things like amyl nitrate to improve the sexual buzz, all the prostaglandins and CMV (cytomegalic virus) in semen that are exchanged in multiple partners. These clearly are not the causative factors in getting AIDS for the heterosexual drug addict or the hemophiliac who was transfused with tainted blood. Yet these factors aggressively increase the virulence of the virus."

"You know," Price continued, "it's like the grease that makes the virus move with smooth virulence."

"These cofactors catalyze the infective state. Of course, none of this was known at the time and was only learned as the epidemic was observed. Still today, statistics from the CDC and the NIH, verify that 97% of those infected with this virus are homosexuals, bisexual males, I.V. drug users or people who received tainted blood. That is 1991 data!" he added. "Nothing has changed in years."

"Peter, I'm very tired. I think it wise we get back on the road, stay out of sight. I'm sure the Agency has already learned of my flight to Albuquerque."

Pete nodded in agreement. "You're right. I'll bet Lt. Tatum has already tried to call me on board my sailboat." Pete shuddered with the thought of being discovered. "We're dead men if we get caught. We must quickly discover what the Agency is doing down here."

Dusk in the desert had already arrived with a surface chill below a red sky marked by a setting sun with its refractive magic. Pete like all sailors knew the adage "Red at night, sailors delight".

They drove northeast from Albuquerque for well over an hour past the Bandelier National Monument and the famous Los Alamos test sight. They pulled off the narrow winding road in Pueblo de Taos, the traditional historic home of the Taos Indians.

Both Ray and Peter were mentally and physically exhausted. In silence, they crossed the Rio Grande Gorge Bridge and settled for a small motel off Route 507. The gorge was flowing slowly nearby with a trickle of sound in the night air.

"This will have to do," said Ray. "Park the Jeep so the plates aren't visible to anyone passing by." Peter found some decent cover in an alley near a dumpster.

"Tomorrow we can check out the Pueblo dwellings and hopefully we'll find some clues from the Anasazi culture and the Hopi. Maybe we'll get lucky. Things might fall together and make sense", offered Price. "I still can't believe anyone would develop a man-made virus to kill whole populations," Peter responded, "especially with no way to control the aftermath."

"They must have a back-up plan. What if this gets out of control? Did you think of that?"

Price turned his head away from the question and peered out the side window into the darkening sky. *"It was just an experiment, it was just a test." He said quietly.*

"Maybe, a kinder heart would conclude; never was it meant to be more than a local experiment on the homosexuals not realizing they had a persuasive political voice?"

"Then, suddenly it got out of hand," mused Price. "They misused my studies and my intentions. I will never forgive them for what they have done!" Price spoke into the now dark sky, turning toward Tierney.

"Pete, this is not the first time a virus was man-made and leaked from the laboratory. The Swine Flu epidemic was no epidemic. It was the first man-made viral leak that I know w i t h c e r t a i n t y ."

Ray gestured with his fist and with a waning fire in his eye. "I'm being killed by my own research and by my own hand. The agency deceived me to believe this would be a temporary and transient viral illness. Like your friendly doctor saying, "It's just a Virus!"

"Come on Ray, don't fade on me now. What about the Swine Flu? "Peter I'm ill and I need my rest. It can wait till tomorrow. Suffice it to say, it never crossed the Canadian border. I've never heard of an epidemic that stopped at a border, have you?"

"There isn't an illness known to man that stops at a border, not even Montezuma's revenge," Pete agreed.

"Others should have asked the same question. Obviously, the swine flu epidemic was never an epidemic. My guess," Price reflected awhile, "Someone in the CDC or the Agency knew what was going on and kept the Canadian Officials informed."

"Pete, it's like dancing or making love. Timing is everything. Sometimes truth is better unknown. We could all go home and let life pass by unnoticed. It would be so much easier." Price was drained. "Tierney, tell me then, why we are risking our necks for some transient expression of truth which no one wants to hear?" Pete reacted quickly. "Because Charles was killed, and Shawn was infected, like you. Because the world is infected and at risk. Someone better damn well better explain, why!"

"OK, Peter, we'll figure it out tomorrow, but not tonight"! The next morning, they drove to the Taos Pueblo Reservation and nosed around exploring, but without success. "We're wasting valuable time. Yesterday we spent a whole night driving around aimlessly. Now, we've learned this is a tourist trap and the Pueblo Indians in Taos have been successful in keeping their traditional ways. We're obviously on the wrong track."

"OK, Ray, I think we should go back to Madrid. I spoke with a guy on the plane about it. It's an unconventional hippie colony, and there may be enough dissent to point us in the right direction. My instincts have not been tracking well lately, but if Madrid is another dead-end then we can back track up north again for Los Alamos and Chaco Canyon. I want to have the cover of night before we snoop around there."

"All right, let's head for Madrid. Pete, what made you suspect a secret project in New Mexico?" asked Price.

"Funny thing about hunches. How do people really know what they believe they know? Nothing scientific about it, but a combination of leads and one day a light goes on. You remember the first shuttle landed in 1981. I recall it as clearly as if it was yesterday. I was glued to the T.V. that day. The shuttle landed in the salt flats. I was so excited I promptly walked back into my office and gave a shot of tetanus to someone that was allergic to it. I was so excited and completely distracted that I forgot what I was doing."

"We can be so preoccupied with ourselves we forget what's going on outside our heads. Other times we can be purposely influenced, by those that play on our distractions. Social strife might be a very good distracter if you have a political agenda. Likewise, hiding the obvious requires some attempt at distractive camouflage."

Pete continued, "Do you the first shuttle where John Glen was promptly whisked away to New Mexico and the Loveless Clinic, or was it the McAfee Army Health Clinic? He was isolated under close medical scrutiny near the White Sands missile testing grounds. This may have been the very first case of quarantine in a modern era. More precisely, it may have been the first public case of reverse quarantine. The purpose was to protect society from an astronaut who might have acquired an unknown space infection."

"Not so strange an idea if one was fearful that their immune system might have been compromised after exposure to the radiation belts and the unknowns within the voids of space".

"Who knows? They could have developed some strange infection while up there," mused Pete.

"The whole idea of reverse quarantine stayed with me and

New Mexico was a natural location, a natural conclusion."

"Ray, it just seems like a perfect place to me. I'm following my nose and I can't really explain why," Peter muttered softly.

"You better be more attentive Tierney, there's a cop following your tail."

Pierce and Tierney had departed Interstate 25 for Highway 14. They had passed the prison at Las Luaas, a low security prison known for its honor system. Entering the gravel road, the Jeep threw up a swirl of dust. They were now headed for Madrid, an old abandoned coal mining town occupied mostly by hippies.

"Where is that cop now?" Pete asked with a growing fear of discovery.

"Still at your six o'clock."

Pete sped up to recapture forward steering as his rear right wheel went off the edge of the gravel road. Another cloud of dust spiraled into the clear air.

To the trailing cop, it appeared the Jeep was evasively speeding with poor control. From that point on it all became automatic, as the squad car turned on his rotating beacons and siren. The squad car radioed dispatch and reported a high-speed chase on the gravel road.

Through his rearview mirror, Pete could see the patrolman on the radio and imagined everyone in the county would be after them. He had not planned on a traffic ticket. It could ruin all their efforts.

"No, I'm not exaggerating," Officer Santos retorted, "the guy is squirreling all over the place. I can handle it, no sense sending a backup squad from the station. You better alert em though."

"And I thought a brown Cherokee Jeep would blend in well, especially with native license plates. We look ordinary, Ray, don't we?"

"Yeah, Tierney, you're a real low-profile kind of tourist. Remember you're just exploring the land of enchantment and the Indian culture. You're into photography and stuff," Ray said with sarcasm.

"Did you bring a camera, Ray?"

"Not me, I thought you were going to take care of everything!"

Pete pulled over on the side of the road, more dust, and the squad car came in behind and stopped. The policeman was still on the radio, probably to headquarters, thought Peter.

He had called in the license plate of the rented Jeep and was awaiting some additional input to clarify the risk. Pete fumbled for his wallet and discovered it was damp from sweat. His postage stamps were stuck together.

"Now they'll run a search through the rental company to find out who I am," said Pete disgusted with himself.

"Do you think the cops will get excited when they learn you're a Navy doctor?"

"Probably not, I've no prior police record. For the moment, we should be OK. It probably depends on if Lt. Tatum has become suspicious."

"Not good, there will be an official record of my passing through the area and it wasn't necessary. Price, it's more important they don't check on you! So, keep your I.D. to yourself."

"Keep your mouth shut, Ray! Don't play mental games with the cops; I know how you love games."

The police officer strode up to the back of the driver's side window.

"So, what's the rush, stranger? You in the habit of speeding?" asked the policeman.

"Sorry, officer, I didn't realize I was speeding and I didn't mean to swerve. I just hit the edge of the gravel road."

"Have you been drinking?"

"No sir."

"Step out of the car with your hands above your head," He ordered.

"What's going on here, officer isn't this a bit excessive?" Peter protested.

Price nudged Pete. "Just do as he says, and we can get out there."

Peter opened the door, stumbled on a stone as he reached the ground. He reached for the door handle to steady his balance. *Great move you idiot,* Pete scolded himself in silence.

"Sure, you haven't been drinken, sailor? Ya know drinken and driven is a great way to get your ass kicked out of the Navy."

"No, officer, I haven't been drinking. Just stumbled on a rock here and how did you know I'm in the Navy?"

"We have wonderful computers here in New Mexico, kind of a high-tech police force you might say, except I'll need to take you in for a breath test."

"Man, this is crazy! I have not been drinking. I just slipped on a rock. I wasn't speeding. My companion is ill and he can't drive...so what do you want me to do with him?"

"Well, excuse me, Mr. Sailor, sir, but your companion is not the problem. We don't take kindly in these here parts to strangers parading in, making a dust storm and calling us crazy. Put your hands behind your back."

Price noticed the sun was starting to set and the melon colors cast off the San Dias Mountains added hues of contrasting reds and oranges. It was easy to see why people loved this country. This however was not the way to enjoy a sunset.

Price struggled to guard his quick lip. He opened the door on the passenger side and walked around the back of the Cherokee. His sudden appearance startled the policeman and he quickly drew his holstered gun, pointing it at Price.

"Hold it mister!"

"Wait a minute, Officer, I was just trying to be helpful," responded Price.

"I said stop, Mister. I mean it!"

Price stopped and remained motionless as the officer redirected his attention to Tierney. He hand-cuffed Tierney and with his gun still drawn and peripherally aware of Price, pushed Pete toward the squad car. He opened the back door and pushed Tierney into the back seat.

"You're next," he said to Price, "get in the back with your buddy. We're all going for a ride downtown to headquarters! You're both under arrest! "Price turned to Tierney. "He didn't say freeze, Pete. They're supposed to say freeze."

"We agreed you would shut up, Ray. Now, just do it."

The cop stood erect, studied his flock with a sense of pride, and stretched his back.

"Fine catch, I'd say, better than fishing."

He turned toward Price. "You look sick, mister. You got AIDS or something contagious? You a fucking homo?" He had handcuffed Price's wrists behind his back and forced both into the back seat of the squad car.

It was a 30-minute drive back to Albuquerque and the police station. Still in handcuffs, both men were ushered into a vacant bailiff's office. The police officer strode over to the duty officer and whispered in his ear.

"All right, sailor, now you get to do the breath analysis test."

The test was repeated three times and still it read zero. The officer was visibly upset with the results and quickly proceeded to jot down a list of charges on the violation registry form.

"OK, sailor, I can get you on speeding, evading arrest and maybe reckless driving, but I want to report this to the military so that you can explain yourself once you get back to your ship!" "I'm not on a ship, officer!" Pete responded.

"Damn Navy!" the officer retorted. "Never where they're supposed to be." I'm still going to report this to the officer in charge at Kirtland AFB, and see what they suggest we do with you, mister Lt. Commander. My guess is they won't know what to do with a seafaring type!"

He called the duty officer at Kirtland and notified them of Tierney's presence as well as Price's.

"Yes sir, they're some sort of medical scientist types."

"No, I don't know what they're doing in these parts," replied the police officer.

"No, they're not on official business, just claim to be tourists looking around."

"Yeah, medical scientist, on vacation, near Madrid, is that believable?" "They haven't been near Los Alamos or the Wilderness, have they?"

"No, I don't think they've been near there".

"Just a sec and I'll check," responded the officer.

The police officer handed the phone to another officer who listened and became agitated. "Don't ask that!"

"You guys haven't been near Los Alamos or the Wilderness, have you?"

"What wilderness?" asked Peter?

"Well, the Bandelier Wilderness, you aren't much of a tourist are you? You got to learn your ports of call, sailor. Yeah, a real navigator you are, must be Jimmy Carter Navy grad." He grinned at the duty officer holding the telephone receiver.

"No, they have just arrived and don't seem to know much about the area. They don't know nothing about Los Alamos or the

160

Wilderness."

"What is going on there?" The police officer asked the duty officer at Kirtland AFB.

Pete listened intently, craning his neck to learn more of the conversation.

"No, sir," responded the cop. "I haven't seen any medical shipments going that way."

"OK, we'll keep a lookout for the heavy trucks going north and I'll let the chief know so no one worries."

"What are they doing up there anyway?" the cop asked.

"Look sir, I'm sorry I asked, you don't have to get nasty...OK, OK, and in a whisper, yes I'll take care of the transmitter on the bumper."

"Are you really sure it's OK to let these guys go?"

The police officer turned to Tierney and Price. "OK, I'll let you guys go, but, we need a hundred-dollar deposit towards the charges. Too many people pass through town, create mischief and then just never show up for trial or pay their fine. It's hard on the city budget, you understand."

"OK, I need to see your papers, leave papers."

Pete gave him a copy from his wallet. The officer scrutinized the paperwork, made a copy for the record and returned the form.

"What is this Cricket, Cricket call sign on Channel 16?"

"Just a Navy code word, officer, you know, nautical talk." Pete was now so irritated that he felt the hair on his neck bristling. "OK, you can pay the bailiff over there and then you're free to go. Your buddy looks sick though. What's the matter, he got AIDS or something?" Pete knew better than to lash back at the red neck cop. He was already in enough trouble, so he restrained his response. "No, officer, he's just dying of cancer. Can we go now?"

They were unaware the Cherokee was tagged with a positional GPS locater newly added to the police budget.

Tierney and Price collected their belongings from the wired cage, signed the log book and let the screen door slam behind them. They found their rental Jeep protected by a secured gate and Dobermans.

Both were silent as they drove north on Highway 25. Their rental Jeep was monitored by Kirtland AFB.

THE LOS ALMOS WILDERNESS:

Tierney and Price drove up the bluff in pitch darkness toward Los Alamos and took a left turn onto a deeply rutted dirt road off Highway 4. They headed for the ancient pueblo ruins in the Bandelier wilderness, a restricted area atop the mesa. They ignored the sign, "Pueblo Sacred Grounds, Do Not Enter!" The pueblo village, imbedded into the cliff walls, was officially registered as belonging to the Sandia National Laboratories which was always heavily layered in security. They both knew better than to stay on Highway #4 and needed to avoid the main security gate.

The duty sergeant noticed the image on the sensors had stopped at the 7,700-foot level. *Probably a stretch and pee break,* he thought.

"Airman Crosby, get Lt. Col. Gray on the line for me. He needs to know we have a potential incursion developing."

"Colonel Gray, we have a possible intrusion. A scientist and a Navy doctor approaching into the periphery of The Box."

There was a long pause. "You're kidding Sergeant, you must be kidding. You'd better be kidding!"

"No sir, just like stray tourists wandering right into a hornets' nest. Sir, I think you better come in and look! It appears real suspicious to me, Colonel. Why would anyone be hiking at this hour?"

"I'll be there in 15 minutes. Find out who they are and where they're from!"

"Yes, Colonel, we already know who they are. Thank you, Sir!"

The Jeep continued toward the southeast and climbed up the road towards Mesa Grande. The sergeant activated a satellite Thermo- sensors for increased resolution.

Tierney stopped the Jeep at the extreme end of the dwindling path. They were on the edge of a valley stretching far below for a good mile and rising to a mesa above.

Both Price and Tierney left the cab, walked to the rear of the

Jeep, and lowered the tailgate. Price reached for his climbing boots, turned them upside down and jarred them against the rear bumper trying to remove any lurking scorpions or spiders.

"No snakes." Price shuddered at the thought.

Something fell to the ground, with a solid thump. *Too big to be a scorpion,* he thought. He focused the red penlight on the solid object at his feet. It looked like some electronic device, a small radio maybe, the size of a pack of cigarettes. A cold chill suddenly struck him like a winter freeze blowing off Lake Michigan. Price placed a hand on Tierney's shoulder and with a finger to his lip directed his attention to the little black box with attached antenna. Both instantly recognized that they were being tracked by someone very sophisticated.

In silence, Peter picked up the box and examined it. It was a Transmitter/Receiver. It had a magnet attached to the back side plus the antenna. A hand etched label indicated "Property of USAF".

Pete placed it back where it was supposed to be located on the underside of the bumper and motioned for Price to follow him to the front of the Jeep.

"Shit, Ray, the Air Force knows we're here and is tracking us. For all I know they've heard every word we've said."

"For how long you suppose?" asked Ray.

"Probably since that sheriff picked us up. This couldn't have been on since we rented the car," said Pete.

Lt. Col. Malcolm Gray arrived at the situation room, sprinted up the three flights of stairs and spoke haltingly between gasps.

"Sergeant, I'll give them twenty minutes to depart the area. Notify the SWIFT patrol and the Cobra Helicopters of transgressors." "Wait a minute, hold that call to the Cobra squadron and get me the
C.O. of this LCDR Tierney. What's his name from the police report? Yes, Lt. Tatum. Get him on the line!"

The situation room was silent as they watched the topographical colored screens. The vertical screen covered the right side of the east wall. They watched as two figures exited the Jeep and walked to the Tailgate. They opened the gate and appeared to be changing shoes.

"Must be climbing boots? Do you think they're going to try and. climb the Mesa?" asked the Sergeant.

"Right into the damn Box. How did they know to go there? Who the hell are these people, anyway? Sergeant, get that Navy

163

Lt. on the line!"

They watched in silence as the two figures stood at the front of the Jeep. They did not seem to suspect anything unusual nor that were they being tracked by Kirtland AFB.

"Sir, the satellites will soon be passing each other for about 40 minutes of lost contact. Shall I notify the Cobra squadron?"

"Just get that Navy Lt. on the line, Sergeant!"

The Sergeant mumbled under his breath, "Nobody goes near the Box, nobody. Hell, I bet the president doesn't even know about the Box."

"Sir, I've got Lt. Tatum on the line."

"Lt. Tatum, this is Lt. Colonel Malcolm Gray at Kirtland AFB. We have reason to believe a LCDR Tierney and some viral scientist are attempting to enter a Top-Secret research center near Los Alamos. Do you know this man?"

"Oh…Yes Sir, I know him. He's in this command. What's he doing there? He was supposed to be on a sailing trip."

"Well, Lt., your man is off course! Excuse me Lt. Tatum, but why are you in charge of a Lieutenant Commander? Isn't that a bit unusual in any military service?"

"Well, sir, not in Navy Medicine. You see I'm a medical service corps manager and we manage doctors. You might say they don't know anything but medicine. So, we control em." Tatum loved the sense of power, no matter how empty the moment.

"I'd say you're doing a lousy job, Lt. Let me speak to your superior and I mean someone, anyone above a LCDR."

"Will the C.O. of the hospital do? He's a

Captain." "Is he a doctor?" asked Colonel Gray.

"Well, Sir, he's a doctor, but he doesn't do any doctoring."

"Then who manages the C.O., Lieutenant?" The Lt. Colonel did not expect an answer to his measured

sarcasm. "I'll have the X.O. call you right

away." "Another Doctor, I suppose!?"

"No sir, a medical service corps manager, like me," responded Tatum. Lt. Col. Gray walked away from the speaker phone in disgust.

He needed answers, not a political pecking order.

Price and Tierney had climbed the Mesa wall and came upon the perimeter fence. It was electrified, but there were no visible guards. They both expected Special Forces to be all over the place. There were no guard houses. Guard towers were not in the design plans, it would appear unnatural. From about two miles it was not apparent that any fence existed because of the use of a silicate fiber mesh. It was a polarized synthetic fence that blocked out internal light like a one-way mirror. From a distance, the fence was invisible. In the background was the pueblo village nestled into the mountainside, just like in the travel brochures from the chamber of commerce tourist information center. They could see figures in the windows. The figures appeared to be wearing yellow flight suits.

There was a drainage ditch near the base of the fence created by an unexpected torrent of rainfall. It took a little work for Price and Tierney to enlarge the ditch. They moved as quickly and quietly as possible.

"The Pueblo compound had been electrified, look at those high-tension power lines, satellite dishes and antennas," whispered Tierney. "Yeah, a real high tech Black project disguised as a sacred Pueblo village and plastered right into a sheer cliff. Not like any you might see in an advertisement for the Land of Enchantment," said Price. "Do you suppose the Primate Research Laboratory from White. Sands is doing AIDS Research testing here?" Tierney asked with the sarcasm of a liberal reporter.

"Nah, I'm quite sure all of this is above reproach. Surely this secret black project would stand the test of public scrutiny. What experiment are these folks studying? Why is it hidden behind the Pueblo Indian culture?"

"Roger that. If it looks like an epidemic, smells like an epidemic, tastes like an epidemic then it clearly cannot be an epidemic. This is political option "C" we're looking at through an artificial fence. No green monkeys, condoms and alternative lifestyle hysteria here." Price seemed to have rehearsed the lines.

"Let's press on Ray. We have a lot to learn! Be careful of those wires!"

"I hope they haven't discovered the Jeep. Did you bring your camera Ray?"

"Hell no, we already have enough trouble. All I need to do is use a flash camera. We would have congress and the whole damn Air Force descend on us."

They both lay low to the cold rocky ground and crawled until close to the walls of the pueblo. Then they carefully pulled themselves up closely against the red adobe stone wall of the pueblo. The search lights were at ground level and cast shadows from bottom to top. The elbow of the wall allowed protection and they found shelter in the shadows.

Price and Tierney slowly rose to tip toes and peered into a lighted window.

There were two men and one woman wearing canary yellow coveralls zippered up the front with a black identification system on their backs. These symbols reflected their sex followed by a bar code and the terminal letters C.T.

A Regional computerized map of the Northeast with New York City highlighted was displayed.

Changing data above the map was distributed under categories:
AIDS Cases: Rate Increase:
 Pop. Subset: Deception Strategy:

10%   Black racial turmoil 07%

women id w/ women's Issues

Deception Strategy:
NYC War on Drugs...methadone program...needle exchange..
    Family values...disruption...City/state initiatives
    Mayoral race...

    Related illness rates. TB, Accumulated VD, Hepatitis
    Homeless issues
    Racial turmoil: election rigging
    Crime organized/gang/prostitution/drugs
    Gun sales, gun laws.
Drugs: introduce new I.V. heroine, target neighborhoods
    Greenwich, Bronx, Harlem, Upper, West Side

A woman sitting with her back to the window was working on data input to a computer terminal. She turned toward the male at the regional map and made some comment about new data for the Southwest Region and the Caribbean.

As she turned, Tierney noticed her breast pocket had an orange label of QR, a very clearly visible R, not an A.

Tierney squatted down again, pulled on Price's pant leg and then whispered in his ear, "What does that symbol **RQ mean**?"

"We know QA was the code name for Quarantine Access. Did you notice the basement entrance in the center of the floor was labeled Kiva-Top Secret?"

"Let's take another look," said Price.

As they peered into the window, the computerized map of the Southwest came up with categorical listings of progress:

Medical Strategy:
Rx...AZT, DDI, ZDV Niverapine, reverse-transcriptase
inhibitor. Vaccine: virus phenotype variants: SI syncytium-
induced NSI non-syncytium-induced Adjuvants:
Genteck QS32-Alum
 rgp 120 Chiron-MF-59+MTP-PE
   -SAF+MDP
Vaccine development:
Viral vectors (adenovirus, poliovirus)
Pox vectors with env/gag/pol
pseudovirons, VLP's
SIV
naked DNA e.g. influenza
Organizational strategy: WHO,
CDC, NIH: Hep. B,C,&
A...Chickenpox Social-Political
Strategy:
Racial pot...SF...LA riots...trials
Financial...Military-Industrial complex...base
closure loan-default S.L.

Male_^{oo}_^{o} C.T., sitting at the regional map, used an electronic pointer to highlight segments of the data. Female ^{ooo}_^{o} C.T., turned toward the standing male at the work terminal who had risen to approach the entrance to Kiva.

They all had bar codes on the back of their yellow coveralls, and this code appeared on their sleeve. He walked to the door to the Kiva, placed his right palm on a light beam and placed his eye close to a red beam near the door jam.

"Agent 73QRCT for entry."

Tierney turned to Price. "My God it's a retinal & voice recognition, palm print identification security system. We'll never get access into this place, maybe we should just get out of here! Have you seen enough?"

"Yeah, it's hopeless!" Price whispered. "Who the hell is behind all this?"

The green blinking entrance light came on the overhead Kieva-Top Secret sign and the bar-coded worker entered alone.

"These guys are not just lackey footmen for the Agency. Who is the Agency?" "I believe RQ stands for Reverse Quarantine suggested Price....we quarantine ourselves from those infected.

"They're monitoring the AIDS epidemic and the political success or failure of various deceptive social strategies. These bar-coded guys are technologists, but they seem involved with more than just passive monitoring, more than mere polling results and measuring catalytic events. What does the QR mean?" asked Tierney.

"Pete, this looks like a test population of QR's who recognize they are unable to change the course of this epidemic but are protecting themselves from the epidemic. These agents are researching the effects of REVERSE QUARANTINE. Protecting themselves and the Agency from the certain death as this epidemic consumes the world. Their only control left is to limit the damage and orchestrate social unrest as a distracter."

"Pete, I think we should get out of here, back to the Jeep. What more can we really do here anyway?"

"I guess you're right, we can't get through the security system so we might as well get out of here, before the Air Force comes looking in their back yard."

They lowered themselves close to the ground and began to crawl back toward the polarized fence, hoping to find the ditch. At the fence Price couldn't find the ditch.

"Where the hell is that hole we climbed through?"

"I can't find it either. Look, Price, you crawl 50 yards that way, and I'll cover the other direction. Just so we don't lose each other, after 7 minutes we will both retrace the covered ground to right where we are now and a bit beyond. If you find the ditch, you crawl through and wait no more than 10 minutes. OK?!"

"OK, don't lose me Tierney, there are snakes out here." "There's
A lot more to be afraid of than snakes Price…don't worry and get moving!"

Seven minutes passed in the cold black air. Tierney thought he had
crawled about 50 yards. He crawled another 10 yards to make sure but still could
not find the ditch running under the polarized fence. He turned back to retrace his
path and over another 50 yards

WHOP, WHOP, WHOP:

The air held the unmistakable sound of incoming helicopters. There
were blinded by dazzlingly intense search lights and loud speakers coming from
the orbiting Cobras circling the perimeter fence.

Peter had no choice. He sprinted for a darken shadow. He had to find the
cover of dark. Then he heard dogs. The canine patrol had been released.

"Price, where are you? Damn,! Where are you?
"RAY!"

Tierney's legs became heavy and sluggish, against a sticky resistance. He
felt at his boots. There was a glue adhering to them, an instant glue for intruders.

"RAY!, Get out of here!" he shouted into the empty night

CHAPTER 10

BUMED at the Pentagon

Tierney didn't need an invitation. The tone of the abbreviated "three-minute orders" delivered to him while in a dusty guarded quarter left no doubt. He would likely be devoured by the sharks at Headquarters. He had never been to the White Plains Testing site and didn't know where the CH-60 had taken him the night before. He would report, under guarded escort before Rear Admiral Hayes. Hayes chaired the disciplinary board of the Bureau of Medicine and Surgery (BUMED). Pete was allowed one phone call and doubted it would remain confidential. He was momentarily surprised to recognize Hayes' name on the summons. He was to report to the same Hayes, who headed Quarantine Access Medical Research and Development at Bethesda.

Hays must be a central player in the theater of damage control. Now he is trying to control political leaks, thought Pete.

Pete believed Admiral Hayes was not the key figure responsible for the epidemic. He must be tasked with limiting the damage from political fallouts damage from political fallout,

He must be just one of many players, thought Pete. Still, Peter felt there was no doubt he would do damage! *Do you suppose he's just a front man?* Pete wondered.

Pete paced the floor circling around a central post supporting the barracks roof at the Marine Barracks Restricted Officer's quarters. Price was nowhere to be found, maybe dead and Pete was once again alone. Without Price he could not collaborate their discovery, much less make any of it public. Pete shuddered. He feared being alone again, lost and without proof. He was in a lion's den. We didn't even have a camera. He could see Price struggling to get off that mesa in the Bandelier wilderness. I tried to stay with him. I told him we must stay together. *The lights from the helicopter must have blinded him.*

I should have known better. He hit his hand against the center post of the tent as he glanced toward the ground and covered his eyes. "I lost my friend Charles, I lost Shawn and now Price. His greatest fears were rapidly unfolding before his eyes.

None would believe him, no one would support him. Shawn had become an emotional ghost. She had left him empty, like a black hole in space. She seemed to care little, might not believe his story nor publish it through her connections with the Boston Globe.

Dying of AIDS did not seem nearly enough reason to abandon me, he felt. *Something is still missing. She didn't believe the condom propaganda any more than Peter.* He cleared his eyes.

He didn't completely believe the tainted transfusion story either. She may be dying, but she might be lying.

He had to call someone, and wasted no time choosing his old tennis friend, Phil Legé, past Navy Judge Advocate. Lege' was well versed in Navy law.

Before calling, he prepared his thoughts and took a long, sigh. Damn hard to summarize all this in an allotted three-minute call. His call would be monitored so he organized his thoughts to be precise and to add urgency in his message.

The phone rang twice.

".....Hello." Phil always had a long pause.

"Phil, it's me Peter. Phillip, I'm charged with security breaches into highly classified areas of biologic weaponry at Los Alamos. They'll nail me to the wall with this one, and I can't tell you who they are, over the phone."

Legé paused, "What the hell are you talking about Tierney!"

"Well, they've created an epidemic. They intentionally used a test virus into the gay community and now they're trying to cover it up. I need help, Phil, can you do anything for me?"

Legé paused and measured his response. He knew the call was monitored. He chose to lead his opponents. He chose to plant a seed. "Pete, you have very few options," said Legé. He paused, and "You better be damn sure of your facts." "I'm sure!"

"OK, if you request a court-martial and attempt to make the proceedings as a matter of public record, the Navy will refuse to allow it to go that far. They don't want it to reach the point of a public disclosure. They will deny you that opportunity. The Military never forgot the lesson learned in the trial of Billy Mitchell. They will never give you a platform to press such a public display. A public audience is the last thing they want. Hmm, maybe there is a better way."

"Where are you now?"

"I'm in a holding tent at The DC Marine Base, next destination, the Pentagon."

"OK, I'll meet you in D.C., as soon as I can. I still think the best solution is not a legal one. We too can play a little power politics. If you have a big gun, you aim quickly and let your intentions be known. I'll catch a flight and see you tomorrow."

"Well, can I file suit against them?" asked Pete. "No, you can't serve the Navy with a lawsuit. They must allow you to file suit. It might not even be the Navy." "We'll talk tomorrow. This call is probably being monitored. It can wait till we speak in person. We need to know who **they** are!"

172

Pete's was interrupted by the Marine security guard who motioned with his right hand to break off, hang up.

"Legé, get back to me... when you get to Washington D.C." He hung up the mounted wall phone and followed the Marine's gesture toward the waiting helicopter, rotors thumping the cool dawn air.

The Marine walked behind Tierney, keeping his distance and gestured with his weapon to move quickly.

Peter stopped, turned around and noted the early sunrise. He had lost Price somewhere and felt he was dead. Price was too frail to escape from the mesa. The Marine nudged him with the rifle. Pete lowered his head and moved quickly to the chopper. The morning sky was a brilliant golden reddish hue. Pete recognized the red sky in the morning as a warning to sailors of troubled seas ahead.

He found a bench seat on the port side and strapped himself in place. He was given ear pieces that were silently muted from the ICS. The wash from the chopper blades at lift off was refreshing. The dawn of a new day would come as they raced toward D.C. There was no escape now. Pete was trapped in the fight of his life and where was Price?

Washington DC - The Pentagon

With a Marine escort LCDR Peter E. Tierney was escorted through the long-tangled halls of the Pentagon. Normally these halls were lined with staid facial expressions, flat affects and head down postures. However, today the expressions became suddenly alert and inquisitively turned at the novel sight of a Naval Officer under guarded escort. These halls usually hummed with suppressed rumors and vibrated with a restrained decorum. Today was different. A Navy Doctor was under escorted guard. Imaginations soared. How could a Navy Doctor so sharply step on his sword?

They entered the chambers of the Bureau of Medicine and Surgery. The motif proved disappointing. Pete had anticipated a grandly appointed showplace commensurate with such a powerful office, but it was soberly disappointing. Nothing approaching the symbolic appointment of the quarter deck on any major U.S. Naval man of war.

He was momentarily guided through a side office while the guards remained outside the double doors. He was briefly alone when a side door opened, Admiral Hayes strode in. He turned toward Tierney, looked him in the eyes with penetrating rage, turned away again and then peered vacantly out from the 4th floor window. Pausing, Hayes then turned abruptly, tossing his cap bearing two rows of scrambled eggs toward the hard-back chair. The hat missed the chair and fell to the floor.

"Just what the hell do you think you were doing Lieutenant Commander Tierney?"

"I'm reporting as ordered, Sir!"

"Lt. Commander, may I set the stage for your prompt accurate cooperation, and complete, total compliance. You, Sir, with some squalid halfwit scientist, breached the security of one of the highest top-secret areas. You were not authorized access to this area. Even in your present capacity with only a confidential clearance, had certainly NO NEED TO KNOW! What the hell do you think you were doing?

Besides that, you evaded arrest and got your friend badly injured." "Price is alive! How is he? Where is he?"

Hayes ignored the question. Rather, he bent to fetch his gold leafed cover and began rapping it against his left hand. The hat repeatedly struck his palm.

"Tierney, do you realize the severity of these charges?" the Admiral admonished with growing annoyance. His dense grey eyebrows furrowed like a CNO clone of Admiral Zumwalt. "Are you really just another errant young staff puke, that doesn't understand the operational needs of the Navy?"

Pete learning Price was alive recaptured his composure and focused on the Admiral's words.

"Admiral, Sir, I am aware of what has been going on from the virology labs at Bethesda R&D, to the experiments in Cuba, San Francisco and now in the Kiva's of the New Mexico experiment."

"Who the hell do you think you are?" Hayes tossed his hat to the leather hard backed chair. It again bounced out and fell to the floor.

"Commander Tierney, we can and shall see that you are punished to the fullest extent of the Law. You will never know what hit you young man. You will never recover from this! You have no idea of the power of this office."

"Admiral, Sir, with all due respect, you are in no position to challenge me. The Navy will not be taking this situation to a court-martial. The Navy would be stupid to place such evidence before the scrutiny of public record. The Navy knows well enough how not to shoot itself in the foot, especially after the lessons learned from the USS Iowa incident. Sir, cover-ups don't work.

A few people in the Navy have learned, the public simply will no longer accept clandestine ops that threaten the health of our society! You need to be a bit more creative, Admiral!"

"Young man, you really do know how to make matters worse for yourself, don't you! You just mined your own harbor. Tierney, do you really believe anyone will ever believe you? There is no evidence to support your accusations. Even if we didn't officially go through a trial, you can be quietly disposed of in some high-risk encounter, or better yet, just simply lost at sea. We can easily arrange that or better, some hazardous special OPS for you, Commander. Maybe we can let you rot in the Amazon or freeze your ass in the Arctic. We can frag your butt sailor!"

"Admiral, Sir, to the contrary. No one will harm me! The entire record of this biologic viral leak and cover-up has left a legacy of death that spans the globe. The Agency has left a trail as wide and traceable as a trip to the bone yard. Sherman's march to the sea was subtle by comparison. Sir, you have created a legacy of destruction the world has never known. There is no way to cover it up"!

"If I'm harmed, or suddenly lost at sea, all this data will be released to the press. It will be selectively leaked, with names, places, and times. You sir, would do well to seek political distance and shelter from this storm."

"Tierney, I'm warning you, no one will believe you! We can destroy you!"

"Nearly everyone knows that something is terribly wrong with this epidemic. The data, the evidence is too compelling to dismiss. The biologic markers are right there to tell any intelligent searcher that the source is nothing less than a man-made biologic weapons leak. Besides the computer trail of Hypertext, if not hard Intelligence Libraries record the legacy. Sir, there is no question they will believe me. How I am treated will determine how fast this story is released, but it will be released. This political epidemic will be exposed whether I am here or not. This disease was no accident, it was no viral mutation! It was a calculated experiment injected into American homosexuals as a test population."

"Admiral, Sir, ordinarily I would say with respect, but your butt is in the sling, not mine!" Hayes turned toward the window overlooking the Potomac. He appeared controlled, his visible position of power commanded respect. He would not lose his composure.

"OK, Tierney, for the moment let's look at this more maturely, let us say, in a rational manner. Let's say just for argument's sake that you have discovered something we at BUMED needed to know about. We, of course, can't condone your breaching security to discover this, but we might be persuaded to...say...overlook your transgression. Am I making myself clear, Commander?"

"Yes sir, go on."

"You're a young man, with a whole career in front of you. We recognize the indiscretions of junior officers, as, well, simply part of the process of growth to more demanding and influential positions within Navy medicine. The Navy wants men of caliber, creative thinkers, leaders and managers. We believe a position might just appeal to you? Well, let's say that I can make your career take an accelerated pace to positions of incredible managerial power and influence. That fellowship in infectious diseases at Bethesda would be a sure thing. After that, maybe a teaching position, maybe a senatorial attaché or the diplomatic corps could be made available." "Go on, Admiral. As you know, Sir, I do love the Navy." Tierney was starting to enjoy the moment.

"Well, I can't be too specific, but I'm sure with a little time and cooperation, this entire episode can be smoothed over. I'm certain; you could become a visible leader for Navy medicine."

"Admiral, since I have gathered so much experience already, do you think I might get involved in the biologic weapon research arena?" Pete probed.

"Well, I'm sure we can consider that, Commander. Yes, hum...I'm quite sure we can check that arena."

"Sir, if I'm to become a player, I need to know what was the motive behind injecting the AIDS virus into the gay population? What was the purpose?"

Hayes studied Tierney's face. It appeared without expression. It seemed non-judgmental. His reddened eyes searched for clues. Could Tierney be trusted?

"You test me, Tierney. Why?"

"I deserve an honest answer. I have lost a friend and will lose two others. I need to know why!"

"Off the record then?" asked Hayes. Tierney nodded.

"The virus was designed to break the economic back of the Soviet Union. No one would have guessed President Regan's SDI would break their economic necks nor that the Berlin Wall would fall. The Cold War became history in a moment. None of us were prepared for the end. The virus was injected into the gays in San Francisco hidden within the Hepatitis B vaccination. It was a local experiment to determine how it might behave. Almost bordering on ethical, just an experiment you might say. Nobody ever expected it to get out of hand."

"We wanted to break the economic back of the Soviet Union. They had 25% of their GNP (Gross National Product) invested in weapons systems. They could not afford to lose another 10% of the GNP to the care of AIDS. We knew this as fact. We could have done it, killing their economy, killing their economy taking care of their people with AIDS. The virus was an economic weapon. It was a National Security Decision. It was only a level II contagion."

"Admiral, Sir, will it allow me to explain the death of my friend, CDR Charles Brewer? Will I be able to explain the loss of his death to his wife Nancy and her child? Sir, will I be required to deceive his wife? Admiral, I also need to know how I will explain the deaths of a million Americans from a man-made disease. Will I manage with the power of this new office you'll create for me?"

"You, self-righteous bastard! Tierney, you're as good as dead. So is your friend, Price!" Admiral Hayes turned to the doors.

"Guard, Guard! Get this man out of here! Get him out of my sight! NOW!"

The double doors slammed open, two marines bolted into the room, approached LCDR Tierney on either side and cautiously grasped his arms. He offered no resistance. They turned him toward the side exit and escorted him from the room, through the small foyer and down a side stairwell to a waiting Brig van. This path avoided the obvious parade through the long gauntlet of prying eyes of the Pentagon.

No sooner was Tierney's departure final, and then Rear Admiral Hayes got on the phone to The Network Agency (TAN).

177

"He knows everything!" said Hayes.

"Then he's a dead man," was the nameless and dispassionate response on the other end.

"Tierney is no dummy; he's already recorded his findings. If he disappears or dies, it goes to press," said Hayes. "It can't go to the Press!" he added. "All right, my wife - my reputation - how will I explain?"

"Tail him, record every conversation he has, every letter sent, every phone call made. We must find his contacts and then destroy the file. He may be bluffing."

Bluffing, Hayes had not considered that a possibility and he laughed with weak reassurance.

"Maybe he is really bluffing." The Admiral wanted to believe it. "He is already in the brig, so surveillance is hardly difficult."

"Close it out Admiral, close this issue out!"

"Admiral, by the way, we can make the arrangement! We could separate him from the Navy and then destroy his reputation. Killing would be much easier. It is important, Admiral, that you avoid a court-martial. It is far too public!"

With a sudden click, the phone conversation was terminated. The Admiral felt a cold wet sweat pouring down his neck. Wiping his neck and forehead, he turned to look out the window, noting the Marine van drawing away with Tierney in secure custody.

Admiral Hayes knew that avoiding a court-martial and the public record was paramount to security. He knew the best way was to simply separate him and then destroy his reputation, if time and circumstance allowed, waste him.

No one man could possibly be such a threat, he assured himself. *Charles Brewer never was a problem; Tierney won't be either. After all the man has no power, he has no credibility.... He's just a damn doctor, an errant staff puke, what possible trail could we have left?* He thought. *What possible threat could such a simple doctor be to our plans? Biologic markers, Hyperlinked computer trails, medical literature trails. Who else knows about Cuba, San Francisco, and New Mexico? What the hell is driving this guy? I must find a way to keep this information from the Navy Surgeon General. Naval medical officers simply do not go to the Pentagon under military guard without lots of high visibility. The rumor mill will quickly capture attention. How will Ideal with the questions* he asks himself?

The Admiral suddenly realized that he was personally at much greater risk than Tierney had suggested. He was beyond his authority in this area and had already shown his hand.

The Agency knew he broke the code and security protocols by calling The Agency Network. There would be no backing away from the Surgeon General, as he was excluded from this informational loop. The Navy wasn't backing this Black Project, only those within the Agency were. Hayes opened a closet for his jacket. He studied himself in the full-length mirror. His reddened eyes betrayed him. His lips quivered.

He witnessed a dead man in the mirror, with no way to change the reflected image.

Hayes realized he was now a target of the Agency. He had enough experience in the Navy to know a dead man when he saw one. The paper trail would lead straight to him, especially for his support of the Cuban experiment and knowledge of the experiments in the Pueblo Kieva's of New Mexico. He was a targeted dead man even if he got Tierney to divulge his publishing connection.

The Admiral felt a damp chill of the night air and sensed there was now more to fear than the early arrival of winter. His official chauffeured white four door Chrysler bearing a gold star on a blue flag fastened to the port bumper arrived at curb side. The engine was left running warming the interior.

His long-trusted driver and attaché, Capt. Samuel, greeted him, opened the left rear door for him, and closed it behind him.

"Anything I can help you with Sir?"

The Admiral didn't respond, just climbed in the back seat and placed his briefcase next to himself.

Capt. Samuel walked to the electronically activated gate thirty yards away. As he inserted a coded identification card the door swung wide. He returned to the silent atmosphere in the freshly cleaned sedan.

He had never seen the Admiral so withdrawn. His usual commanding presence kept danger at bay. Samuel glanced in the rearview mirror. Hayes was rubbing his grey eyebrows peering out the window at passing traffic.

Samuel entered the beltway traffic pattern. They were only a few miles from the Pentagon when it slowed to a crawl, bumper to bumper. Traffic advisors on the radio offered no short cuts around the mess. They were better off on the METRO. Samuel was distracted by a flash in his side mirror, a motorcycle darted between the traffic lanes of stalled cars, the only way to travel in such a mess he thought. The air conditioner was on high with a low fan setting. The radio was off at the Admiral's insistence. They were struck in traffic and the blue flag with one star did not help. The digital clock read 1745. A motorcyclist wore a grey helmet with a pitch- b l a c k visor. Looked muscular and wore a zippered coverall as he later recalled. Nothing seemed unusual for the rush hour.

The rear window exploded shattering the glass. There was a second blast. Samuel hit the brakes and turned right hitting an adjacent Ford pickup. Horns screamed out from all sides. The front hood and right fender was smashed as Samuel's head rebounded from the impact. He wasn't sure what happened.

"Are you alright sir?" he asked.

"Sir, are you alright?" He couldn't see the Admiral in the rearview mirror and the horns masked his voice. He turned his head toward the right placing his forearm on the seatback.

The whole back seat was filled with glass and blood spattered across the seat and opposite door. He opened his door and jumped out to open the rear door. The window was gone. The metal frame peppered with shot. He opened the door. The Admiral fell, slumping to the yellow separator line. The left side of his head was gone.

"Oh shit! Admiral, Admir..,as he searched for his carotid pulse. Captain Samuel looked up the roadway. Traffic was jammed as if glue had fallen from the sky. The motorcyclist darted across three lanes onto the right-hand shoulder and exited on the off ramp.

Samuel went for his cellular phone but knew there was nothing else that could be done. The Admiral in his charge was dead.

Chapter 11

Held in Quarters Restricted Officers Quarters Marine Barracks, Washington D.C.

"Lt. Commander Tierney, you have a visitor," said the Marine guard. "He is a retired, Commander Legé from Washington State."

"Thank you, corporal, send him in."

"Pete, it's really good to see you, but what the hell happened to you? Can we talk?" asked Legé.

"I'm not certain of anything Phil, except that you are here. I need some expert advice. You must have caught the red-eye special."

"Did you see this morning's Washington Herald? There was a drive by execution near the Pentagon."

"No," replied Pete, "fill me in, let me see that," he snatched it up and looked for better lighting.

It was Rear Admiral Hayes!

"Shit, I just talked to him last night!" Pete exclaimed.

The whole of D.C.'s beltway was awash with rumors, according to the newspaper. Most of the rumors tried to answer the question,

Why was an Admiral in BUMED (Bureau of Medicine) assassinated? No one could possibly imagine a medical type knowing enough privileged information to represent a risk to anyone.

"Phil, we are not safe to openly discuss anything here," wrote Tierney on the edge of the newspaper.

"Wait here," directed Phil. "I learned this trick while stationed in Turkey."

Legé walked to the front of the restricted quarters and spoke with the Marine sergeant at the desk.

"The taxi driver will give you his car keys. His meter is running and we will be in the back of his cab. We need privacy to prepare a legal response. You can guard us while we sit in the back seat."

The guard nodded approval and rested his rifle with the piece at his side.

Tierney told Legé everything he could as time allowed.

"They just can't kill my friend Charles Brewer and get away with it. They almost killed Price. God knows how many have died from AIDS, maybe 300,000 by now and a million infected. They can't! I won't let them get away with it!"

"Admiral Hayes tried to bribe me!"

"That is obvious Pete," said Phillip, "only a select few in the upper echelons of the Navy are aware of what's going on here. Otherwise Hayes would not have been killed. My guess is, Hayes spoke of your meeting yesterday to someone in the Agency. The only reason you are even alive today, my friend is that you played the right hand."

Legé continued, "They obviously don't want publicity. They don't want any paper trail. They're stuck having left a trail, like a big ugly oil slick."

"Pete, your biggest risk will be trying to get the final chapters of this story to your source for publication.

"How are you going to get the story published?"

"The Agency will bug every call, check every correspondence analyze every cryptic event, maybe even past encounters, looking for your publisher. Killing your connected lady journalist will seal the leak and both your coffins. You're both as good as dead."

"If the Agency can terminate your contact with Shawn then my guess is that they will undercut the accuracy of your information. You know the drill. They'll try and make you look like a fool or an incompetent, if it's published. However, I'm convinced your accuracy will bear the test of public and scientific scrutiny." "What about this trial for breaching security of the top-secret quarantine experiment in New Mexico?" asked Pete.

"First, they can't try you without going to a court-martial as I'll not let you accept Non-Judicial punishment. Second, the top-secret experiment of Reverse Quarantine in New Mexico has the blessings of the Agency Network and select member of the military. It's an illegal black project and the Navy will not claim it as part of their sanctioned authority. It's not the Navy. It's the Agency. The Navy will distance itself. They want no part of this, and no part of you."

"From the Navy's standpoint, the sooner you're out of their hair, the better. We'll still have to play some legal moves, show that we understand the game being played," said Legé. "It would be helpful if your lady journalist had some influence with a senator or two."

"No, I'm afraid she has no such connections in high places."

Pete sensed he had to find Shawn quickly. He had to get Phil Legé to do some fast-talking legal work. He hoped the Agency would disappear now that he had legal counsel, but it was unlikely.

They discussed ways to approach Shawn, safe ways, low visibility ways. Phil felt he could safely make contact at the toll booth outside the Marine gate as it would not be tapped. Even if trailed by surveillance this would not likely be a traced call. He planned to deliver the summarized data describing the New Mexico experiment.

"Tierney, for the moment you'll be safe in confinement, under Marine guard. I'll do some leg work and prepare the information package for delivery. Once you contact Shawn, I can transmit it on a pulsed cryptic fax to her editor."

"Phil, I'm afraid you'll get her targeted for a quick kill with frequent phone calls. It needs to be hand delivered. I can't trust her from a distance. I need face time with her. After all, she turned her feelings off, instantly! I do not have much confidence, I'm feeling insecure, if you know my meaning."

"Doc, you might be right. There's no time for second guessing. Besides, I'm getting real sick of your lost lovelorn tales. There's a lot more at stake here than your damn feelings!

"You better get your head on straight, Pete. I didn't come all the way out here to listen to this shit! Screw your feelings, Tierney. Sort it out!"

"OK, Phil, OK, I'll do my best. I've come too far and there's nowhere else to go," Pete reassured Phil and remained silent.

They nodded understanding and opened the rear doors of the taxi. Tierney started to return under guard to his quarters while Legé talked to the taxi driver.

"Take me to the Office of the Judge Advocate General, and then we'll go back to my hotel."

"Wait a minute, driver would you give us some more time." "No problem, Mac, my meter is running, I've got all day." He pulled the collar of his jacket to brace his neck from the cooling autumn air mass and walked away from the taxi. The guard handed him the keys.

As they climbed back into the back seat, Phil asked, "Pete do you know anyone on the Hill that might play power broker, possibly someone like a congressman or a senator from your area?"

"The only person I know is 7th district Representative Fred McDewey, who is a self-proclaimed expert on AIDS in Africa, East Asia and the Pacific Rim."

"What do you think of him? Can we trust him?" asked Legé.

"No, my guess is that he's an insider to the Agency. Some time ago I met him at a bash in Seattle. He made some crack about Sand Point being part of a social experiment. I thought it was just the scotch talking, but the timing coincided with the old Madigan Army Hospital being considered for use as a quarantine holding station. The Sand Point Naval Station was on the chopping block, for donation back to the civilian sector," Pete recalled.

"It was the way he said it. Well, like this will surprise everyone. There was an off comment, something to do with social planning. I don't trust him! He spoke of the rate of AIDS in Uganda being controllable if only monogamous heterosexual couples used condoms for the next ten years. I couldn't believe the shit head felt that was a success story. Imagine, a stable rate of AIDS in married couples using condoms is considered a success. What totally misleading political jargon! Sex is the one pleasure of life in Uganda. Sex with a condom is like sex without sensory input… very tough to find pleasure. Mind you this guy is the unchallenged congressional expert on the subject. You can bet he has central information than is not obvious to us. No, I don't trust him!"

"OK, Pete, legally we have 72 hours in which some preliminary papers must be served. As a Naval officer, you must be formally charged with a crime to be held in custody. Once again, I don't think they will try via a court-martial, even under the cloak of closed proceedings. You could appeal any decision made forcing it to an open procedure, one of public record. Public attention is your ally, not theirs."

"What do you want me to do Counselor? They can screw with me, they could get to Shawn, and they could cover up the trail to New Mexico. A lot can happen in 72 hours!"

"Just let me sort out the options, Pete. I've had little sleep. I want to record our efforts to date and file some papers. As you realize, I'm probably targeted by the agency just for considering representing you. Just the association with you could get me killed. It will become obvious when and if I choose to represent you."

"What do you mean choose to represent me?"

Damn lawyers, thought Tierney, biting his lip with annoyance. He rubbed his neck. *I tell 'him the secret of the century and you consider representing me.*

"OK, OK, Phil, just give me your best advice. For now, I'll chill out, and stay calm with this gun slinging Marine grunt at my side." "Have a little faith, my boy. I know someone I can trust on the Hill. A salty old' Legal Eagle", I worked for some years back. We did some high vis work at the US Justice Department. He's on the Senate Judicial Committee and should know about 'Black Projects'. "Black Projects?" asked Pete.

"Yeah, the Bandelier Box on the mesa is a black project secretly funded and bypassed by the normal Department of Defense funding processes. This is Top Secret on the same level as Psychological Operations."

"A Senator Clarence Dowell, on the Senate Intelligence Oversight Committee, from New Mexico might be of help. Do you suppose he knows about this black project especially since it is in his own backyard?"

"Look, Pete, I've got to get moving. Don't worry. For now, don't contact your lady friend or anyone else you care about. Everything you do is monitored. You have time to think about ways to approach this while I try to position us legally."

"I don't like the odds Phil nor being held at gun point. Just get me out of here! Do you think you can save my career? My father had almost twenty years as a Naval aviator, my two uncles were line officers in the Pacific theater. It's just Navy medicine that is all messed up. I'd like to save my career. It's kind of a family tradition.

"Within 72 hours they'll conduct a Pretrial Confinement hearing to justify holding you. They can't hold you without due cause. You're unlikely to be at risk of flight, and no one would expect you to engage in any serious misconduct, you know, threatening stuff. So, you're safe for the moment. Organize your thoughts and I'll get right back to you.

"First, I want to see if I can collect on an old debt from Senator Clarence Dowell. A gracious favor, as we say in the Orient. With his seniority, he probably has a stately home in the suburban D.C. area. I'll be able to find him."

Lege' paused and looked worried. He frowned and tossed his yellow legal papers into the briefcase on the bench seat beside him. He closed the briefcase with a final snap.

"By the way, did you list Shawn on your Page Two, in case of death?" Lege' asked.

Everybody knew that a Page Two was the official Navy form listing significant others like children and spouses who would inherit insurance money if the sailor died. Page Two was privileged information. Some guys listed a mistress as they knew that no one would ever get to see the document. It had tightly controlled access and was protected by privacy acts. Not just anyone could get to this information, but the Agency could.

Pete looked away trying to avoid the question. He instantly realized he had placed Shawn in harm's way. He had listed Shawn, with her address and phone numbers. The Agency would have no trouble obtaining this information. He couldn't protect her.

"Phil, I listed her on the Page Two."

"Ok, we'll have to live with it. We'll think of a way out. Got to go Pete, keep the faith." Legé hailed the taxi driver who was pacing the curb. Pete watched the taxi as it sped away with his tennis friend plotting the next move.

The cold air was refreshing as the guard briskly ushered Pete back to his quarters.

They still might not be able to find Shawn if we're careful how we contact her. She was rarely at home and had recently been in the hospital. I must give Legé her new address. He must warn her!

Damn, he didn't tell me where he's staying. Pete knew time was running out. He must contact her, but how?

Annapolis, Maryland

Nancy Brewer ordered a chicken teriyaki salad and ice tea. Granny C. had her favorite steak, eggs with an English muffin, and a side order of pancakes. She had a bit of diabetes, was mildly overweight but looked great for seventy-three. She was quick to smile and easily bored. It was 10:45 and the breakfast menu was still available. The sidewalk Denny's restaurant was within three blocks of the Naval Academy. In the background, they could hear the cadence of midshipmen chanting while jogging in unison.

"What have you learned?" Granny asked.

Nancy took a deep breath. "I just read the testimony of a Norwegian Flight Surgeon, Dr. Johannesburg. He was sent with the marines on a humanitarian U.N. Mission to northwestern Cambodia. The Norwegians were sent to an area designated sector C. Their deployment occurred just after the Berlin Wall came down in 1992."

"Go on." said Granny. She glanced at her watch. It was 10:50 am.

"Well, as you know, Norway is sexually liberated, not many hang-ups, like in the U.S. Despite a tolerant liberated culture, the country only reported 268 cases of AIDS. There was no difference compared to the U.S. All were in homosexual males, I.V. drug users or blood recipients from the above. There was no 'explosion' of heterosexual AIDS as the statisticians and social planners predicted."

"So where do the marines fit in?" asked Granny.

Nancy took a sip of her iced tea, looked at her watch. It was 10:53. "After the marines returned from Cambodia there was a significant change in the disease spread. Heterosexual women started to represent a larger percentage of the pie. The young flight surgeon pleaded with the government of Norway did blood tests before and after the deployment. The officials refused, saying they had to protect the privacy rights of the marines."

Granny played with the white salt shaker containing rice to absorb the Chesapeake humidity. She aligned it like a chess piece next to the matching pepper shaker.

"Granny, half the Norwegian marines were given liberty call in Bangkok before they entered Cambodia. The government knew eighty five percent of Thailand prostitutes were infected with the AIDS virus."

"I don't believe it." Granny reacted.

"They call 'them Female Sex Worker's, FSW's." Nancy added.

"You mean, the Norwegian government knowingly allowed the Marines to get infected? Then they returned home with the infection to their wives."

"Yes, and under the guise of privacy rights. I would have suspected the issue of privacy to be the hallmark of American thinking, not Norwegian. Since when has privacy become an international slogan?" Nancy brushed bread crumbs from the table like distractions from the big picture. "The details are clouded, but we know expansion of the epidemic in Norway is clearly traced to the marines returning home from the U.N. Mission. Dr. Johannesburg did all he could, to s t o p i t , b u t the powers that be would not listen."

"Sound familiar?" Granny nodded and paused.

"Yes, just another government tactic, encouraging the epidemic to fester and expand."

"Now, we have the data of tainted blood transfusions in France, Japan, Rumania, Germany, and the United States. We have the Uganda connection and now the Norway connection." Nancy summarized with a tone of sarcasm.

"Have you been able to contact the New Mexico Senator?" asked Nancy.

"No, but I've done some homework." Granny adjusted her split lensed glasses lowered on her nose and peered over the frame.

"I've learned a little of the local politics from West Virginia. Senator Rockefeller is the leading proponent of health care reform. He wants to push military medicine to the forefront for humanitarian efforts abroad." Granny paused and leaned forward on her elbows.

"There is a hell of a lot of funding available in Refugee Medicine. With the cutbacks, the military is hungrily looking for ways to save their jobs."

"Sounds like they're going to use medicine as a tactical weapon system." said Nancy.

"Exactly, military medicine is becoming the political tool for applied international power since we've run out of enemies threatening American borders. Refugee medicine is the foothold in the door for applied foreign policy, the Trojan horse of the 90's. It's becoming a national security issue."

"Money is in short supply and the military is happy with a mission, any mission. Makes sense." said Nancy.

"There is more at stake than an epidemic. There are budgets crashing, bases closing, carriers going to the floating museum and jobs lost. Peace can kill the economy. "We can't afford peace." Granny added.

She looked at her watch and took a sip of her orange juice. The waitress was coming with an aluminum serving tray at shoulder height. "It is part of Truman's law, "if you can't convince em, then confuse em. Today's facts are tomorrow's fallacy." Granny stressed. "Medicine has become a tactical weapon system. Who would of thought, in our lifetimes?" Nancy glanced at her watch. It was 1100 hours.

The Denny's restaurant had made the fifteen-minute service deadline. There would be no more free meals.

CHAPTER 12

Understanding at The Vietnam Memorial their whaling wall

Washington D.C.

Fall had come with a vengeance; the leaves were swirling around with orchestrated chaos and moist winds off the Potomac added a biting chill to the evening. The Vietnam monument gave a cold finality to the coming of nightfall. It formed a stark setting for Phillip Legé to meet with Senator Clarence Dowell.

"What's this you say, Legé, an experiment in quarantine going on in the Pueblo village outside of Los Alamos?"

"No, Senator an experiment in reverse quarantine and social deception." "What makes you think I don't know about this project?" he added with an air of annoyance and growing hostility. "Nobody in my state does anything without my knowing."

Legé was confused. *First Dowell suggests he knows what is going on, but doesn't. His body language says no. I bet he doesn't know anything.*

"Senator, we have ample evidence demonstrating, No, we have clear convincing evidence of a black project, in your back yard at Los Alamos. There are a select few who are informed; my guess is that you are not one of them. Those that are included are called The Agency Network, TAN. It functions within a subtle subculture of government. It is not a legal organization nor officially recognized by our government. It makes decisions for mass global and national immunization programs, and with the experiments of quarantine in Cuba has expanded its goals. It has been instrumental in orchestrating international conflicts between prominent and respected international groups such as the Pasteur Institute and the US contingency in the AIDS testing market. It plays on social conflicts."

Phillip paused. Dowell looked frightened - his intensity stiffened. The toothpick in his mouth stopped moving and lay passively on his lower lip. He attempted to speak, cleared his throat and paused again.

"Sir, you should not feel professionally offended. You were kept in the dark about these unethical projects. This started as a monstrous mistake, a miscalculation. It has now become a global epidemic. You want distance from it, not familiarity."

We know only a small amount of what has happened, but I have a client, a Navy doctor, who has discovered the cover-up while trying to solve the killing of his friend."

"Sir, The AIDS epidemic is man-made. The New Mexico experiment is an attempt to isolate a select population of the Agency network from the wrath of this disease. The command center at Mesa Grande was coordinated in your state because of the proximity of major institutions of higher learning, experimental test sites, in military establishments. It's si m pl y a pe rfe ct place for secret experiments using political science methods."

"What do you want from me?" the Senator asked as he braced himself against the brisk, winter winds.

"First, I need your support in protecting my client from Navy prosecution. Second, we must make public these events. This publication will be made through a reliable source that cannot be disclosed. The story will be leaked through a respected newspaper outlet. We need you to add heat and credibility to the investigation, by publicly asking probing questions to expose these experiments in

191

New Mexico. We need your influence to stay the legal hand of the Pentagon and to place the kind of pressure on them that they will understand."

"I want to meet this Navy Doctor!" insisted Dowell.

"That will be easy to arrange, Sir! Right now, he's held in quarters in D.C. charged with breaching top secret security, but that will be hard to prove, especially if the black project itself is secret. If they can't admit it exists, then how can it be breached?"

"You've been away too long, Counsel. There are ways to get rid of Navy doctors that are an embarrassment. And, it does not require paper trails. I hope you haven't forgotten some of those lessons since you retired from the Navy."

The senator paused.

"Legé, I somehow knew your leaving the beltway madness would come back to haunt me. You should have stayed a Navy pilot," he said sarcastically. "You were less dangerous as an aviator."

Dowell had a deep sense of gratitude. He had been left out of the informational loop, left out because he was an honest man, a rarity on the hill. Dowell admired and respected Legé's insights.

"You can count on me Legé. Keep me informed of your plans," said the Senator. He then added after reflecting, "There are a great many secrets here. Anything can happen secretly in Virginia, Maryland and D.C. Langley is a great location for clandestine activities.

It's a rustic setting, dissolved w i t h in trees, headquarters of the CIA, including a special library in the woods. Your young doctor may not be the only one who has become suspicious. Others may be tracking the same problem and we are not aware who they are." Legé nodded in agreement and understood that his message registered with the Senator. He judged Dowell as an astute statesman and a powerful man.

Dowell pressed further, "Legé are you aware of what's going on at the Armed Forces Institute of Pathology? It's a huge complex at Walter Reed and the only nuclear bomb proof building in Washington D.C. The walls are six to twelve feet thick - in a huge concrete bunker. The only comparable structure is the Navy hospital in Sigonella, Italy. Sigonella is the blood bank for the entire European theater storing 40,000 units of blood. Has this Navy doctor, done any snooping around at the Armed Forces Institute of Pathology?

I'd follow that trail if I were him."

"Senator, I don't know if he's had a chance to get there. He obviously will not be able to extend his investigation further."

"Senator, you need to inquire about the Armed Forces Center of Medical Intelligence in Fort Detrick. It's loaded with black projects and we can't get access. Tierney could not get near it and the CIA probably can't get into it either."

"You're quite right Phillip. I may need to put my nose in that hornet's nest myself."

It was getting dark and they started to leave the black marbled Vietnam Wall that had allowed a nation to begin healing. It provided a similar site for morning and grief filled prayer not unlike the Wailing Wall in Jerusalem. They walked briskly in opposite directions, the names and rows of names passing by in a shadowy blur, like the nameless already lost to the epidemic.

Phillip felt secure that Senator Dowell did not know about the project in New Mexico, he also felt that the senator would be politically supportive and would be catalytic in the investigation. He simply could not have known about the experiments surrounding quarantine. Dowell had been excluded from the information loop.

Phillip made an amendment note: *.I will need to coach the Senator before he goes public. Having him visit Tierney, while in confinement would be the high visibility we need.*

It might cause TAN to reflect on its own security. It will send a message to those that can brief the Senator. He learned this first hand from Tierney, not to make assumptions regarding inside information, e.g. a viral leak causing AIDS.

Lege' knelt down next to the Memorial Wall before his departure and ran his fingers across the deeply etched stone. It was dark, and he didn't need to see, but caressed the name... **Damitio.** He was a high school friend that never returned from Viet Nam. Were it not for such a friend, he would not have survived the ejection from his crippled A-6 Intruder. Lege' knew what it meant to owe his life to another. He worried of Tierney's survivability.

Annapolis:

Nancy Brewer was emotionally unsettled. Her anger had calmed some since the funeral. A smoldering distrust of any government agency remained suppressed, just below the surface. She had relocated to Annapolis, Maryland into a second level three-bedroom apartment complex that was close to her family yet far enough away.

It was 10:00 on the first Saturday morning of the month. There was a knock on the door. In winter blues Lt. Deborah Krane introduced herself. She was a legal officer who said she represented the forensic pathology department of the Armed Forces Institute of Pathology. She flashed her I.D. card.

She was an attractive woman except for her eyes and a smirk cornered in her lips that suggested more than the words she spoke.

"Mrs. Brewer, we are deeply saddened about your husband's death."

Nancy nodded and stood in the doorway for a prolonged moment of indecision. She realized she was blocking the door, but then invited the Lieutenant inside. It was her social habit to offer a cup of tea. She recognized the legal insignia above the two stripes on her sleeve. "We know you have not received any financial c o m p e n s a t i o n or benefits since the funeral," she explained. "The suicide note had prevented the activation of the SGLI Insurance for $200,000, and all benefits were placed on hold pending the decision of legal counsel and the benefits department."

"Yes, I'm aware of the lack of support by the Navy, Lt. Krane!" Nancy responded with an edge to her awakened bitterness. "Why are you here?"

"Although your husband died under less than honorable conditions, we have been asked to reappraise your husband's overall Naval commitments. On behalf of the US Navy, I am prepared to reinstate all your benefits as a surviving widow."

"Lieutenant, you're not suggesting for a moment that I am not a surviving widow, are you?"

"Mrs. Brewer, I must remind you, committing suicide is a crime in the military. It's officially considered destruction of government property. Need I remind you that we have absolutely no legal obligation to reinstate any benefits! I don't wish to be harsh."

Nancy again noticed a subdued smirk in her facial muscles. It appeared the Lieutenant was enjoying herself.

"What is it that you want?" Nancy asked again.

"We wish to reach a mutual understanding and that you will accept these benefits as an expression of our support for the family of CDR Brewer."

"So... go on, Lieutenant!"

"And we want a mutual understanding. We want to see you redress your interest in the autopsy performed on your husband. This is merely a formality, you understand. Often, it's necessary to sort of allow the grief process to take its course before we terminate the case, rather, the investigative procedure."

"Well, Lt. Krane, I'm not at all certain I understand your suggestion. It seems to me if we have an understanding as you call it, that I should understand, but I don't."

"Mrs. Brewer, I have been given the authority to reinstate your benefits as a surviving Navy widow. To do this my command needs the assurance that you will not continue to press for the autopsy reports or the reason he committed suicide. We are willing to settle this matter right here and now. Your child will have the financial security of knowing their father provided for them. Of course, that includes educational benefits that are due when a military member is killed in the line of duty."

"Then he was killed while serving his country. It was not suicide!"

"That is not what I meant, Mrs. Brewer. Officially your husband committed suicide and all the pathology reports will confirm this fact. We are willing to overlook this tragedy as a suicide. It is not unusual to change the paperwork to reflect a loss of life while in the service of the country. For us it is a mere paperwork formality." "The pathology report has confirmed this as factual?" "Mrs. Brewer, you're being difficult."

"Should I have a lawyer here to help me?"

Krane's eyes narrowed and pierced Nancy's question with professional ridicule. "No Madam, I am a lawyer. You can trust me!"

"Are these the papers to sign?"

"No ma'am, just your verbal agreement will suffice as our agreement. This tragedy will pass and I can advise and convince higher authority of your sincerity in this matter."

"Is there anything else, Lieutenant?"

"No, we just don't want to drag your husband's reputation and name through the legal process. It might appear unseemly."

"Lt. Krane, this has the ring of a bribe to me? Are you quite certain I should not have a lawyer present?"

There was no answer from the Lieutenant. Rather there was deafening silence as the two women appraised each other's position while sipping tea.

"May I consider this proposal over the next three or four days?"

"Well, certainly, of course. In the meantime, I have the authority to pay you your husband's back salary and for the next month which is $35,000." She opened her brief case and it was filled with small bills.

"Lieutenant, I will think about your offer. In the meantime, I have no trouble accepting his wages as they are due to me and our child."

The Lieutenant was stunned. She had been instructed to get a commitment not give the money away. She arose in silence, swallowed, and readjusted her uniform. She felt she had been trained to be quick on her feet.

Well maybe she could explain this to her command. After all, she succeeded in part. If not, she could concoct a story that might sell while she drove back to Washington D.C.

"All right, Mrs. Brewer, I'll give you three days."

Nancy escorted her to the door. She watched the white Chrysler turn the corner. She walked straight into the kitchen and phoned Granny C. As she dialed she recalled Lt. Krane's vehicle did not have an official USN license plate.

"Sounds like a bribe to me, Nancy. You got to be very careful. Do you have a lawyer?" asked Granny.

"Just come over, for all I know my phone is bugged. No, on second thought, I'll come over there and maybe we can talk more freely. Give me 20 minutes!"

When she arrived, Nancy was not in the frenzy Granny expected. Rather there was a smile on her face and an intensity of purpose in her eyes. She exuded the confidence that comes with insight. It was as if a weight had been lifted from her shoulders.

"What happened, Nancy, what happened?"

"The Navy is trying to bribe me. Keep me out of the investigation around Charles' death. Pure and simple, it was a bribe. They killed Charles and want to shut me up. They admitted, in an off handed way, Charles was killed. They don't want me nosing around stirring the pot. It sounds like the autopsy report was doctored. That lawyer tried to bribe me. She was working on her inner bitch."

"So, what are you going to do, Nancy?"

"I thought about my options while driving over here. Say no and risk getting killed and leave my daughter orphaned, or say yes, take the money and keep snooping, while maintaining a low profile. Then, find a lawyer."

"How can you possibly do that?" Granny responded.

"I'm not sure I can do anything. I can only hope to buy some time, hope to uncover something tangible. And God, I've got to find Peter. I know he was searching in Cuba and I know he is in danger. At least I know Charles was killed, and never doubted that he was straight.!" She paused, turned away scolding herself in silent doubts as she asked, "Why did I have two blood tests to prove to myself that I was not HIV positive?"

She looked in the mirror, and a pulsating torrent of tears followed. Mrs. G. held her closely.

"Something will break child, but right now you need a lawyer!" "I must find Peter. Shawn Carole might be able to find him." "You're better off with a lawyer. Does Shawn know a lawyer?"

"I don't know, but Pete knew a lawyer, a tennis friend, a Frenchman, Phillip Lege' I think. How could we find him? They played tennis at the local racquet club in Bremerton and Seattle."

She picked up the phone and called directory assistance getting the phone number. She called the racquet club and asked for the phone number of Phillip Lege.

"We have a member by the name of Phil Legé, but we can't give out phone numbers. We must protect our member's privacy," responded the clerk with a protective lilt to her voice.

Nancy pulled out her personal directory of the area and was unable to find his name. She slapped her forehead; "I forgot, he's retired and no longer practices law."

"If he's retired, doesn't practice law, how can he be any good to you Nancy?" asked Granny. "He knows Peter. He might know where he is. If Pete were in trouble he could use Legé for advice. I'm absolutely sure of it."

She looked up Shawn Carole, no listing, and she called directory assistance in the Seattle area. The listing was in Queen Anne area

under S.N. Carole. She called and left a message. Nancy was
certain it was Shawn's number as Pete's voice made the recording.

Do you have a friend in Keyport we can call and have them go to
the tennis club, take his name off the roster?" Granny suggested.

Nancy called Mary Rush in Keyport, a close neighbor she
could trust.

"Mary, I need you to go to the Bremerton Racquet Club and get
the phone number of a Phil Legé. You must pretend you're
interested in joining the club. You'll probably get a tour of the
place, and like most clubs the tennis members will have a Find a
Partner Bulletin Board. His name should appear in the same area as
Pete's name, sharing a common level of play. I desperately need
Legé's number. Can you do that for me?"

"Piece of cake, call you right back," said Mary with enthusiasm.

Granny was excited with the idea of an information search and
started to advise Nancy of options. "If this threat by the Navy lawyer
was an empty threat, then you would be making concessions that
aren't necessary."

"You better explain that" Nancy probed. "OK, well, if this truly
was a suicide, then it could be argued that Charles lacked legal
responsibility for his actions. If that were upheld, then you would
not be threatened with the loss of indemnity compensation. In
short, you cannot be responsible for your husband's crime. Either
way it would become an empty threat, an empty bribe."

"You're absolutely right, Granny. I need a lawyer, but I need
one I can trust."

The phone rang and it was Mary. She had Legé's phone number.
She laughed, it went exactly as planned. Phone numbers were posted
publicly for everyone to see. She was lucky. Her escort at the club had
to excuse herself to use the restroom. She returned and surprised Mary
as she was closely scrutinizing the bulletin board. She asked what she
was looking for. Mary had fun with just about everything. She said
she was looking for a male partner that might play at her level.

Nancy immediately called Legé's home and was disappointed
to get his answering service. She left an urgent message and her
phone number.

"I need to find Pete Tierney and have critical information about
the death of Charles and this epidemic."

CHAPTER 13

Senatorial Influence

Senator Clarence Dowell arrived at Marine Barracks Washington D.C. The trip was not scheduled on the calendar so no one on Capitol Hill is aware of his itinerary including his secretary. She knew only that he would be out of the office all afternoon. The arrival of the Senator was not to be secret much longer. A dark sedan arrived at the Marine Barracks with the senator.

The gate sentry was startled and promptly allowed his official passage through the gate. It was a short drive before the limo arrived at the Officers Restricted Barracks. These huts were 1940 vintage, all white wood structures with a well maintained simple utilitarian front lawn and shrubs. The Marine sentry called security and made certain the Officer in charge was briefed on the senator's arrival.

Pete responded to the knock at the front door and was stunned to find a senator seeking his audience. Certainly, word would quickly spread up the chain of command to the base CO the rumor mills of D.C. would come alive and stirring with questions. The Pentagon bristled with attentive sensitivity to any Congressional inquiry. Pete and the senator would not be free to speak openly in this environment.

"Senator, it would be safe for us to speak freely in your car, I learned this in Turkey," Pete said with a wink. "Have you been speaking with my attorney Legé"?

They walked to the dark sedan, the driver was excused and both Pete and legal counsel sat in the back seat, across from each other.

"The windows are reinforced, and buffered to prevent sound vibration off the glass," the senator reassured Pete. "Some CIA filter he explained. I was better in political science than science," he added.

Pete nodded and smiled with approval.

"Commander Tierney, I am here because Phillip Legé is a good friend. He tells me of your troubles in New Mexico. As the Republican Senator from New Mexico, I need to know what you discovered. What were you doing there in the first place?"

"How do I know I can trust you, Senator?"

"You don't know, but you need a friend in high places. Nobody else is coming. There are very few honest people on the Hill. Legé will petition the military court system in the morning to let you return to your command. That is about 24 hours from now, when you are released you will become one very big target!" "Yes, Sir, I understand," Pete said with a sigh of fatigue.

"You will probably be ordered to some strange, distant place where people end up disappearing. Your parent command will likely cut unkind orders. They will devise something to quiet you, or dispose of you without a shred of paper to mark your exit."

Pete knew what happened to sailors who fell out of favor and were listed as lost at sea.

"Senator, there's a lot more at stake here than simply my safety."

"Then tell me what you know, Tierney, or I won't be able to place the right pressures on the Pentagon and the other machinery within government."

It took over an hour for Tierney to explain the details of his discovery and of Price, Shawn, and Charles Brewer. The senator listened intently, rarely interrupted, and then only to guide his thinking.

"I believe you, Pete. What can I do for you?" asked the Senator.

"I need to find Shawn. I must see for myself how she is and I must get the rest of this story to her and her editor."

"I knew you would ask about her," said the Senator.

"After last night's meeting with Legé, I've had her traced and located. She's very ill and is dying of AIDS. She just survived another bout of AIDS related pneumonia. She had been hospitalized for the past two weeks. She was released five days ago and promptly flew to Boston. I don't know for sure why, but I'm led to believe that she is staying in a small flat in the borough of Chelsea."

"Oh, my God, she's really bad. I must see her." He shuddered at the thought of her losing vitality, her spirit, and life itself. "She doesn't look well, Pete. You had best be prepared, son."

"Will you help me get out of here?" he pleaded. "I'm so ashamed I doubted her!"

"You will have to await release from confinement. You will undoubtedly be escorted under military guard; well...I'm not sure quite yet where they will send you Commander."

"Senator is there anything you can do for me, like at the Pentagon or Naval headquarters?" asked Pete.

"Rest assured I'll create lots of visibility. The military will be very careful to treat you properly."

"Not good enough, Senator. With the whole of New Mexico on stage and in the lime light, Sir... publicly it will look bad. It could look even worse for you, even if you're only remotely aware of what's happening. They'll say you should have known or worse, did know. We must expose the agency network and I need to know what happened to Price!"

"Price was released from the hospital." Pete paused awaiting the Senator's response. The Senator's eyes revealed no alarm.

The Senator was too professional a politician to display a reaction.

"You have my pledge Tierney. Unlike most of Washington, my word is good."

Pete paused, "Senator, Price and I, recorded our findings, and transferred them to a data disc. It was Price's idea. It was transferred to our source in Boston, rather to Shawn's and her source. We forgot to bring a camera." "Is that to the Chelsea district?" asked Dowell, thinking aloud. He continued, "So that's how she fits in the picture. Your trump card, except, she is dying! Isn't that risky Pete? To invest

So much in a woman that's dying. I mean, if she is suddenly found dead, your story is worthless and you're as good as dead yourself!"
"I know, but she will get it printed. I trust no one else with the story, Itrust her with my life. You see, Sir, it's easier to understand if you knew her. She will get the information to the editor in Boston, whatever agency she uses! I'm sure she will make it despite her illness."

Pete added, "She already has the raw data of the past month." "If she's strong enough, I know she'll get it into hard copy and to the editor! Senator", Tierney paused, "I must find her before it's too late!"

"No, Tierney, you can't, the Agency is already scouring the country looking for her. You were foolish and listed her on your Navy personnel and officer record. They, however, were unable to find her because of her hospitalization. Privacy rights in regards to hospitalized AIDS patients are closely guarded. Even the gay activist and insurance companies have trouble getting that sort of information and resort to tapping into diagnostic codes to draw inferences. Tierney, the activists are snooping all the time."

Pete tried to ignore the details.

Well, if nothing else the timing of her discharge from the hospital may distract the Agency, thought Pete.

"Where do you think she might be in Boston?" asked the Senator. "I'm not sure. I've got a fax number, that's all. Her grandfather was a policeman that walked a beat. When she was a kid, she liked to visit him at the precinct and would pretend she was lost looking for Officer O'Malley. Of course, he showed up for his little granddaughter and after a mild perfunctory scolding, would take her out for an ice cream cone. It was a different time, a more trusting, peaceful time." "Senator, I suggest you start at the police station and look for some adjacent apartments, say near a deli, or ice cream store. That's in the borough of Chelsea," Pete added. "Would she use an alias?" Dowell asked.

"Probably O'Malley, or O'Killalea, her mother's maiden name," Pete said.

"We'll find her for you, Pete. We'll ensure the data is processed for printing. I will ask some pressing questions at the Pentagon and of the Department of Defense about this Black Project in my home state. That will get some butts twitching and heads rolling, you understand my meaning, son?!"

"Yes, Sir but, I must find Shawn, and Price," Pete insisted. "I'll talk with Legé and see if he can make some legal maneuvers. It will help if he files legal pressures in the system. The paperwork alone gets people excited and forces issues."

The door of the sedan opened. The Senator remained inside and Tierney shook his hand. He had a dry warm and firm hand. He felt he could trust this man!

Pete turned and walked back to the confinement shack. He noticed the sky; the clouds were billowing up in a dark anvil formation. His left shoulder ached from an old parachute training injury.

The barometric pressure must have fallen. We're in for a big storm, he thought, *a big storm!* He smiled.

Senator Dowell hit the chamber door to his office in the Capitol Annex and bolted through the waiting room. His secretary had seen her boss in action before but was startled as he stormed through the door. She followed him into his inner office where he tossed his winter coat across the room and missed the standing hanger.

He was a powerful man, in build, in manner and in political persuasion. Things happened the moment the inner office door closed. Almost like a conductor of an orchestra, the music began.

He rolled down a wall mounted map of New Mexico and adjacent states. He circled the Four Corners area with a grease pen, intersecting the North-West corner of New Mexico.

"Alyce, I want you to get me the head of security at Los Alamos Laboratory and the White Sands testing site."

She began recording his requests.

"Then I want to personally talk with a scientist held in jail at Los Alamos by the name of Raymond Price, and I want papers drawn up to place him under congressional restraint and my personal protection. If there isn't such a thing, then call someone like Justice Brown for the proper terminology, like an umbrella for a material witness, protective clauses, whatever it takes. It has got to be legal, so make it legal. Get Price moved to, he paused in thought, to, Oceana Naval Air Station. I don't want Price and Tierney in the same place. It's too risky. Put Price under security and I'll make a trip down there to meet with him." " Yes, sir." She kept recording.

"I then want the Secretary of the Navy, and the Chief of Naval Operations on the phone, and that's before I talk to the Surgeon General of the Navy, whoever the hell that's supposed to be. No, I want to see both of 'them in person, together. We'll test this accountability principal, this captain of the ship rhetoric. See if it really applies or is an empty theory. Put the Joint Chiefs of Staff on the, Things To Do List, but follow up with a call to the Center for Disease Control. I want to visit the director and get a feel for who is pulling political strings on this AIDS thing."

He paused in thought, paced around a coffee table.

"I want a list of every newspaper in the Boston area and I want the phone number and name of the chief editor. I also want to know who owns the newspaper and their political persuasion."

"Get me a map of Boston and a list of every police station, deli, and ice cream store and apartment complex in the city. First we'll focus on the Chelsea district.

"I also want to talk with Phil Legé. Let's find him. While you're at it, get the Commanding Officer of the Marine Barracks on the line." The Senator stopped pacing in circles and walked to the coat hanger, properly replaced his coat and hat, positioning them with a sense of finality.

The secretary looked dazed, overwhelmed despite her knowing Dowell well.

"Senator, are you sure you're, all right?" she asked.
"Thank you, Alyce, I'm quite all right!"

"Is not the shared four corners area of New Mexico, Colorado, Arizona and Utah where the Hantavirus epidemic broke out?" he asked.

Alyce shook her head, she hadn't heard about it.

"Senator, you're thinking out loud again. You know better."

"Yes, your right again, but I wonder if it's related." He stroked his grey mustache. *Forty-eight people were infected with Hantavirus and over fifty percent died. It was a virus discovered in the Korean War that infected thousands of our troops and almost fifty years passed before it inexplicably reappeared In the four corners area. Seems to me, they invented a cure within a month. Is that not a strange coincidence,* He thought?

Judicial Office Pentagon

Phil Legé approached the military court and filed a petition for dismissal on behalf of Lieutenant Commander Pete Tierney. The petition filed was for prompt dismissal of all charges, administrative discharge from the US Navy under honorable conditions. He would otherwise ask for a full official hearing, a general court-martial along with a complete Congressional Inquiry.

With this petition, Washington D.C. and the Pentagon became abuzz with speculation and rumor. The Washington Post had picked up a story of laundered moneys, something to do with black projects and viral studies of an experimental nature. It was quite enough to delay any military response of a more visible nature, such as, a special court-martial. It would warn the Flag officers to be attentive and avoid involvement, and it would make the agency's gurus think twice before reacting.

Chelsea, Boston

Shawn had not yet updated her editor as she had just received the newest disk via Fed-Ex from New Mexico. She sat at a breakfast nook adjacent to the apartment window. It was on the third floor and overlooked a black iron balcony railing, fire escape and the cornered alley way as it intersected the street below. It was a cloudy day with a brisk winter wind scattering debris below. The brick apartment building was 1920'svintage.

Surely, she felt, *her grandfather Patrick O'Malley had walked his beat along this street, night stick in hand, with his generous laugh. He probably would have greeted those kids she saw playing street hockey.* They avoided the narrow alley way as it was cobblestoned. Their play offered a pleasant, rhythmic change to the noise of passing vehicles.

She had unpacked two nights ago, but still was unsettled. It might have been her stomach normally troubled by flying eastward, but it was the illness consuming her. It would not let her stomach settle. Her cough had returned, and the drenching cold night sweats did not allow a semblance of rest.

She positioned her lap top computer near the jarred window where she could feel and absorb the breeze of life outside. The digitized material from Pete only spoke of him and Dr. Price meeting in New Mexico and planning some excursion into Pueblo dwellings. She knew they were in danger. She did not know of how much danger.

She felt the only way she could protect Peter was to record and edit the information. She must present it properly to her news agent at the Boston Globe. She knew it was dangerous and it would expose The Agency Network.

She felt her body dying rapidly. It was a strange sensation, like being imprisoned in a foreign, unfamiliar decaying cell. It was abandoning her, right before her very eyes. It forbade a full breath, it was a fatigue where life had lost its color and was being drawn into an agonal stage of darkness. There was a sense of unfinished business, an incomplete conclusion. She wanted to touch and feel Pete. She wanted to feel him inside of her again, but her love would not allow the momentary fleeting pleasure of such an experience.

It's better to die than to kill him with my love! She vowed. *Besides I'm too tired,* and she laughed inwardly. It simply is not meant to be.

She had lied to Peter about the blood transfusion in France. Yes, she had a transfusion, but it was after the tainted blood had been properly screened. She had ruptured an ovarian cyst, but it was not Pete's fault. So, it was only a partial lie. She just couldn't tell him that when she did the article on the Bastille, that it was a dark unlighted alley where she was raped. She knew the man was a criminal, who had escaped, smelled like a prisoner and a drug user. He had tracks all over his tattooed arms. She couldn't get away from his arms as he groped and tore her dress away. She knew she could never tell Pete what happened. It would kill him.

She placed her head into the pillow beside the bed and cried. It still hurt after so long a period.

An hour passed and when settled, she called her editor and arranged to drop off the latest material. They agree to meet that evening at an Italian Restaurant. She glanced out the window to check the alley way and intersecting street. She felt confident that no one knew where she was located, not her editor, not even Peter. She checked her watch. It was time to shower and get dressed.

Washington D.C.

"Senator, I have Los Alamos on the line." said Alyce.

The Senator picked up the phone. It was the Los Alamos Director.

"Sir, we have nobody here by the name of Raymond Price. What is the purpose of your inquiry, Senator?"

Dowell had an incoming caller ID system which gave a display of the source of the initiating phone call. The caller was not the New Mexico 505 area code, but rather was 301, which he recognized as Maryland. While continuing the call, he recorded the number; 301-555-1324 on a yellow sticky pad.

"I'm sorry, he said. You must have been misinformed. I made no such inquiry. Maybe you wanted the Democratic senator?"

After some trailing remarks, he hung up, knowing that he had not convinced whoever called. He chastised himself for not sounding more convincing. He never had a good poker voice, and he knew this to be a liability on Capitol Hill. Still, he felt it a clever verbal exchange.

"Senator, I have your private investigator, from Boston, Sir, on line one," Alyce, said over the intercom.

"Thank you, Alyce, put him on."

"Yes, I understand you have located Shawn Carole, and she is in a 3rd floor flat in the center of Chelsea. The three hundred block of Hamilton St., above the New Age Deli."

"Good work, thanks! But, I've another project for you. I need you to track down a phone n u m b e r ...301-555-3124".

"Senator, there is more."

"There is?"

"Yes, Sir."

"Well spit it out George!"

"Sir, The Department of Defense in 1992 requested $60 million for its research program and last June announced its intentions of building a laboratory for testing viral pathogens at the Dugway Proving Ground in Utah. Senator Erin Hutch blocked plans for the facility because of public pressure and fears of genetically altered pathogens with no possible cure."

"Are you certain of this George?" Dowell asked. "Yes, we've a solid paper trail. The army is now trying to find a place to develop a facility with less rigorous containment facilities. They're playing with anthrax, encephalitis virus and toxins." "I'll talk with Senator Hutch about this George." "Anything else I need to be aware of?"

"Yes, sir, The Government Accounting Office has verified that duplicate research is being done at the National Institute of Health and the CDC."

"George does the whole damn country know about this? Am I the only one left out?"

"No sir, the whole country, thinks it's got something to do with condoms, monkeys, accepting, homosexuals, you know, diversity. Some in the Pentagon and the President know what the hell is going on!"

"Shit, George! I can't believe I'm paying you for this!" "I know, my father told me, I'm not worth much!" "Nonsense George, you've been a great help. More than you know."

Senator Dowell hung up and recorded necessary information including Shawn's phone number. With a sigh of relief, he learned no one else appeared to have found her. At least there had been no visible surveillance. She also appeared very ill.

"Alyce, would you get Phillip Legé on the line for me?"

He will need this information and can pass it on to Tierney when they make contact. The fewer phone conversations we have the better, he thought, *especially since all calls will be monitored at the officer's restricted quarters in DC.*

"Alyce, have you heard from Dr. what's his name, the director from the Center for Disease Control? Dr. Ernest Brush, was a political presidential appointee to the CDC. Alyce just then received his call. She patched it to the senator. "Dr. Brush, I need to speak with you about a very important matter, when can we meet?"

"Well, Senator, I have an opening this week, say Wednesday?"

"No, Doctor, you don't understand. I need to talk with you now, rather openly and frankly, about some epidemiologic intelligence!" "Senator, what state did you say you represent?"

"New Mexico," he reacted with irritation.

"Oh, well sir. Can I can get back to you after; after say I well, say uh...clear my schedule. I think next week will be more open."

Brush's reluctance and hesitation said more than the conversation. Dowell read this as a delaying tactic that he feared would ultimately prove a long-term avoidance technique. *The doctor must be a TAN member*, the Senator thought. The doctor was a presidential appointee. There was no way to know how high this might go.

"Alyce, I want you to put that private investigator onto the Armed Forces Medical Intelligence Center at Fort Detrick. They deal in viral production stuff, black information. I want him to track its relationship to the Black Project near Los Alamos. Track it like a blood hound.

Understand? I need a wire diagram of who owns the CDC."

"Yes, sir, I'll get right on it."

"Alyce, I thought there was a Presidential executive order in 1969 by Nixon, discontinuing all offensive biologic weapon research. I want a copy of that order. I want to know who is acting outside this directive. Shit, someone is conducting a war without the approval of congress or the Presedent!"

"Yes, Sir,...But."

"Oh, I've gotten word that Price is on a helicopter for Oceana, as we speak." "Good, set aside some time for me to go to Virginia, by tonight." "On United?"

"Sure, why not, Alyce, that's fine."

Quantico, Marine Air Base, Virginia

Legé felt relieved that the legal petition had properly been filed within the allotted time frame. The hearing was docketed for tomorrow. He called the Senator and learned Shawn's whereabouts and health. The senator spoke of his suspicions toward the CDC.

Chelsea, Boston:

Shawn had some warm memories of a happier and more complete time, a more physical time when she and Pete were at the hotel in Seattle across from the new public Library.

She returned to the reality of the present moment. She was still at the breakfast nook overlooking the streets below.

It's no wonder I have these thoughts. She resumed her writing and wondered what was happening to Pete. What could he be doing?

She went to the kitchen for a cup of tea. It helped awaken her from day dreaming. She positioned her chair and returned to the work at hand.

The phone rang three times before she could get to it. It was Pete. His voice was breathless and she could hear him shiver in the cold. He was in a telephone booth and she could hear the heavy roar of traffic passing. Pete explained he was near Logan Airport.

There was a familiar ring of pleasure at hearing his voice, almost like being next to him sharing a pillow. The memories recalled scents that linger, including his voice that had a rhythm and harmony which she dearly loved.

She knew she had never stopped loving him. Each encounter built a new emotional bridge. Their love had deeper roots neither could explain. She just was no longer free to love him physically the way she wanted. The pain felt deeper than her heart could bear. They agreed to a meeting at an Italian restaurant in Chelsea.

Funny to find an Italian restaurant in an Irish neighborhood that had evolved into a Puerto Rican neighborhood. She laughed.

NAS Oceana

Oceana NAS was the east coast home of to the F-14 Tomcats and F-18 Hornets. Raymond Price had been placed under heavy security. He wasn't quite sure where he was, except he recognized the ocean as he flew in on an H-60 and saw a carrier USS Carl Vinson in port (CVN-70) which he recognized as at Virginia Beach. He didn't know why he was being moved and he was tired. The cots in the facility were hard and the chill unforgiving. Wool blankets helped. The view from his window exposed the Navy installation built in the 40's with an above ground steam pipe system for heating and Naval air presence.

There was a knock on his cell door. "You have a visitor, Doctor Price." said, the Marine guard.

A large man entered, with grey wavy hair, a mustache and a quiet manner but a bounding voice.

"Doctor Price, I'm Clarence Dowell, Senator from New Mexico. I'm a friend of Pete Tierney." He displayed a wide smile. "I know it's hard to believe, being from the government and all, but I'm here to help you."

"OK, go on Senator, what do you want?"

"Tierney is being held in custody at the Marine facility in Washington DC. I need to understand this man, Tierney. What drives a doctor to abandon everything including his career and follow an instinct that exposes the lies of respected medical institutions and the government?"

Dowell paused and studied Price, who appeared ill, very thin and fatigued.

"I also need to understand why if you know so much, they have chosen not to kill you?"

"I had little to lose." Price said as he measured Dowell.
He appeared honest and sincere.

"Senator, have a seat." They both sat down on the ends of the cot as there were no other accommodations. Price pulled a wool blanket over his lap.

"There was a Frank Olson who was killed by the CIA in 1953. The CIA denied involvement. Olson was a top germ-warfare researcher from Fort Detrick, New Jersey. He knew too much. Fort Detrick, is where the Armed Forces Institute of Medical Intelligence is located, and we know they later developed and produce the AIDS virus and swine flu." Price explained.

"Twenty plus years after the death of Frank Olson, President Ford invited the surviving family members to the White House and apologized for what happen to Olson. The government paid $750,000 to the family in hopes of settling their claim against the CIA. This is a matter of public record."

"We researchers learned from Olson to keep backup files on our work. Just in case something happened to us. I made it known that my research was placed in a safe deposit vault, to be opened if I met an untimely death." Price offered. "So that is probably why I'm alive".

"You're a political animal Price, covering your backside." said Dowell, with some admiration.

"I also suggested to them that I had AIDS, and I look like I've got it, so it's believable. They went out of their way to make sure I didn't die early, protecting me. They thought I was a goner more than once. The front-page story on the news had them sweating! "So Senator, I lied to stay alive, and gambled they wouldn't know how to challenge me."

"What about Tierney?" asked Dowell?

"Now Tierney, is a different matter. He is driven to find out who killed his friend, and deceived a nation.

He is trying to save his profession from the politicians who see it as just another industry to control. He has lost friends to this disease and he is pissed!"

Dowell nodded, stood and shook Price's hand.

"This experiment in New Mexico was dead wrong and not of my doing. I don't know this internal Agency group TAN, but I'll do my best to expose them. You have my word on it."

Price extended his hand and they felt each other's commitment with a firm handshake.

"The public's memory is very short senator. This is a real danger. I fear, the longer the epidemic continues to spread, the more the Agency bets there is less of an outcry. We are avoiding it becoming just a disease for the history books. And I don't want them to hide it under the cloak of racism or homophobia."

Dowell nodded in agreement. "A Short memory indeed."

"Senator, let me know how I can help?" asked Price.

"For the moment, I think it best to keep you under protective custody. I'll have them place you in more refined quarters and ensure you can contact me."

"I must catch the flight back to New Mexico. Tierney is probably heading to Boston to meet with an editor and his lady friend."

They shook hands again. Price felt secure in Dowell's sincerity. He knew that even senators were mortal, and it was late in the evening when Dowell arrived back at his office. He found Alyce busy at her desk. She was chewing an apple and pointed to a message on her desk.

Dowell scanned the note:

The Private investigator traced the phone number...to Frederick Maryland. He couldn't get inside, he needed a top-secret clearance to get into the Armed Forces Institute of Medical Intelligence.

CHAPTER 14

Boston Connection

Tierney and Lege' had agreed to meet at the Cucina de la Sorelli Italian restaurant at 8:00 pm on the west side of Clove street. Phillip Lege' assured Pete it would be safe and made every effort to keep secret the time and location. Pete would deliver the last bit of evidence confirming the Black Project in New Mexico. The Bandelier Wilderness reverse quarantine experiment would expose the Agency network and expose this subculture within government. Peter needed to find Shawn and objected in futility to a flight attendant for the delay in landing. The DC-9 was finally allowed to reenter the pattern and made final approach for landing at Logan International Airport. Shawn finished a shower at her Chelsea flat. She stood with a terry cloth towel wrapped around her, opened the towel and examined her figure in a full-length mirror. She had become accustomed to seeing her body dying before her eyes. Her skin drew tautly over prominent boney margins with atrophic muscle remaining. She felt life slipping from her frail body as she paused in witness to her own death reflecting in the mirror.

No matter, she was determined to appear presentable in Peter's eyes and to make the short journey from her third-floor flat without drawing unwanted attention. After all, it was not a great distance, only a brief walk, she assured herself. She felt secure in knowing that no one knew where she was located. Only Pete and her editor at the Boston Globe knew her whereabouts.

Pete hailed a yellow cab at Logan International and directed the driver to a department store in Cambridge. After paying the driver, he entered the storefront passing through women's wear, jewelry, underwear, and finally luggage before exiting out the back door. He hailed another cab for Chelsea. It took an hour of aggressive, testy Boston traffic before he arrived in the borough of Chelsea.

He paid the driver and found cover in the Carr Coffee and Book Store on Clove Street. Sitting on a worn leathered bar stool, he peered through the painted store front window, his elbows resting on the long bar abutting the window as he examined the street activity. A group of kids played street hockey several blocks away. The shouts of young voices and the clap of hockey sticks made it an ordinary Boston winter day. Growing dusk approached as shadows grew with long tangents and street lights began to glow.

The coffee was hot and steamed up Pete's glasses. He removed the horn-rimmed spectacles, studied the condensation and thought how different his career might have been if he had 20/20 vision. He would have become a pilot, a Navy pilot, just like his father. Wiping the moisture on a napkin, he realized that were it not for this physical malady, he would not have become a doctor. He surely would not have found himself in this political-medical mess. Replacing his glasses, he checked the time. It was already 7:30 pm and it had begun to rain. It was time to scout out the area despite the down pour. Pete left a small tip, paused and added more for fear the waitress might remember him. Doctors are notorious bad tippers and he needed to avoid his identity.

As he left the front door, he spotted a waiting cab and hailed the driver. The cabby reached over the front seat and flipped open the right rear door inviting him to enter. Pete slipped into the back seat finding protection from the cold rain. The penetrating chill distracted him momentarily from the urgency of seeing Shawn. He startled at the menacing appearance of the driver who wore a black leather jacket adorned with silver spikes protruding from shoulder straps and accompanied on the right with brass knuckles. Almost with exaggerated comic relief. Right out of the south side of Chicago thought Pete. A lesson learned long ago, never take the B-Train south.

"Where to, Mac?" he was asked with a New York accent.

"La Cucina de la Sorelli on Clove St. You look serious in that jacket," Pete probed almost in jest. "Keeps the bad guys away", he responded.

The man fumbled with his earrings and turned toward Pete, tossed his black hair, stiff from inattention. "Chelsea isn't what it used to be. I do what I do, to make a living. The gangs, the mob, drugs, the blacks, the Chicano's, I'm fair game and I must let them know it won't be easy. It's my business suit and it's worked so far!"

"Would you recognize a government agent, if you saw one?" Pete asked.

"In an instant, a piece of cake, they stick out like a hard on." He wiped his nose and stuffed an orange rag back in his jacket.

Pete knew he had the right cabby. He needed a professional, someone who was street wise and experienced. This cabby would do nicely. He could smell trouble without looking for it and there was plenty to find.

They drove in silence going in wide rectangles, initially going west, then north, then east and back south along Clove. The Italian restaurant appeared inviting and secluded. There were three cars, two foreign, one Mercury Cougar parked adjacent to the restaurant. The cabbie parked on the vacant east side of the street. Three men approached the restaurant, all from different directions. One dressed in a grey suit and red tie, carrying an umbrella, another in a dark trench coat with collar pulled up around his ears and carrying a briefcase. He stopped at a telephone booth, scanned the area and made eye contact with a third man who was black, his dress was threatening and ill kept. He wore a black watch cap pulled over his ears and a tattered plaid coat. They each nodded to each other so slightly and singularly began walking toward the restaurant. There was a fourth man, who appeared hurried, about 5' 10", wore glasses and carried a leather briefcase, had a bright golf cap and wool pullover.

Pete said, "The guy with the golf cap must be the editor from the Boston Globe."

The cabbie nodded. "What ya talkin about man? If the gofer is the editor then those three must be agents." He pointed.

A blue Chevy van with shaded side windows pulled up to an intersection, made a 180 degree turn and smoothly parked against the curb outside the main door to the restaurant. A small antenna slowly rose from the left side of the hood. It remained at idle and appeared menacing.

"Shit man, what's going down here?" asked the Cabby.
"Don't know. You better move on round the block." said Pete.
"Hey man, ya better have a big tip waiting for me."

He began driving slowly around the block again.

"Keep your eyes open for a young woman, about 37, wears glasses and is very thin." Pete instructed.

The cabbie shook his head, reached over to the meter and plunged a lever to double the rate. "That ok with you mister?"

Pete nodded approval as he rose again to a full sitting position. They rounded the north corner again and were coming back down on Clove. Everything seemed momentarily quiet. He noticed a slight black woman hurry to catch a frail woman who had slumped against the brick wall.

"Pull over, pull over now." Pete commanded.

"God we're right next to the restaurant, we're in plain view," Objected the cabbie.

"Just do it!"

It took only a moment for Tierney to recognize the black woman. It was Nancy Brewer attempting to help the stricken woman. Pete flung open the rear door, shouted to the driver; "Stay put, this is real." He rushed to the scene. The cab was now across the street on a diagonal between the blue surveillance van and the restaurant blocking the view of the van and those in the restaurant

"Nancy, what are you doing here?"

"Peter, Oh Peter, Lege' your attorney told me I could find you at the Italian restaurant, but this woman fell." She turned toward the frail woman slumped on the sidewalk against the brick wall.

Pete knelt beside the woman and pulled her hat back from her face. It was Shawn. "Oh God, Shawn, Shawn." he whispered to her.

She attempted to moisten her lips, but there was no moisture left. "Peter, I didn't want to draw attention. I've missed you so." Although her lips were dry, her eyes moistened with tears, she was pale. He felt her pulse. It was rapid and shallow. Still her eyes were alert. Pete felt she was not dying, not just yet. "Shawn, I don't want you to worry, I'm not going to lose you. I think you will be ok."

"Pete, all the information you gave me is already with the editor, Richard Weiss. He is privy to everything you have sent me and has it ready for copy. I love you!"

Pete rubbed his eyes. "I know, I know. Just, don't you worry, you'll be OK."

Nancy turned to Peter. "Tell the cabby to call an ambulance. No, we better not call. The damn ambulance will cause too much commotion. Let's put Shawn in the cab". As he was about to lift her, she handed over a few updated briefs.

Nancy also had a small portfolio of classified information. "We must get these to Weiss in the restaurant and past the three agents inside the restaurant".

"You can't go in! The Agency is just waiting for you to show. They will kill you and the editor." said Nancy.

"I've got to get what is left of the cover-up to the editor. How else will anybody ever know the government has hidden this epidemic? Three hundred thousand people have died of a man-made epidemic and a million more will follow. The government is fucking with us!"

The cabbie pulled up. "Hey man, ya want me to call the POlice. I can use my radio." He was holding up the hand-held transmitter.

Nancy grabbed Pete and shook him. "Look, I've got more data in my brief case, about the Navy experiments in Cuba, the African experience, the Bonn and the Norway connections. It's all right here. This includes the transfusions of bad blood in France and in the USA. Thirty thousand people deliberately infected by an arrogant attitude, a policy that has spread it around enough to affect everyone."

"Nancy, they will kill us to keep this information quiet. All that is between us and the devil, is this cabbie."

217

Pete turns toward the cabbie. *This guy has no idea of what is going on much less what is at stake? He knows nothing of the importance.*

"Nancy, there is no amount of money I could give that guy to enter that restaurant and get the editor out of there." said Pete. Let's get Shawn in the cab and both of you out of here. Take the briefs with you and I'll get to the editor."

"Pete, you're crazy! They know you, all they want is to find and kill you. No story, no worry and no paper trail. Walk in there and you're a dead man."

"Cabbie, I've got a deal for you." Pete said.

"I need your jacket and hat. I need you to take this lady, Shawn to the hospital with Nancy. You must keep guard over these papers." Pete handed him the entire portfolio of documents measuring the international maneuvers of the Agency Network.

"If you do nothing else in your life, you must guard these papers. Do you understand?"

"I've got to get the editor out of the restaurant."

The cabbie nodded. He pulled off his black leather jacket with the spikes and gave the brass knuckles plus his cap to Peter.

"I'm going to the hospital. You don't owe me a thing man!" he said. He drove off with Nancy and Shawn and then suddenly stopped.

"Shouldn't I wait for you somewhere?" he asked.

"Go a few blocks north and wait. I may send someone your way." Pete said with an empty sense of conviction.

Pete was now alone on Clove Street with the ominous blue van between him and the editor of the Boston Globe.

Pete felt the chill of the wet evening air penetrate his body and he began to shiver. He placed his hands in the leather pocket as he cautiously walked across the street toward the van. He felt a wad of snotty rags in the jacket. The other pocket had a pair of dark shades.

"Shit, that's all I need, this crap on my hands."

He walked to the rear of the van which was running at idle, bent over and stuffed the exhaust pipe full of the snotty rags. Wiped his hand on the right leg of his pants and pulled out the dark glasses and put them on. *Might slow them down, he thought.*

He entered the double doors to the restaurant, and searched for the editor.

Smart guy, Pete thought, sitting over in the far corner with his back to the wall. Pete scanned the room and noted three agents planted at opposing corners, all with good visibility. Pete knew that they would not expect him in disguise. He walked to the maître de and asked for a copy of the menu. Then he walked with the menu to an adjacent telephone booth, examined the menu and dialed the phone number on the menu.

"Cucina de la Sorelli, May I assist you?"

"Yes, thank you. I am meeting with a gentleman at your restaurant. He wears a bright golf cap and I need to speak with him. Can you patch me through on your phone?"

"Well, yes, by all means. Uno momento, Prego."

The phone was delivered to the editor, who was startled at being recognized by a phone call. He knew only that Shawn was aware of his presence.

"Hello, Hello."

"Mr. Weiss, do not look around. Appear as if you are on a routine business call. I am Shawn's contact and I know we are both in grave danger. The Agency has targeted you, they are across the room and ready to kill you. I am Peter and I'm in the phone booth across the room. Don't look this way! I need you to feign having received an urgent message and leave the restaurant. I want you to exit through the front door, go north as quickly as possible.

There is a blue van outside that may follow. It is not friendly. Avoid it. I will leave the restaurant and turn south. Meet me at the Old Naval Hospital in Chelsea. You will not get another chance. You must trust me. I'm Pete Tierney and Shawn is my friend. Look for a cabbie with two women, one is Shawn."

The editor hung up the phone. Replaced his hat, left a tip and exited the room without the slightest of glances to the periphery of the room. The agents were stunned. They made moves to exit in varying sequence to avoid the appearance of an ordered departure. Pete watched their eyes and their moves. They scanned the room and seemed desperate. The two with briefcases seemed to toss them about as if empty, but Pete guessed they were bombs looking for a target. Pete hung up the phone in the telephone booth, replaced his dark glasses and headed for the front exit.

As he arrived at the door, the black agent with the watch cap simultaneously tried to exit. The dark glasses did not hide the anger in the black man's eyes. He burst through the door and watched the editor break into a run. The black man looked at the van and gestured with his right arm.

"Get em, ass-hole!"

"Excuse me." Pete said as he brushed against one of the agents. He hurried thought the front door and headed opposite the direction of the editor.

The black man hailed his other two agents and recognized Pete as a plant. He hailed the van.

"That's our man pointing towards Peter who was now in full stride down the street. The black man tossed his nitroglycerine satchel at Pete as he ran for cover.

The van accelerated to catch the editor. The engine coughed and the van lunged forward with the thrust of a popped clutch. The editor in the golf cap rounded the corner. The door of the van flung open and a man jumped out, firing an automatic rifle. His aim was off from backed up Carbon monoxide exhaust fumes. The smell of gun powder penetrated the air. Pete dove for the street curb and for cover. The satchel was tossed high into the air just past the van, reached its zenith and was on its way to the ground. It landed on the curb.

Pete fell to the street and tried desperately to get behind the parked Mercury Cougar. A massive blast of orange flames erupted. Adjacent cars exploded. The van struggled to get away but was engulfed in the flames. The explosion engulfed the van which came to a halt. The store front window exploded. The whole damn block was ablaze.

The cabbie waited, two blocks north on a parallel street. The editor stumbled as he turned the corner and grabbed a light post to steady himself. He spotted the cab with Shawn in the back seat. The back door flew open and he jumped inside as they sped away. The cabbie turned toward the stunned wide eyed panting editor. "Almost as bad as New York, eh? Here is a pile of classified documents for you." Shawn smiled.

It was December 12th. The Boston Globe reported the News of the day. This was no ordinary day. The Headlines read: Mob like bombing, seven dead in Chelsea: Government denies involvement. AIDS link suspected, full story to follow.

CHAPTER 15

Press Time

Congressman Dewey steadied his hand against the cool iced glass of scotch, rubbing the condensation with his index finger. He brought the scotch to his lips and slowly swallowed the smooth liquor, feeling the warm rush and its reassurance.

The makeup artist teased the congressman's hair and added grey contrast to the temples and eyebrows. Grey added a bit of dignity, he thought. He applied his artistry in concert with the silent rhythm of Dewey's hand searching for the scotch.

Alfredo added shadowing under the cheek bones. Removing twenty-five pounds with makeup and lighting was beyond even his acclaimed magic, but he gave his best effort.

"Ten minutes to stage time." announced the manager.

The phone rang. Dewey's aid in a double-breasted suit picked it up, listened, covered the transmitter and handed it to Dewey.

"Yes, Sir, It's Senator Orting."

Dewey held the receiver to his ear as the makeup artist adapted to this latest positional change.

"Yes, Sam, what can I do for you?"

"Make it look good tonight! Stan Razor, the anchor will grill you afterwards and he won't hedge."

"Don't worry Senator, I've trained for this very moment, been coached on every possible question." said Dewey.

"Remember to think calmly, smile and change the subject with a statement. The President is going to be watching, he's worried."

"About the bombing?" He probed, but Sam did not respond to the question.

Dewey jiggled the ice in the scotch glass. "It's OK, I've been targeted before. What about the news reports of the bombing in Boston? Anything new I need to know? Should I suggest that it is related to a gang killing?"

"We're working on a response. The situation team is weighing options. We think it will blow over, just another crime in the inner city. We are not sure yet, we might be able to make it look racial."

"The President is working on the Haiti thing again and will be sending military medical teams back to Guantanamo Bay. Just give them a good speech and limit your responses to Razor."

"I can handle it." Dewey said as he placed the glass back on the damp cork tumbler.

"Any word on the Navy doctor? What do you think he knows?"

"We're working on it Dewey. Just concentrate on your performance. "Three minutes!" announced the manager as the red light came on over the dressing room door.

"Sir, we have to get rid of the glare on your forehead" The makeup man moved nervously against the clock while searching for the right tanning powder.

"OK Sam, I've got to go. Show time as they say."

"Anything else I should know?" Dewey asked after a long pause.

"Let's walk." said the stage hand.

"No, I don't think so." said the Senator. Remember, the President is watching."

Dewey hung up the phone, looked in the mirror, adjusted his tie and thought, *I've got to start working out on that exercise machine. I can't hide an extra chin anymore.*

Congressman Dewey arrived at center stage, where the podium shielded his bulk. The podium was in the State Department foyer often used to address the news media. All major networks were present for prime-time viewing, with lights and cameras poised.

Dewey scanned the transparent heads up display allowing an orator to read a prepared speech while appearing to focus on the camera and audience. This same head up display was copied from the F-18 cockpit. A pilot needs to keep his head out of the cockpit as much as a politician needed to keep his image unblemished.

Air: THREE, TWO, ONE.

"My fellow Americans, Representatives and Senators, this is a time for change.

It is a time for compassion, a time for leadership and a time for visions.

As leader of the House Appropriations Committee, I take pride in announcing a national joint bipartisan effort to confront the AIDS epidemic.

Within the next three years we will establish regional Quarantine Centers. A prototype of the communal support center will begin in my home state of Washington. The US Navy has donated the Sand Point Naval Air Station for use by voluntary citizen groups who either have AIDS or are infected with the HIV virus. The medical community is invited to establish support facilities within these confines.

The insurance industry is financially supportive of this endeavor. We lobbied hard for their support. All who meet the criterion of acceptance to this social commune will be paid a salary and given meaningful work. Their sexual practices will be confined to the commune and to the residences therein.

This new national policy will be funded by a new Humane Health Service Tax base and new legislative actions will generate a special funding program.

We will establish a new Health Policy, a New National Health Insurance, and a New Management Bureau of Civility.

We are going to solve the AIDS Problem and do so humanely. We will do the right thing, until a vaccine of promise is developed.

I'll now open the podium for questions."

Razor stood and held the microphone. "Why Congressman has it taken thirteen years before quarantine was considered a viable option? Isn't that closing the barn door much too late?"

"As you know Stan, the issue of civil rights and freedoms are sensitive issues. The gay rights of sexual expression, the charge of homophobia and lobbying has paralyzed a response of the CDC. Now we have a clearer vision."

"Sir, then my question is: Why has it taken thirteen years to develop a clear vision? Why are you pointing a finger at the CDC which doesn't make policy?"

"We believe it has to do with politics, and the insensitivity of the Ford and the Carter era. "So, Congressman, you're suggesting the democrats and republicans didn't have a voice in politics for thirteen years? You can't seriously be suggesting this is a political disease?" Razor thrived on conflict.

Dewey covered the mike with his left hand, wiped a drop of sweat from his forehead, then his lip.

"Dan, give us a break, I think we have a new program with vision. The President is fully supportive. We finally have a humane solution. Give us a chance."

Stan had another question, but Dewey turned away.

He pointed to the next newsman who was waving rolled papers.

"Congressman, what do you know about a group called TAN, The Agency Network?"

Dewey's mouth dropped.

"The Boston Globe reports a cover-up of the AIDS Epidemic and connects TAN to the recent bombing in Chelsea MA.

Do you have a comment sir?"

"Sir I don't know what you're talking about. I have no further comments." Dewey felt his world start to crumble.

NEWS BULLETIN:...FLASHED: across the bottom of screen.

IS AIDS EPIDEMIC AN EXPERIMENT GONE

WRONG,
FULL STORY TO FOLLOW.

CHAPTER 16

Year 50 A.E.
After the Epidemic
2030 A.D.

The large auditorium at the Medical Universiteé of Paris, France was hushed with anticipation. Rumor suggested a new demonstrated technique would be displayed and it seemed that new medical technology had long ago been invented.

The Department of International Contagion was sponsoring a world-renowned professor of infectious disease. A doctor emeritus and professor from the University of Vienna, Austria.

Professor P. Tierney was an invited epidemiologic, historian of international acclaim. He was not the guest speaker but had the privilege of presenting the global overview prior to the demonstration by Nobel laureate Professor Emeritus Rene'-Louis Fouchee' of the Pasteur Institute.

The world and the medical profession had seen remarkable change in the two generations who had grown up in the shadow of the Great Epidemic. There had been an incredible record of change in the past 40 years. It was no wonder the audience was abuzz with interest.

There had been the dramatic technical advances associated with the mapping of the human genome. It seemed to be an era unto itself. For the millions of genetic codes, only some 173 codes were now identified with known diseases. Every new born child was DNA coded prior to birth and again at birth. The serial genetic coding was transposed to a bar coded identification which every adolescent and adult now carried on their person. These genetic codes were used for international identification. In the United States, the Social Security numbering system had long ago disappeared. The Social Security System had gone bankrupt by 2030 AD (50 AE) as predicted, but now, more importantly, so many had died during the epidemic that a nine-digit code was excessively optimistic. If the problem before was overpopulation, it now was a scarcity of diverse peoples and cultures.

Medical care and technology had become graphically distanced from people. Now computer surveys had replaced the archaic physical examination. In fact, placing a hand on a patient was an unsterile subjective encounter requiring disciplinary action, if not legal measure, applied during the epidemic. It became an outgrowth of the feminist movement of the nineties. There were gender specific physician's first and designated specialties second.

Genetic splicing in utero had become a refined procedure. All genetic diseases had been controlled if not eliminated. Even behavioral and most psychiatric illness were now eliminated before birth or subdued by genetic modulation to less virulent or controlled disorders. The prototype of behavior modification applied to substance abuse and deviant sexual predators. Sexual preference aberrances were all addressed as now standard procedures. Gene splicing and intra-regulatory social directives were considered necessary to control the Great Epidemic in history now known by the historical reference as the period of "Social Strife".

Medicine had become a political and social management tool, an extension of the Federal Administration's policy directives. This had dated back to the Rodham-Clinton White House Charter Letters. Their entire profession's role was redefined as public servants -

beholden to the State. Public doctors became politically used. An entirely new ethic, still reluctantly accepted by tradition, was: Your health was public property. This was deemed 'necessary' because of the Great Epidemic and the era of Social Strife. The principal of privacy had become autonomously tied to the needs of the state. Privacy became an historical term relegated to the attic. Nobody was happy with the present state of managed medical policy.

The world and the US had become sparsely populated compared to the 20th century.

Tierney strode up the steps to the podium. The audience came to a complete silence, hushed by the man's reputation. He was instantly recognized, like the Salk of a different era.

"The world we have known has shrunk a great deal since the Great Epidemic," he began.

He asked for the first holographic slide a global map depicting Southern Europe and Africa extended to the Cape of Good Hope, under a common currency and a common European ancestry. Black Africa dwindled to an endangered species. The land masses of the world had not changed much, except the southwest border of the United States and the Baha peninsula had disappeared underwater in the Quake of 2030. The Western Pacific Asian community was now mainly Chinese or Japanese ancestry. The Philippine Islands and native cultures had almost disappeared. The epicenter of these geographic changes was a combination of geothermal faults, shifting plates and cultural changes that followed the Great Epidemic. Muslims dominated much control over cultures.

"Much has changed in our world," Tierney continued, stroking his white moustache. Japan and earthquakes plus dissolving nuclear energy plants have destroyed their heritage.

"The Great Epidemic of AIDS made us a responsible, but less diverse social people. It made us a global community. This example of social strife, as we all now fully understand, became the greatest example of deception for political gain. We learned governments, and not just ours, seek control of the minds of men by confusion of ethical values. We still find the loss of almost an entire ethnic continent of Africa as the legacy of such times. The black population that survives does so almost as an endangered species. Our goal is to see it thrive. It is a sorry legacy from our past."

Tierney continued, "For an old man, I am still pretty swift,

227

although I walk a bit slowly now. I still laugh. And I still cry about those <u>that have touched me deeply</u>. There were many people who helped me bring this message to you. Most have died, and I shall always feel deeply grateful to them. This was no easy journey, but an honest journey. I wanted you to know that telling a story as important as this is the ultimate journey of man. This world will regain its footing, its values, and its direction. There is hope for generations to grow and prosper. But there is an imperative to never forget: Those that seek to influence do so for a reason, and you must decipher their message before it becomes your legacy. Power may corrupt completely, but only you can be deceived completely. Wake up my fellow colleagues, your efforts have greater merit than you suppose. You must become alert to the weakness within all of us. We all are subject to compromise, which is what the Agency seeks and thrives upon. There is a fearful element within us all - a weakness to become a part of the Agency and share its agenda. It is like a cancer within."

The next hologram projection revealed a united China whose population remained stable, intact reflecting the Confucian tradition. However, Hong Kong was now the capitol center of trade and commercialism of mainland China.

Japan's population literally had exceeded its landmass before the epidemic arrived a decade later destroying 67% of her population. She remained an island empire, self-contained and rebuilding with her traditions intact.

The Arctic and Antarctic land masses were unchanged from the late 20th century. The ozone layer was intact and unchanged over the past half century.

Continuing he added, "The unique island populations of the Western Pacific, by contrast, have become a lost culture with mere hopes of rekindling their Polynesian heritage. The cultures of the Sandwich Islands, including Hawaii, Guam, Midway, struggle to rebuild. It's the same story for the Marquises islands, Cook and the Solomon Islands."

"Thailand was devastated very early in The Epidemic and has never been able to repopulate.

"Ladies and Gentlemen, we have witnessed an historic epidemic, like no other known to mankind. This began as a controllable event, and then became a political catastrophe disguised under political euphemisms and correctness of discussion.

"We as a profession, played ball passively, and lost our soul. In the process, we abandoned our ethic - and didn't realize it. We became part of the problem. Worse, we became a spokesman for the Agency that deceived us and the world. Political correctness is a disease far greater than any epidemic. Independent thought is the critical balance needed and that is your charter. You must challenge any movement that is without truth and is Godless! Prayer is our greatest strength.

"With that final note, let me introduce Professor Rene'-Louis Foucheé."

AWARD

Professor Rene' Foucheé removed his stethoscope from the thin women's abdomen as his right hand exited from the zippered aperture of her gown. It was opened from the top of her sternum, to the symphysis pubis bone of her pelvis.

The international medical audience remained stunned and hushed in recognition that something different was happening. There was a sense of anticipation the dawning of a new day; a new era was being demonstrated. The thin but finely proportioned thirty-year-old woman arose from the flat table and zipped up her gown to avoid exposing her breasts while turning toward the audience. The passive sensory dynamic table, slowly followed her movement and adapted to her new posture, like a clinical voyeur. There was a visible blush to her cheeks, if not a new glow. Her frailness seemed something of the past, almost as if the human touch had given her a sense of caring vibrancy. The sensory monitors that surrounded the stage displayed the usual hemodynamic and diathermic color coded visual displays of functional vitals.

Professor Foucheé, moved slowly to the podium.

"My distinguished colleagues of international medicine, this woman has so kindly displayed great courage in allowing me to demonstrate the process once practiced, called a physical examination. Young medical students originally learned a studious hand on process of inspection, palpation, percussion and auscultation after a history of substance was taken. This historic process was often referenced in old literature as telling more about a suffering individual."

229

"However, for brevity's sake, all her sensory input has been transmitted to the peripheral video colored and tridimensional monitors, and as you can plainly see, this woman has a localized left sternal audible systolic grade 2/4 murmur and an associated third heart sound in what used to be termed a hyper dynamic precordium. Her breasts are a bit engorged, as you can discern from the thermos- grams and sensory indirect transducers indicate a pre-lactic hyper-secretory state. We purposely disconnected some of the sensor systems to limit your usual information base. We wanted to challenge the paradigm of your thinking and sense of observation. She has an un-sustained lift of the precordium and no palpable thrills. More importantly she has this peculiar firm, even hard, mass in her abdomen."

He then pushed the podium sensory differential diagnostic button and twenty-seven possible causes instantly displayed on the central stage monitor. Associated were percentile predictions of accuracy, international matrixed political costs of care, percent survivability, burdened effects on society, altered managed effects if multiples of complexity are calculated in a Gross National Product. And, the odds of it being infectious and communicable, directly inferred by what was now well recognized as the Quarantine Probability Scale.

Professor Foucheé then asked three questions of the crowd:

"First, does this require quarantine as a contagion? Second, is this life threatening and to which population? Finally, what is your diagnosis?"

The individual armrest integrated functional analysis systems were activated by the medical audience and the summary tally was observed to compute the summary of opinion on the middle display of the central overhead monitor.

The professional audience remained stunned at the exhibition of a young woman being examined by the exploring hands of a physician. He was using instruments that had disappeared from use for at least two generations. He had placed his hands upon her breasts and had listened through this strange black rubber hosed device stuck in his ears.

Tierney, turned to his female companion, and with raised bushy and silver eye lashes quietly whispered, "I bet she's not ill at all, but filled with life." He smiled, and the twinkle in his eye had only grown more magnetic through the years.

She whispered in his ear, "Nonsense, even your mind is old, you aging old fart. You're too used to mystery solving, everything in your life. It has been a search for political deception. This is not another deception. This woman is dying of metastatic ovarian cancer," said the elderly professor of OB-Gyn.

The medical consensus of the international congress of physicians was indeed Ovarian Metastatic Cancer.

Professor Rene' Foucheé returned to the podium and remarked at length on the correlation of data that was before all peripheral monitoring systems.

Foucheé continued, "My dear colleagues, this woman, has so kindly allowed us to reflect on our humble human nature. She may not be ill at all. Rather, she is pleasantly pregnant. The history that was missed on the initial questionnaire would have made this the highest diagnostic and obvious priority. The heart findings are all physiologically characteristic of pregnancy, not a disease, although pregnancy in the past was considered a disease."

"She is not contagious, and we can thank our stars that she is bringing new life to this changed planet. I will close this demonstration with an admonition that we have as a profession abandoned personal commitments to intellectual honesty. We have done this for many reasons. Some of which are reactionary, but the most pressing politically popular distractions were one of believing that when we put our hands on a patient, it suddenly became an OBJECTIVE finding. Nothing could be further from the truth. You, I will attest, cannot place a hand on a patient and not be affected, as will they. This is then is a subjective encounter. You must interpret the subjective as an artisan of medicine.

I believe it has been clearly demonstrated here today. This is what medicine is about. You cannot become used by managers as a technical tool of political expression. That is why we are proposing that you consider embracing the concept of human medicine as a discipline of science and of the humanities. If you are not actively communicating in the humanities, it will continue to be mismanaged by the purview of politicians who know nothing of medicine. This has been the legacy we have all witnessed. You are not hard-core scientists; you are scientists of the humanities. With that in mind, you must remember to always touch the patient. The power to persuade will become part of your necessary armamentarium. You need to learn to touch from the past and apply it to the human sciences.

"If there was a time in history for separation of Church and State, over three hundred years ago, the time is long past for separation of Medicine from the State. AIDS should never have been allowed to become a Political Disease."

Rene' Foucheé, paused and then stepped aside from the podium. The audience remained silent for some time and then stood and applauded warmly. No one has experienced such a personal hand on contact in almost a quarter century. Most physicians hungered for personal contact, as did the patient.

Tierney, returned to the podium using the steps on the left side of the stage. He shook Professor Foucheé's hand and whispered in his ear. Then Tierney turned to the audience who was still applauding. He motioned with elevated hands for quiet and after a few minutes the audience stayed its enthusiasm with respect and found their seats. The feeling was akin to a bolt of lightning entering the arena.

"We have set the right stage for a new beginning," he said to Rene'. They both gave each other a respectful nod and shook hands again. Pete then returned to the podium.

The audience was quiet again, and now anxiously attentive, hoping for more.

"I feel privileged to address this international audience and to have witnessed the first hands on physical examination in almost 20 years. If that is not enough history in one night, then I propose still another first. Tierney paused and turned toward the far corner of the stage, where a figurine was draped with a dark cloth. It stood almost human size and was on a pedestal. A black elderly woman was in attendance.

"This my friends, is a symbolic trophy to a new era in medicine and in our world...it is a trophy to the Humanities of Medicine, it is a trophy to honesty in research, it is a tribute to those that have died in the epidemic. It is a trophy to those we have loved. It is a trophy to honesty in medicine. It shall always bear fruit and be symbolic where political interference is aborted and clarity prevails. It is a statement that compromise is not the measure of truth, but a reflection of conflict without loss of principals. Compromise is not what medicine is about; truth is what medicine is about, applied to those who live in compromise. This trophy has a very personal message. It shall be called the Noel Prize of Medical Humanities. May we have the unveiling?"

The black female attendant tugged at the dark olive-green cloth. It fell cleanly away from the statue, and before the audience stood a life-sized statue of a woman in flowing bronze dress, swirling with her dress flared as if in the physical dance of life. She appeared to be dancing, or skating, simply turning for a better gaze. She was slim, with full breasts and a cautious waist that invited handling. Her arms, raised celebrating truth. Her clothing was gently flowing and demonstrated her perfect bodice. Her eyes were of bronze, but had light from within almost like a Rembrandt. She seemed alive although only in spirit.

Her posture was poised as an artisan painter as she had a brush in her left hand and a palate in her right. The brush was raised to measure her subject which, of course, was ever present, although not seen.

"May I read, the inscription?" Peter paused in hesitation; he brushed his eye, for a tear seemed near. His throat would not clear and seemed filled with dry cotton. He swallowed several times, recapturing his composure. It seemed so odd...the loss of Shawn was decades ago.

He could not read the inscription. He turned toward the elderly black woman who had removed the olive-green cloth. Their eyes brightened with the recognition of each other. It was Nancy Brewer. She was an old woman, as old as he.

Peter reached out his hand and it was not enough. They hugged in an unhesitant embrace.

Pete whispered in her ear. "Nancy, would you read the inscription? I don't feel able."

Nancy turned toward the crowd with her hand in Pete's. "The inscription reads..." she paused, "For an uncompromising Honesty and Truth in the Medical Humanities, and for those that believe despite political pressure continue to keep separate Medicine from the State." "With Warm Memories and A Hug" Shawn Noel Carole.

THE NOEL PRIZE:
    FIRST AWARD TO...
       Professor Emeritus Peter K. Tierney MD in year 2030 A.D.

Pete held his breath, swallowed with difficulty and wiped a tear from beneath his glasses. He knew their love lived. He could never have buried it. He could only feel it, touch it. He loved her still. Being an old man did not make it distant.

"Nancy, what ever happened to Price?" Peter whispered and gestured to depart the forum of the stage. He placed his arm around her still slight waist and guided her to the eaves.

"I wrote and called him for several years and heard nothing." "Oh, Peter, I thought you knew." Nancy motioned to a bench near the stage entrance where they sat down.

"Ray Price moved to New Mexico. He fell in love with the people, their mountains and the sun sets. Some hunters found his body up on the mesa and called the sheriff. The corner said it was a snake bite. Probably a coral snake, because it happened so quickly."

Pete broke into a smile and laughed. "That was the only thing he feared, snakes. It seems, we all succumb to our greatest fears.

Glossary of Terms and Acronyms:

Navy jargon adds a dimension of reality and lacks nonsensical communications, Transmitted messages are abbreviated, and it becomes very interesting to dissect their meanings.

AFB: Air Force Base
AFIMI: Armed Forces Institute of Medical Intelligence. Located at Ft. Detrick, Maryland.
        Tracks global health threats to military and civilians.

AFIP: Armed Forces Institute of Pathology. One of best pathology labs in world. Collects DNA identity of all members of service in case of death.

AIDS: Acquired Immune Deficiency Syndrome…acquired, as takes some active event to get infected.
 AZT: an early antiviral drug.
BOQ: Bachelor Officer's Quarters…. temporary housing for an officer in transit.

CDC: Center for Disease Control at Atlanta, GA
CO: Commanding Officer e.g. Bangor SUBMARBASE =Sub-Marine Base, Bangor, WA.
NAV BREM HOSP = Navy hospital Bremerton

DNA: Deoxyribonucleic Acid. Our genetic identity.

Fort Dix, NJ. A biologic research laboratory.

GITMO: Guantanamo Bay Naval Base occupied & owned by US in CUBA

HIV: Human Immune Deficiency Virus that causes AIDS

HMO: Health Maintenance Organization

HTLV: Human T-lymphocyte virus. These Lymphocytes (white cells) are especially vulnerable to HIV.

ICS: intercom system

JAG: Judge Advocate General....lawyers who are legal officers in Navy.

Kaposi sarcoma: a dermal (skin) cancer associated with an AIDS infection.

Mail buoy: a factitious mail drop departing any port that entices new officers or enlisted to embarrass themselves by running to deposit a love letter home.

MAMC: Madigan Army Medical Center Tacoma, WA

MC = Medical Corps...a Navy doctor.

MSC: = Medical Service Corps. An administrator that services the medical corps.

NIS: Navy Investigative Service

Navy Officer Ranking:

> Warrant Officers = many experienced warriors that arose through the enlisted ranks.
>
> O-1 Ensign...newest officer on block.
>
> O-2 Lt.-JG. (junior-grade)
>
> O-3 Lt. (lieutenant)
>
> O-4 LCDR, Lieutenant Commander
>
> O-5 Commander (first senior grade officer eligible for a command)
>
> O-6 Captain usually in command of something.
>
> O-7 Flag rank beginning with Rear Admiral

OIC : Officer in Charge

OPS: Operations

ROTC: Reserve Officer Training Command, usually at University levels

SIV: Simian (monkey) Immun- Deficiency virus

SSBN: Subsurface Ship Ballistic Nuclear = Trident species called "boomers with ICBM's".

SSN: Subsurface Ship nuclear…generally an attack submarine.

USAMRID: US Army Medical Research Institute of Infectious Disease at Fort Dietrick, MD

SGLI : Life insurance program for service members where we list recipients we want our assets to go in case of death. This information is secretly kept

USS Iowa incident 1989 Turret explodes killing 47 sailors. Navy initially attempted to blame Homosexual sailors for misfired episode.

References:

"And the Band Played On" Politics, People and the AIDs Epidemic How the epidemic was allowed to happen in San Francisco under Mayor's watch. By Randy Shilts
"The Coming Plague" by Laurie Garrett Chapter 11
"The River" by Edward Hooper, discusses the source of AIDS. This first mass vaccination in 1957 with OPV/ AIDS theorizes viral contamination of vaccines. Louis Pascal wrote of contamination and ignored by academia. No accountability by so called medical science, but hugely related. First case of Immune deficiency in Manchester Sailor involved with vaccination program. No one recognized this new disease with his death. Pascal quoted…. "then the whole medical scientific establishment covered it up…" "The very first batch gave us AIDS". Note pg 100-101.
Rolling Stone Magazine, March 19, 1992, links to Polio Salk vaccine. Although in technical error was on the right track. Author Tom Curtis discredited on some details, but valid in that was not from green monkey, but African Chimp harvested from kidney culture substrate.
Statistics to date:
Thirty nine million have died of AIDS, 1.7 million in USA and many more expected. AIDS is a disease of mankind affecting the globe and it occurred in a climate of a biologic warfare race with the Soviet Union. The source of this pandemic is hugely important.

"Decameron" by Giovanni Boccaccio 14th Century…how ten survived an epidemic by Reverse Quarantine.
United States Special Virus Study (1962-1978) with 15 annual reports, some recovered, 6 missing. Study was coordinated by Pentagon and administered by National Institute of Health (NIH)

Notes :

Cross References: